UNDERSTANDING SOCIAL NETWORKS

Understanding Social Networks

THEORIES, CONCEPTS, AND FINDINGS

Charles Kadushin

OXFORD
UNIVERSITY PRESS

OXFORD
UNIVERSITY PRESS

Oxford University Press, Inc., publishes works that further
Oxford University's objective of excellence
in research, scholarship, and education.

Oxford   New York
Auckland   Cape Town   Dar es Salaam   Hong Kong   Karachi
Kuala Lumpur   Madrid   Melbourne   Mexico City   Nairobi
New Delhi   Shanghai   Taipei   Toronto

With offices in
Argentina   Austria   Brazil   Chile   Czech Republic   France   Greece
Guatemala   Hungary   Italy   Japan   Poland   Portugal   Singapore
South Korea   Switzerland   Thailand   Turkey   Ukraine   Vietnam

The author and publisher gratefully acknowledge permission to quote from or use previously published material under
copyright. Elsevier Limited granted permission to use material from the author's published articles in *Social Networks*
and for permission to quote from Borgatti, Stephen P., and José-Luis Molina. 2005. Toward ethical guidelines for
network research in organizations. *Social Networks* 27 (2):107-117; Kalish, Yuval and Garry Robins. 2006. Psychological
predispositions and network structure: The relationship between individual predispositions, structural holes and
network closure. *Social Networks* 28:56-84.; and Valente, Thomas W. 1996. Social network thresholds in the diffusion of
innovations. *Social Networks* 18:69-89. Taylor and Francis granted permission to quote from Granovetter, Mark, and
Roland Soong. 1983. Threshold models of diffusion and collective behavior. *Journal of Mathematical Sociology*
9:165-179. Wolters Kluwer Health granted permission to quote from Rothenberg, Richard B., Claire Sterk, Kathleen E.
Toomey, John J. Potterat, David Johnson, Mark Schrader, and Stefani Hatch. 1998. Using social network and
ethnographic tools to evaluate syphilis transmission. *Sexually Transmitted Diseases* 25 (March):154-160.

Library of Congress Cataloging-in-Publication Data
Kadushin, Charles.
Understanding social networks : theories, concepts, and findings / Charles Kadushin.
    p. cm.
Includes bibliographical references and index.
ISBN 978-0-19-537946-4 (cloth : alk. paper)—ISBN 978-0-19-537947-1 (pbk. : alk. paper)
1. Social networks.   I. Title.
HM741.K33 2011
302.3--dc22   2011014668

7 9 8

Printed in the United States of America
on acid-free paper

For Ghislaine Boulanger

Contents

Preface

WHEN I WAS a graduate student, before the term "social networks" came into general use, Paul F. Lazersfeld introduced his students to the idea of personal influence as a major factor in decision-making. Robert K. Merton had his seminar students read Georg Simmel line by line, among other matters explicating the ideas of triads and social circles. These teachings formed my introduction to social networks as problem-solving tools in understanding why people went to psychiatrists and how elites were organized. Hans Zetterberg insisted that social theory could and should be systematic. I am grateful to these mentors for getting me started on what became the study of social networks as key methodological and theoretical insights that could help to unpack social phenomena. I remain as much interested in the impact of social networks on social structure and cultural content as I am in the study of networks themselves. This book reflects that bias.

The Cohen Center for Modern Jewish Studies at Brandeis University, my colleagues there, and especially the director, Leonard Saxe, were extremely supportive while I was writing this book making time and intellectual space for the effort. Deborah Grant, managing editor of the Center, turned the manuscript into readable prose. Katherine Ulrich was a meticulous copy editor. I am grateful to the Brandeis Libraries for their wide subscriptions to electronic journals and data bases, making it easier to download an article than to go to my own library and find the hard copy version. Peter Prescott provided sage advice about publishing.

The social network field is so broad that it is almost impossible for a single individual to encompass it and get everything right and make things understandable to the non-mathematically inclined. To the extent that I managed at all is because a number of people have helped and encouraged me. Foremost is James Moody who reviewed an earlier version of the manuscript and gently pointed out omissions and commissions, and gave me feedback from a class to which he assigned that earlier version. Thomas Valente introduced me to Oxford University Press, provided me with an early draft of his very useful book *Social networks and health: Models, methods, and applications,* and was helpful in many other ways. Claude Fischer reviewed the chapters on concepts and several others as well. Others reviewed one or more chapters and are acknowledged in a footnote at the beginning of each chapter. They include: Richard Alba, H. Russell Bernard, the late S. D. Berkowitz, Andrew Braun, Michael Brimm, Cynthia F. Epstein, Linton Freeman, Bethamie Horowitz, Dani Maman, Amalya Oliver, Stuart Pizer, Robert Putnam, Gary Robins, Theodore Sasson, Leonard Saxe, Tom Snijders, Barry Wellman, and Douglas R. White. Remaining errors and infelicities are of course my responsibility.

My wife, Ghislaine Boulanger, who knows well the pangs of authorship, supported me throughout.

Fishers Island, July, 2011.

UNDERSTANDING SOCIAL NETWORKS

1   Introduction

"NETWORKING" SEEMS TO be on everyone lips. No one simply goes to a party anymore. They go to network. For many people, the World Wide Web exists for the main purpose of making connections. Networking seems familiar yet mysterious, accessible yet arcane. Social networks, however, have been at the core of human society since we were hunters and gatherers. People were tied together through their relations with one another and their dependence on one another. Tribes, totems, and hierarchies may have come later. Kinship and family relations are social networks. Neighborhoods, villages, and cities are crisscrossed with networks of obligations and relationships. Beyond kinship relations, people in modern societies are dependent upon one another for such things as picking up the mail when one is away, help with fixing the lawn mower, or recommendations for good restaurants. Nonetheless, it is said that urban Americans are becoming more and more socially isolated. The metaphor of "bowling alone," rather than in clubs, leagues, or with friends, describes this picture of isolation and disengagement (Putnam 2000). But rather than disappearing, neighborhood and village-based groups celebrated as the heart of nineteenth-century America have become transformed from social relations and networks based on place or kinship into communities oriented around geographically dispersed social networks.[1] The telephone and automobile started this revolution and were, not surprisingly, popular in rural areas where there were great distances between households. We have been "networkers" for millennia.

Networks are not the same thing as "networking," or actively using a network to make connections to further one's personal goals. A network is simply a set of relations between objects which could be people, organizations, nations, items found in a

Google search, brain cells, or electrical transformers. Transformers do not "network." In this book we are concerned with *social* networks, and what passes through these networks—friendship, love, money, power, ideas, and even disease.

Has the internet, itself an example of a huge network, changed the rules of social networks? Less than has been claimed. Though people's networks contain substantial numbers of friends, neighbors, relatives, and workmates who are locally based, social networks are supplemented by new internet-based media. It is not a matter of one replacing the other; rather, the "internet fits seamlessly with in-person and phone encounters . . . The more that people see each other in person and talk on the phone, the more they use the internet" (Boase et al. 2006). Social networks are resilient and constantly adapting. Large "mass societies" remain bound by personal ties.

So while the mass media may have "discovered" social networks—a few years ago the *New York Times* celebrated social networks as one the "new ideas" of 2003 (Gertner 2003)—what is relatively new are systematic ways of talking about social networks, depicting them, analyzing them, and showing how they are related to more formal social arrangements such as organizations and governments. In 2008 alone, *Science Citations Index* found 1,269 articles on "social network" or "social networks." In the last 10 years, the total figure is 6,304. The growth is linear. Since 1984, there has also been rapid growth in the number of substantive areas to which social network analysis has been applied, from train schedules in China to the HIV epidemic. The popular press and blogs have been deluged with writing about social networks. Recently, Google listed over 52 million entries for "social networks."

Nonetheless, there is something mysterious about social networks. We live surrounded by them, but usually cannot see more than one step beyond the people we are directly connected to, if that. It is like being stuck in a traffic jam surrounded by cars and trucks. The traffic helicopter can see beyond our immediate surroundings and suggest routes that might extricate us. Network analysis is like that helicopter. It allows us to see beyond our immediate circle.

This book aims to take away some of the mystery about social networks by explaining the big ideas that underlie the social network phenomenon. I concentrate on the concepts, theories, and findings of the social network field. Intended for readers with no or a very limited background in mathematics or computers, this is not a "how to do it" book. There are many useful books that help the reader, often assuming the aid of an instructor, to analyze, deconstruct, and display social networks with the aid of computers. Here I attempt rather to explain the concepts, theories, and findings developed by network experts. Because I am a sociologist, the book has a structural social science bias, but it also takes account of people and their motives. I hope it will be useful to social scientists who encounter social network research in their reading and wish to know more about it and to students new to the network field. I also hope it will be useful to managers, marketers, and others who constantly encounter social networks in their work life. Maybe avid social "networkers" will find it useful. Graphics are important to the network field. So when there is a mathematical basis for network ideas and findings, I try to present them as a graph.

There is a lot to cover, and if the rapid growth of the field is any guide, the coming years will see even more work. There are two contrary trends in any field: investigators build on the basic work of others and stand on the shoulders of giants (Merton 1993), but at the same time they strive to make previous work obsolete. While recognizing that the social network field is moving swiftly, I attempt to select material that serves as basic building blocks and examples of best practices that will allow the reader to understand and evaluate new developments as they emerge. By the time the reader has finished the book, there may well be important new discoveries in understanding social networks and their myriads of applications. Social network sites are burgeoning systems that in the hands of ordinary people as well as revolutionaries may—or may not—be changing the course of history. Yet sound research on these sites is still in its infancy. My hope is that this book will give you the concepts and ideas to understand research and accounts of developments in social networks that are now almost unimaginable.

A few examples that dramatically capture the current state of the art of the field are the best way to begin to understand what social networks and social network research is all about: getting connected; networks as information maps; leaders and followers; and networks as conduits.

Getting Connected

Everyone could be connected, if only we knew how to reach out beyond our immediate horizons. One of the signs of the growth of the social network field is the very idea of "networking,"[2] especially with the aid of the internet. Making connections through social network sites and the internet is ever increasing. It is not confined to adolescents looking for more friends. As of December 2008, 75% of the U.S. adult population used the internet. Of these, 35% now have a profile on an online social network site, up more than fourfold from 8% in 2005.[3] Seventy-five percent of adults 18 through 24 have a profile and almost 70% of students and teenagers, suggesting that as these cohorts age, the total proportion of the U.S. population using social network sites can only rise.[4] Almost 90% of adults use their online profiles to keep up with friends, and half use it to make new friends. Internet-based social networking is more common among urban dwellers who perhaps might feel otherwise more isolated. Facebook, founded in 2004 as a social networking service for Harvard students, is currently (2010) valued at $50 billion dollars. According to the research firm ComScore's 2009 *Digital Year in Review*, it has surpassed MySpace and attracted 112 million visitors in December 2009, up over 100% during the year. As of July 2010, Facebook claimed 500 million active users worldwide. Twitter, publicly released in August 2006, is a social networking service that enables anyone to post messages of no more than 140 characters, known as tweets, to people who sign up as self-designated followers. ComScore reported 20 million visitors for Twitter in December 2009, up tenfold from the previous year. Google, the leading search engine that aids social networking services, is also based on network ideas first developed for citation analysis in the 1950s. All these sites and services are free to the user.[5]

Social network sites have profound implications. Suppose the number of "friends" you have on your profile is a modest 100. If none of them is a friend of the other, then two steps removed, you have access to 10,000 people (100 times 100), who can also reach you. Three steps removed there are 1,000,000 (100 times 100 times 100). Soon, the entire world is a potential friend, for better or for worse. No wonder you hear from people who want to be your friend, many of whom you have never before heard from. There is some danger in this, for you may be exposed to more people than you may have desired. The world is indeed "small." The implications for network theory will be expanded upon later in the book in a chapter on the "Small World."

As "social networkers" hope, these connections can be useful. Connections have the potential to give a person access to valuable resources such as: referral to jobs by people out of one's immediate circle who might know of jobs one's close friends are unaware of (Granovetter 1973); ability to rise in the social ladder of occupations (Lin and Erickson 2008a); help with personal problems (Thoits 1995); referral to a good restaurant, book, or movie (Erickson 1996); or someone who can pick up your mail when you are away (Fischer 1982). These networked resources that you do not own, but to which you have access through your friends and acquaintances, are called "social capital" (Mouw 2006).

Networks as Information Maps

Social network analysis reveals what is hidden in plain sight. When you buy a book from Amazon, the site tells you what other books those who bought your selection also bought. I myself have succumbed to this marketing application of networks and bought books I might not have otherwise considered. Using network analysis principles, Valdis Krebs, an organization consultant who specializes in social network applications, exploited the Amazon data to create on his blog[6] a map of books related to the 2008 presidential campaign. Below is his map of books bought by the same people (figure 1.1). The

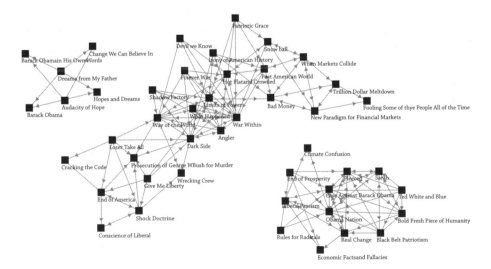

FIGURE 1.1 Books Bought by the Same People in the 2008 Presidential Campaign with the kind permission of Valdis Krebs

arrows show, for example, that people who bought *Dreams from My Father* also bought *Change We Can Believe In*.

There is an Obama cluster of books in the upper left corner; a Democratic campaign cluster in the middle, and a Republican group on the right. There is no overlap between the clusters. In 2008, the reading population of America was polarized, a significant augur for subsequent political polarization. *Rules for Radicals,* by radical community organizer Saul Alinsky, does not fit the partisan tone of the rest of the books in the Republican cluster and was bought by people who bought anti-Democrat and anti-Obama books. One supposes that they wanted to learn about some of the successful grassroots organizing principles of the Left. "Tea Party" organizers?

Network ideas are useful for displaying data such as who bought what book but are especially helpful in making sense of news that involves connections, such as who was involved in what banking deal, who was tied to Madoff's Ponzi scheme, or who was in the network of 9/11 highjackers. Newspapers and Web news sites increasingly use them. Displays of networks on the Web are especially useful because they can be interactive, allowing further information about the points in the network. We can not do this in a book, but figure 1.2, provides an example from *Slate* of the network implied in the Mitchell Report[7] that connected baseball trainers and players involved in providing

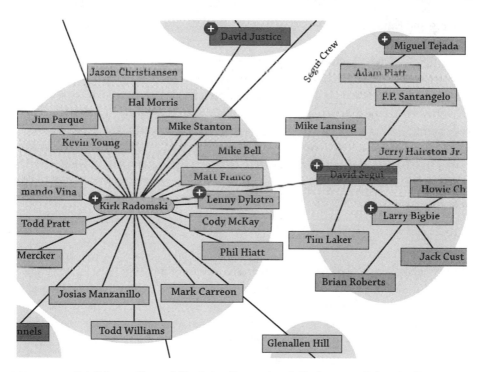

FIGURE 1.2 Detail from a Network Depicting Connections in Performance-Enhancing Drug Usage in Baseball.

With the kind permission of Washingtonpost.newsweek Interactive (WPNI), publisher of Slate Magazine

Slate: The steroids social network. An interactive feature on the Mitchell report. By Adam Perer and Chris Wilson Updated Friday, December 21, 2007, at 11:12 AM ET. The figure is produced by *Social Action* software developed by The Human-Computer Interaction Lab of the University of Maryland.

or using performance-enhancing drugs. The full network diagram gives at a glance the information contained in the lengthy report.

We are all familiar with another kind of network display: the organizational chart that shows who reports to whom and who is responsible for what. One of the earlier applications of social network studies was to discover how workplaces and organizations really worked and what made for leadership. The formal chart cannot possibly account for workplace complexities, and strict adherence to them is usually a recipe for stasis. One of the latest buzzwords in management is "Network Organization," meaning an organization that is explicitly non-hierarchical.

What is a formal organization and what is an informal network has been the subject of a recent Supreme Court case.[8] A man convicted, under federal racketeering laws, of breaking into safe deposit boxes claimed that his loosely organized group was not really an organization under the law. For the majority, upholding the conviction, Justice Alito wrote, "The group need not have a name, regular meetings, dues, established rules and regulations, disciplinary procedures, or induction or initiation ceremonies." The core group was "loosely and informally organized, lacking a leader, hierarchy, or any long-term plan."[9]

Leaders and Followers

Not long ago, Valdis Krebs started to utilize Twitter. Then there was a "denial of service" when Twitter broke down. He began to wonder about the failure of such services as Google, Facebook, and other sites that rely on a single site. They play with what he calls the betweenness paradox. Ultimate control when they work—total failure when they don't. Figure 1.3 from his blog[10] shows a network with a number of obvious failure points. Take out one point, and many others become unconnected. This is also true of covert intelligence and terrorist networks. Take out a key point, and the network becomes ineffective.

Networks as Conduits

Networks are conduits of both wanted and unwanted flows. Physicists who recently became interested in networks, social and other, were intrigued by the rapid failures of the North American electrical power grid leading to massive blackouts. Although the failures were eventually traced to one or two individual electrical transformers, it was determined that the design of the power network caused those failures to cascade into a system-wide breakdown (Watts 2003, 19–24).

Obesity can be an "epidemic." Network magic is no more evident than in the study that shows that over time, obese people are socially connected with other obese people (Christakis and Fowler 2007, 373). Network diagrams covering a period starting from the year 1975 show that the tendency of obese people to be mutually connected

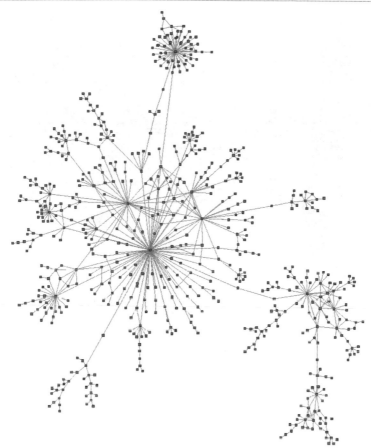

FIGURE 1.3 Kreb's Followers on Twitter. Copyright © Valdis Krebs, with his kind permission

dramatically increases over time. This illustrates two of the major propositions of social networks: homophily—people with like characteristics tend to be connected; and influence—connected people tend to have an effect on one another.[11] The example of body mass is unexpected since that does not appear at first glance to be a social characteristic. But network analysis reveals that it is. These investigators showed, with the same Framingham study, originally intended as a prospective study of how heart and hypertension problems develop, that non-smoking, a "good" attribute, also tends to be contagious.

Marketers are always trying to find ways to reach and persuade individuals in a mass society. Personal contact is most effective, if one can find a way to start a snow-ball rolling. Borrowing from epidemiology, marketers call this "viral marketing." In the network below (figure 1.4), researchers tracked recommendations for a Japanese graphic novel and illustrated the spread in a dense network. The full story is complicated, and viral marketing does not always work, but the investigators found that

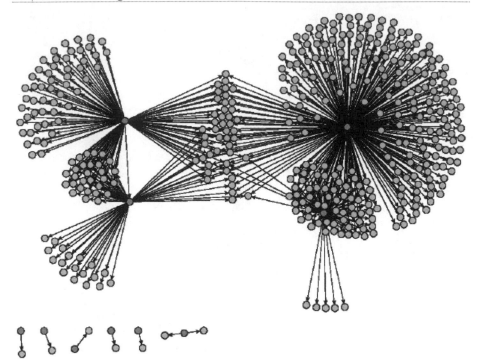

FIGURE 1.4 Personal Recommendation: Viral Marketing for a Japanese Graphic Novel

Jure, Leskovec, A. Adamic Lada, and A. Huberman Bernardo. 2007. The dynamics of viral marketing. *ACM Trans. Web* 1 (1):5 doi>10.1145/1232722.1232727. © 2007 Association for Computing Machinery, Inc. Reprinted by permission.

"personal recommendations are most effective in small, densely connected communities enjoying expensive products" (Jure, Lada, and Bernardo 2007, 36).

You can see how the recommendations for the novel fanned out from a few key points in the network.

The Point of View

I have described just a few striking aspects of social networks. This book seeks more systematically to locate social networks within the general enterprise of social science. The structural point of view in social science sees the patterning of connections as both a cause and a consequence of human behavior: I hang out with people who share my ideas; but by virtue of hanging out with them, my ideas become more and more like their ideas.

This view differs from a purely structural analysis of nonhuman networks. The massive power failures that affected the North American power grid in August 2003 were not a failure of individual transformers but a failure of the very patterning of the power network, that is, a design problem in the way the whole network was structured. Transformers, of course, have no "motivations," though when their functional designed parameters are exceeded as a result of system overload, they fail and in part become responsible for a blackout.

Human networks are also subject to structural analysis. But there is a difference. Human networks arise as a result of acts by individuals and organizations. The networks created by these acts in turn produce networks that have consequences for individuals and social organizations. Social networks evolve from individuals interacting with one another but produce extended structures that they had not imagined and in fact cannot see. Individual interaction takes place within the context of social statuses, positions, and social institutions, and so social networks are constrained by these factors. The social statuses, positions, and social institutions, however, can themselves be regarded as connected networks. These networks are constantly emerging and as a result affect and change the very institutions and organizations from which they emerged.

Understanding a feedback system requires that one starts somewhere. The book is based on the assumption that social networks begin with people. One could of course argue, as indeed some do, that the network patterning itself produces individual motivation such as status seeking. But we prefer to start with people rather than with large social systems and build up from people and small groups to larger social systems.[12] After explanations of key social network concepts in chapters 2, 3, and 4, chapter 5 deals with the psychological foundations of social networks: people, their motivations to form connections, and the cognitive limitations that affect the size of their social circles. We build on this with chapter 6 on small groups and leadership, which shows how these elementary building blocks draw on basic characteristics of individual motivation. Chapter 7 on organizations shows how patterning in small groups affects the function and structure of organizations. We then move to considering whole social systems. Chapter 8 explains how the "small world" works and its implications. Chapter 9 covers diffusion through networks of artifacts, ideas, attitudes, and disease. Chapter 10 on social capital summarizes some of the utility of social networks as assets analogous to economic capital. In the end, most social network data comes from people. Since there are ethical issues in revealing personal connections, chapter 11 deals the complications and ethics of gathering network data about people. The Coda, chapter 12, sums up the ten master ideas of social networks.

As a rule, we generally eschew explaining a phenomenon by pure patterning and structure. There is a constant feedback between structure and behavior. Because of this feedback, network analysis gives us powerful tools and concepts to unravel matters of concern to classical social theory, though to be sure, this is a work in progress and we have a long way yet to go. Some of the questions that are addressed, though hardly solved, are: What is the relationship between basic personality constructs and social relations? How do groups form? What is the nature and source of leadership? How can we best describe the way social positions relate to one another? What is the nature of authority in organizations and society? What are the ways of constructing efficient organizations that benefit their stakeholders? What is the nature of community, and how are people world-wide related to one another? How do new ideas spread and develop? What are the basic social resources of individuals and societies and how can they best be utilized? From time to time, we will reference classic social theorists to see to what extent social network ideas illuminate the problems that they posed. In this view, social networks are not only structural abstractions and the study of networks is not an alternative to classic ways of understanding society, but is a way of gaining greater insight into social life. Though networks also characterize the inanimate world such as electrical power grids, social networks have to be understood, to quote E. F. Schumacher (1973), "as if people mattered."

2 Basic Network Concepts, Part I
INDIVIDUAL MEMBERS OF NETWORKS

Introduction

Social network theory is one of the few theories in social science that can be applied to a variety of levels of analysis from small groups to entire global systems. The same powerful concepts work with small groups, with organizations, nations, and international systems.

Chapters 2–4 introduce elementary network concepts, the "score-card" without which you cannot distinguish the players. In addition to defining the concepts, the chapters provide some flavor of how they are used and how they are linked to basic ideas about networks. This chapter introduces concepts concerning relations between the units that comprise a network. Chapter 3 discusses concepts that describe a network as a whole. Chapter 4 addresses where to draw the line—partitioning whole networks. We begin with a definition of a simple network that connects pairs or dyads. We conclude the chapter with a discussion of triads, the most elementary network in which the structure of the network really matters. For networks, dyads and triads are the analogue of molecules. Dyads and triads will give us a handle for understanding larger networks.

With dyads or pairs we are interested in why people come together—why they form a dyad in the first place. As with all network theory, we will see that a feedback loop is at the heart of network processes. There are forces such as propinquity—for example being in the same place at the same time—that bring people together; but at the same time, the dyad creates consequences for its members and for the whole network. People who are connected with one another tend to be physically proximate. People who are near to one another also tend to share the same characteristics, values, and social statuses. This relationship is one of the reasons, for example, that desegregating neighborhoods or integrating schools can be particularly challenging. Regardless of how the connection happens, once people are linked, there is a tendency for them to acquire the same characteristics, values, or social statuses from one another. Chicken-and-egg problems abound in social network analyses.

The discussion above concerns "people," but the concepts apply to all levels of networks including groups, organizations, and even nations. Some illustrations and a few elementary propositions will be offered for each concept. Further applications of the concepts, as well as more complex concepts and propositions, will be developed in later chapters devoted to specific topics. While all the concepts have formalized means of measurement, and often several different ways to measure the same concept, the aim of this book is to develop the concept itself and show how it is applied in theoretical statements and in substantive findings. Measurement issues will be noted and referenced, but the mechanics of the analysis is mainly reserved for other literature.[1]

What Is a Network?

We begin with a more precise definition of "network": a network is a set of relationships. More formally, a network contains a set of objects (in mathematical terms, nodes) and a mapping or description of relations between the objects or nodes. The simplest network contains two objects, 1 and 2, and one relationship that links them. Nodes 1 and 2, for example, might be people, and the relationship that links them might be as simple as standing in the same room. If 1 is in the same room as 2, then 2 is in the same room as 1.[2] The relationship is in figure 2.1a is not directional.

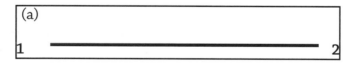

FIGURE 2.1A Simple Relationship

There are also directional relationships (figure 2.1.b) such as 1 likes 2.

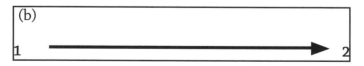

FIGURE 2.1B Directed Relationship

In this simple network of "liking," the relationship could be symmetrical.

Nodes 1 and 2 like one another, or their liking is mutual. The liking network below (figure 2.1c) is similar to the first one of standing in the same room together, but has a valence or a flow. Mutuality is a tricky matter, however, and not all that easy to achieve, so mutual networks tend to be limited. A prevalent tie between dyads is *anti-symmetric*. Father and son, boss and employee are examples. The relationship is by definition different, depending on which way you look.

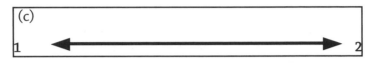

FIGURE 2.1C Symmetric Relationship

There need not be just one relationship mapped between nodes 1 and 2. For example, 1 and 2 might be in the same room and might also like one another. When there is more than one relationship, this is called a multiplex relationship.

Aside from their directionality, or lack of it, relationships might be more than the sharing of an attribute or being in the same place at the same time. There can be a flow between the objects or the nodes. Liking, for example, might lead to an exchange of gifts. Flows and exchanges are very important in network theory.

At one level, this list of concepts of relationships between pairs of nodes is now logically complete. But consider a network (figure 2.1d) between pairs that operates via an intermediary node. For example:

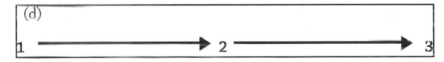

FIGURE 2.1D Relationship Through an Intermediary

Node 1 is connected to 3 via 2. The relationships shown above are directional and not reciprocal. They might be transitive or they might not be. If the relationship is transitive, it means that if 1 loves 2, then 2 also loves 3. Possible, but not likely. Transitive relationships are more common in an official hierarchy. Node 1 gives a message to 2 who forwards it to 3.

One can describe the network distance between pairs of nodes in terms of the number of steps or links between them. There are obviously two steps between 1 and 3. But if 1 also likes 3, as shown below (figure 2.1e), the network is said to be transitive or balanced and mutual and, in this case, all three nodes are directly linked.

The network depicted in figure 2.1e is a "sociogram"—a term invented by Jacob Moreno (Moreno 1953 [1934]), who is regarded by many as a key founder of modern network studies. It is also what mathematicians call a graph. There is a branch of

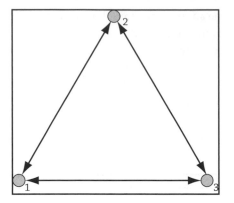

FIGURE 2.1E Sociogram of Three Nodes, All Mutually Related

mathematics, graph theory, which allows sociograms to be manipulated mathematically (Harary, Norman, and Cartwright 1965). The depiction of relationships as sociograms allowed observers almost instant insight as to what was going on in small, not overly complicated networks. The addition of graph theory to the tools for understanding networks further allowed for understanding and manipulating much larger and more complex networks. In this introduction to network theory, we will dispense with the mathematics of graph theory but will rely on its insights and findings. The simple network of three units is called a triad. This simple network turns out to be the building block of more complex relations and will be discussed at the end of this chapter.

Many network analysts, and much of the software for manipulating networks, prefer to work algebraically with networks when they are depicted and expressed as matrices. Below (table 2.1) is the same sociogram but in matrix form. In network terms, we call this an adjacency matrix because it shows who is next to whom.

The numbers, 1, 2, and 3 on the top line and the first column identify the same nodes as in figure 2.2. The number 1 on the second line indicates a connection between the nodes. Node 1 "chooses" nodes 2 and 3. Node 2 "chooses" nodes 1 and 3. Node 3 "chooses" nodes 1 and 2. The dashes indicate that in this graph or matrix, self-choice is not at play, though in some networks self-choice can be an option. For example, candidates in an election can vote for themselves.

TABLE 2.1

The Adjacency Matrix that
Represents Figure 1

	1	2	3
1	-	1	1
2	1	-	1
3	1	1	-

Sociological Questions about Relationships

Though all of our examples thus far have been social, in principle, we might as well have been talking about electrical currents. There is a branch of network theory that deals with such matters, though electrical circuits tend to be considerably simpler than social networks. But consider. At each level of analysis—individual, organization, or nation-state, for example—what are the conditions that make it more or less likely that a path will exist between two nodes, that the nodes will have the same attributes, that they will be reciprocally or mutually related to one another, and that triads will be balanced? The answers lie in social theory. We now introduce some elementary hypotheses about these conditions.

Social scientists have investigated three kinds of networks: ego-centric, socio-centric, and open-system networks. Ego-centric networks are those networks that are connected with a single node or individual, for example, my good friends or all the companies that do business with Widgets, Inc. (the favorite name of organizations studied in business schools). However, a list is not necessarily a network. In popular discourse, especially when social support is discussed, any list is called a "network." It is a network in a basic sense because even if no one on the list is connected with one another, each individual is at least all connected with the person being supported. The support may include help with a job search, comfort during an illness, or a loan of money or a lawn mower. A person with a large number of good friends whom he or she can count on is commonly said to have a large "network." This network cannot be discussed in social network terms, however, unless we know whether and how these people are connected with one another.[3] It is obviously one thing to have a supportive network in which most people know one another and a very different matter if the people are unknown to one another. Ego networks and how they extend further to links beyond the starting point are discussed in the next chapter on whole networks.

Socio-centric networks are networks in a "box." Connections between children in a classroom or between executives or workers in an organization are closed system networks and the ones most often studied in terms of the fine points of network structure. These were the ones with which Moreno began his studies. Open system networks are networks in which the boundaries are not necessarily clear, for they are not in a box—for example, the elite of the United States, connections between corporations, the chain of influencers of a particular decision, or the adopters of new practices. In some ways, these are the most interesting networks. Later chapters in this book, one about the "Small World" and one about diffusion, explore these open systems in some detail.

CONNECTIONS

We now examine some of the social situations and forces that make for connections between one node (e.g., a person, an organization, a country) to another.

Propinquity

At all levels of analysis, nodes are more likely to be connected with one another, other conditions being equal, if they are geographically near to one another. Individuals are more likely to be friends if they are geographically close (Feld and Carter 1998). In a pioneering study of the propinquity effect, Festinger, Schacter, and Back (1950) demonstrated that in a new housing project for World War II veterans, persons who lived near to one another were more likely to become friends. Persons in corner housing units were more likely to be socially isolated than persons in units that lay between other units (ibid.). Further underlying the importance of location, a study of networks in the United States of people who serve together on several different corporate boards of directors (these are called "interlocking directorates") found that "[i]nterlocks are concentrated in firms headquartered in the same locale" (Kono et al. 1998). Being selected to serve on boards of directors has more to do with local upper class structure, being acquainted with people because one has run into them at the same clubs, than with simple friendship. Though some of the same network principles (in this case propinquity) apply for individual persons, corporations, or countries, how the principle plays out may differ for various levels of analysis. Trade between countries, other things being equal, is more likely if the countries have common borders. But, for example, "averaged over all EU countries, intranational trade is about ten times as high as international trade with an EU partner country of similar size and distance" (Volker 2000). Economists tend to define propinquity in terms of cost of transportation rather than the actual number of miles between nodes or sheer border crossings when tariff is not an issue (Krugman and Obstfeld 2000).[4]

Propinquity can also be more broadly defined as being in the same place at the same time. There is a distinction between co-location, which puts people simply within range of one another, and co-presence, which implies a social relationship that is within the framework of a social institution or social structure (Zhao and Elesh 2008). Common interests (e.g., music) and common arenas or foci for meeting (e.g., mothers at the playground) are another mode for drawing people together (Feld 1981; Feld and Carter 1998; Kadushin 1966). Studies of elites show that persons are more likely to have a connection, relationship, or friendship if they went to the same prep school at the same time (Domhoff 1967). Of course, these individuals may merely share an "old school" tie (they went to the same school but at different times), in which case we are talking about homophily, a different kind of propinquity.

Homophily

Homophily (from the Greek, "love of the same") is a concept introduced into social theory by Lazarsfeld and Merton (1978 [1955]) that embeds a folk proposition: "birds of a feather flock together." More formally, if two people have characteristics that match in a proportion greater than expected in the population from which they are drawn or the network of which they are a part, then they are more likely to be connected (Verbrugge 1977). The converse is also true: if two people are connected, then they are more likely to have common characteristics or attributes. There is also an implied feedback: over time, relationships tend to sort out so that they become more homophilous. I have said "people," but the homophily principle, like propinquity, applies equally to groups, organizations, countries, or other social units.

Individual-Level Homophily

At the individual level, persons are more likely to have a connection, friendship, or association, if they have common attributes (Lazarsfeld and Merton 1978 [1955]). While common norms are promoted through common attributes, so are common attributes likely when association or friendship occurs as a result of co-location and commonly situated activities (Feld and Carter 1998).

Lazarsfeld and Merton distinguished between status-homophily, which can be ascribed (e.g., age, race, sex) or acquired (e.g., marital status, education, occupation), and value-homophily (e.g., attitudes, stereotypes), which has also been termed homogeneity (Hall and Wellman 1985). Common attitudes can be based on patterns of relationships (Erickson 1988). Numerous studies have documented the tendency towards homophily in a variety of social networks (McPherson, Smith-Lovin, and Cook 2001). But a critical research and theoretical question is which characteristics, attributes, or activities are selected in a given situation to be salient candidates for homophily. For example, the extent to which the situation values "race" or defines it in terms of skin color will affect whether common characteristics such as skin color will be related to children's choice of one another as friends in a classroom situation (Hallinan 1982; Hallinan and Williams 1989). Because of the principle of homophily, social network analysis thus almost invariably involves the sociology of class, gender, ethnicity, and nationality as well as cultural values. Some of the sorting out and clustering of networks is of course the result of visible attributes, but some is the result of less visible ones. To make the less visible more visible, dating and matching services offer checklists through which they attempt to bring people together.

There are two kinds of causes of homophily. Common norms or values may bring nodes with common attributes together, or the reverse, common attributes and contacts may lead to common norms, and this holds true for both individuals and collectivities (Burt 1982, 234–238). For example, a study of adolescent girls found that students belonging to the same clique tended to have similar scores on various measures of behaviors such as binge eating, alcohol use, dietary restraint, and so on. But we do not know whether adolescent girls hang around together because they share similar habits, or they have become similar to each other while hanging around with one another (Hutchinson and Raspee 2007). In general, research on homophily investigates the conditions under which homophily is likely to occur—which factors in a social system encourage which kinds of similarities and leads to particular ties (McPherson, Smith-Lovin, and Cook 2001). This is even more complex than it seems because homophily is a process. To reiterate, if people hang out together they tend to have the same attitudes, and if they have the same attitudes, they tend to hang out together (Erickson 1988). Chicken-and-egg situations always create difficulties, and a major part of Lazarsfeld and Merton's original formulation was devoted to Lazarsfeld's essentially unsuccessful attempts to sort this out.

A second cause for homophily is structural location. Two nodes may have the same attributes because both operate in the same arena, and again, vice versa (Feld and Carter 1998). While similar pairs tend to form a relationship, the availability of similar attributes is a function of social structure. I am more likely to find people interested in solving mathematical problems in a physics class than in a class on English literature. But people drawn to mathematics are more likely to choose a physics class that an English class. By studying the email interactions, over a year, of a population of over 30,000 students and staff in a university, Kossinets and Watts (2009) were able to determine that individual preferences for like persons and common social location both produced homophily. But modest initial preferences for similar others became amplified over many email exchanges into stronger patterns of homophily; similar interests led to similar locations in which similar interests were more available. The feedback between network structure and individual preference thus becomes especially noticeable over time.

In sum, if people flock together, it appears that there are four processes involved: (1) the same kinds of people come together; (2) people influence one another and in the process become alike; (3) people can end up in the same place; (4) and once they are in the same place, the very place influences them to become alike.[5]

The principle of homophily exemplifies the tendency of social networks to be "unfair" and makes "social engineering" to counter prejudice and segregation more difficult. For example, in one study of social network engineering and race, a police academy attempted to facilitate racial integration by populating squads with a selection of recruits that reflected the demographics of the larger cohort (Conti and Doreian 2010). The academy also instituted fixed seating. As observed and surveyed over the training period, squads "worked to increase levels of social knowledge within and between races through time as well as the level of friendship at the end of the academy. The fixed seating arrangement worked in the same fashion but as a weaker force. Social knowledge and friendship were highest for pairs of recruits in the same squad and were adjacent in the fixed seating—both within and between races" (ibid., 42).

Interaction led to greater understanding, but not to a complete elimination of conflict around race: "expunging underlying attitudes regarding race is another matter. Throughout the academy, an underlying tension regarding race existed and was expressed with racist remarks (recorded as part of the ethnographic data)" (Ibid.).

Homophily and Collectivities
Hypotheses about homophily are straightforward for individual persons, but somewhat more complex when it comes to collectivities. At the organizational level, whether similarity leads to a greater likelihood of a tie depends on the kind of a connection, as well as the on the industry.

Consider Ford, Chrysler, and General Motors as having common characteristics: they are automobile manufacturers and are geographically adjacent to one another in Detroit. But common characteristics and geographic propinquity do not necessarily lead to a tie. For example, Ford does not sell cars to General Motors. On the other hand, when engineers and managers move from one company to another, a tie develops between the automobile companies. Similarly, software firms in Silicon Valley cultivate ties to one another through their practice of regularly licensing software to one another and also exchanging personnel. Geographic co-location is of course covered under the heading of propinquity, but through the principle of "external economy," it also leads to homophily via structural co-location. External economies, as the name implies, are "the economies that a firm can obtain through the use of facilities or services 'external' to itself" (Hoover and Vernon 1962). This leads to the classic situation of "birds of a feather flocking together" to take advantage of readily available services and hence lower transaction costs.[6] The being in the same place at the same time, at once a factor in homophily also makes relations with one another easier. It is no accident that firms that compete with one another and thus have very similar attributes are also geographically close (Uzzi 1996). We will have more to say about this principle when we discuss social circles of organizations.

The corporate examples suggest that power in a relationship is not irrelevant. Given that there is a dyad formed by virtue of homophily, and that the dyad connection itself creates greater homophily, what is the role of power or mutuality in the dyad? We often observe that in any relationship at any time one of the pair has an advantage over the other. When are the relationships equal; when is there mutuality?

Dyads and Mutuality

We have seen that in directed graphs or networks, there can be four possible relationships: none at all (they are not connected), A relates to B, B relates to A, and A and B both relate to one another. We are concerned here with the fourth relationship, reciprocity or mutuality.

The concept of mutuality implies first, that relations are reciprocal, that is, they involve a give and take between the two parties; and second, that power or asymmetry in the relationship is of little or no consequence. Mutuality is strongly affected by the social and cultural structure within which the dyads are embedded. For example, in elementary school, girls are more likely to reciprocate friendship choice than are boys. Girls may be more socialized to emphasize personal relationships therefore develop more intimate friendships (Shrum, Cheek, and Hunter 1988). The doctor-patient relationship can be a close one, though guided by professional norms. But the relationship is inherently anti-symmetric. Recent developments in psychoanalysis, however, urge a more mutual relationship between therapist and patient (Mitchell 1993). The American husband-wife relationship is another one in which norms of mutuality have been changing, though to be sure women still do more housework and have greater responsibility for child rearing.

Under what conditions, in what kinds of networks, can we expect that nodes will have a mutual relationship? One can try and address this question by looking at the likelihood that a particular network or social system will be composed of more or fewer mutual relationships than one might expect at random (Mandel 2000; Wasserman and Faust 1997). Mutuality begins early in life and is a key factor in human development.

As such, mutuality is strong factor in the formation of children's friendships (Schaefer et al. 2010).

While at the level of individuals it may be difficult to sort out mutuality, at the organizational level this task may be easier. Organizations can share an attribute—two organizations that confront illegal drug problems, for example. In this respect, the police and psychiatric clinics can be said to be in the same network. Then we examine the nature of flows between them. Do the police send people to psychiatric clinics; do the clinics send people to the police? If both are true, how does this reciprocal relationship work out in practice? Is there more than one relationship between the police and psychiatric clinics? For example, do they "exchange" clients (a flow), and are they both members of the mayor's task force on fighting drug addiction (a shared connection); and if so, how does this multiplex relationship affect them? Answers to these apparently very simple questions can result in complex analyses of the roles of different organizations in dealing with drug problems. Just as a reminder, there are also relations between units larger than organizations. There is an entire branch of economics that deals with trade relations between nations (Krugman and Obstfeld 2000).[7] The advantage of organizational or national research into reciprocity is that data are from databases that trace transactions of one kind or another and hence do not suffer from people's faulty memories. For example, contrary to the theory that argues that the hierarchical structure between core and peripheral countries are becoming more and more solidified, the reciprocity between countries in the global telecom network was found to have increased between 1989 and 1999 (Monge and Matei 2004).

There are a large range of propositions and studies about pairs of relations, most of which assert that the greater the similarity of the attributes of the pairs, the greater the likelihood of there being a flow between them (see homophily, above). While this may be obvious, consider that most "coalition building" consists of creating mutual flows between pairs that do not share many attributes. There is a major movement in public health and in drug- and alcohol-addiction-prevention programs that attempts to build community coalitions in an effort to have an impact on drug and alcohol consumption. The proponents remain optimistic. Foundations and the federal government continue to fund these programs, yet careful studies show that "overall the documented research evidence for positive coalition or partnership outcomes is weak, or, in stronger language, conspicuous by its rarity" (Berkowitz 2001, 220; see also Kadushin et al. 2005). Although "obvious" to network analysts who understand that bringing pairs together in the long term when they have quite different characteristics is difficult and rare, this elementary fact of pair relationships is apparently poorly understood.

Balance and Triads

As noted, network analysis really begins with triads, for they are the beginnings of a "society" that is independent of the ties between a dyad:

In respect to its sociological destiny...the dyadic element is much more frequently confronted with All or Nothing than is the member of the larger group. This peculiar closeness between the two is most clearly revealed if the dyad is contrasted with the triad [in Simmel's German, 'associations of three']....Where three elements, A, B, C, constitute a group, there is, in addition to the direct relationship between A and B, for instance, their indirect one, which is derived from their common relation to C....Discords between two parties which they themselves cannot remedy, are accommodated by the third or by absorption in a comprehensive whole....Yet...no matter how close a triad may be, there is always the occasion on which two of the three members regard the third as an intruder. (Simmel 1950, 135)

In Simmel's view, the third can be non-partisan and a mediator, but can also be "the Tertius Gaudens" (the third who enjoys; Simmel 1950, 154). The third can line up with one of the two others and thereby gain his or her own advantage or can act as a broker between them and make a broker's profit. This latter possibility will be taken up at greater length when we consider Burt's "structural hole" argument (Burt 1992). Simmel also observed that the most certain way of compromising a secret between two people is to add a third to the "secret."

The addition of a third member to a dyad thus, perhaps surprisingly, vastly increases the complexity of relationships and sets the stage for our examination of whole networks in the next chapter. One important set of ideas hinges on the balance between the three members of a triad and leads to the classic "Balance Hypothesis." Intuitively, just as there is the aphorism "birds of a feather flock together," there is also the saying that "a friend of my friend is a friend of mine" and "an enemy of my friend is an enemy of mine." Beyond intuition, this can be more formalized as: "In the case of three entities, a balanced state exists if all three relations are positive in all respects, or if two are negative and one is positive" (Heider 1946, 110).

For example, the earlier network illustrating a triad shows all three relationships to be positive. But if A dislikes C and B also dislikes C, then it follows by the balance hypothesis that A and B like one another. Heider further contends based on the principles of Gestalt psychology that there is a tendency over time toward balance; "[i]f a not balanced state exists, then forces towards this state will arise." And further, "[i]f a change is not possible, the state of imbalance will produce tension." Even in an apparently simple network, the minimum structure for a "society," matters can be more complicated than they seem.

Martin suggests that given two emotional states (love and hatred) and extremely rational participants, there must be strong institutional support for the balance to emerge, for the simple reason that the "laws" of balance assume a reactivity that is the opposite of what would consider rational. Take the principle, "my enemy's friend is my enemy. It is a poor sort of enemy who allows himself to be guided by this maxim" (Martin 2009, 45). Martin explains that if A and B are enemies, it is good strategy for A to try to make friends with B's friend C and all of B's friends, thus leaving B completely isolated.

Whatever the chosen strategy, triads are analogous to molecules in a periodic table of elements. While there are only a handful of elements found in nature, molecules combine to form complex chemical structures, according to certain rules (in the case of triads, rules include balance, transitivity, homophily, and circles or foci, among others): "The triad census is thus a 'periodic table of social elements' and similarly able to categorize and build social structures."[8]

There are actually 16 possible configurations of triads, as shown in figure 2.2. We offer the figure for reference because of the great amount of work than has been focused on this, the most elementary network. Most of these analyses are beyond the scope of this introduction. Still, as we shall see, there are some interesting consequences to the possible arrangements of the triads and their nested dyads. In the next chapter on whole networks, we will show how different arrangements affect the interpretation of cohesiveness in a small club.

The first character in the triad name gives the number of mutual dyads. For example, there is one in triad number 3. The second character gives the number of asymmetric dyads, for example, 1 in triad number 2. The third character gives the number of null dyads, that is, no connection between pairs, as in the very first triad in which none of

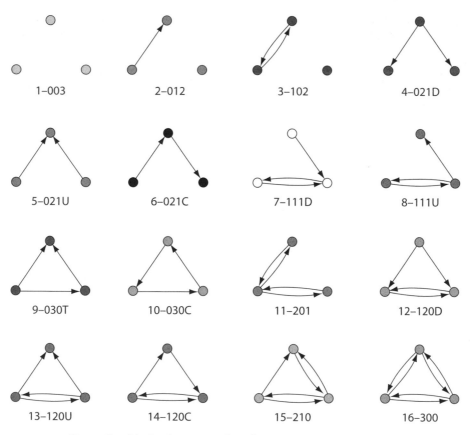

FIGURE 2.2 Sixteen Possible Configurations of Triads

the nodes is connected. The fourth character, if present, distinguishes between triads which are otherwise identical. For example, there are two 030 triads, number 9 and number 10. Number 9 is Transitive and number 10 Cyclical. Numbers 7 and 8 look alike except that in 7 the asymmetric pair has a Downward arrow or connection sign, and 8 has an Upward arrow.

The arrangements may seem obscure, but the census or count of configurations can be compared with the chance distributions of these configurations in any network and yield important insights about the network. In general, the triad census, that is, the distribution of the 16 types of triads in an actual network, the "local" processes in the network, has been very useful in evaluating theories about the global attributes of the entire network, especially since some theoretical structures of a network may be contradicted by the distribution of the triad types in a particular network. A network of interpersonal choices must have only certain kinds of triads. From the balance hypothesis, it follows that friends are likely to agree about a third party—if one of them likes a third party, both will like that person. And close friends agree more strongly about a third party than friends who are not particularly close. Configurations (numbers 7 and 8) that conform to this hypothesis should be statistically more frequent in a social network than configurations that do not. This balance tends to be supported in a wide variety of social networks in which the nodes are people (Wasserman and Faust , 596). International alliances also seem to follow the hypothesis (Antal, Krapivsky, and Redner 2006) Another property of triads related to the balance hypothesis is transitivity: if actor P chooses actor O, and actor O chooses actor X, then P is likely to choose X. For example, triad number 9 contains one transitive relationship, triad 12 contains two, and triad 16 contains six transitive relationships. In contrast, triad 6 is intransitive. Statistical tests "are very supportive of the proposition that interpersonal choices tend to be transitive" (Wasserman and Faust ,598). Intransitive triads are very rare.

Nonetheless, balance is only one theory about choice in a network and does have its limitations by postulating rigorous rules for relations that in messy social life do not always hold.[9] Homophily and its extensions are another cause of connections and, though related to balance, homophily takes account of the social and cultural structures in which a network is embedded. Social circles and foci of activities (see earlier discussion) are other reasons for relationships.

While the distribution of triads seems at first to be a limited idea, the prevalence of different combinations of triads can reveal a great deal about the entire network. We shall see in chapter 5 how transitivity defines the boundaries of a small group. Indeed, the plan of this book follows the heuristic that networks are built up from smaller components.[10] There is a class of network models that utilize the dependence of types of dyads and triads on various attributes of the actors within the network that are extremely useful in shedding light on the social processes within these networks, though work in this field is just beginning to receive wide application (Robins and Pattison 2005; Snijders, van de Bunt, and Steglich 2010; Wasserman and Robins 2005). We observed previously that tendencies toward reciprocity start early. So too do transitivity and balance. In the same study of preschoolers and social networks cited earlier, "children were more likely to select others as play partners when those ties increased the number of transitive patterns in the network" and "[t]hroughout the year, children became increasingly likely to form relationships with the friends of current friends"(Schaefer et al., 67).

Where We Are Now

We began with some simple definitions. A network is a set of nodes and a map showing the relationships between the nodes. The simplest network is a dyad. Relationships in a dyad can be undirected, mutual, or directed. When there is more than one relationship between a pair, such as coworkers and friends, it is called multiplex. Relationships are transitive when what holds for A to B, also holds for B to C. Triads begin to introduce a true social system. Finally, a description of social networks does more than merely list friends or supporters but rather reveals the extent of connections between them.

Socially interesting aspects of networks occur when homophily and propinquity are introduced. Sure, "birds of a feather flock together" but how this phenomenon occurs for individuals and for collectivities and under what circumstances forms the basis of social analysis, whether the subject be friendship patterns, corporate overlap, or international trade. Especially interesting is sorting out feedback and "chicken-and-egg" issues. People become more similar when they hang out together; but they hang out together in the first place because they are similar.

While there are major tendencies for balance in triads, other principles may also be at play. Groups and individuals may strategize to avoid the consequences of balance and try to make friends with enemies. People come together in different foci or social circles in which not everyone is symmetrically related to the others and yet they are a relatively cohesive unit.

Although triads are perhaps the analogue of molecules for networks, there is an even smaller unit—the dyad. Whole networks consist of many dyads—the basic building block of networks with which we began. Each connected triad is, as we have seen, composed of three dyads—within the pair the choices or connections are either reciprocated or not. A further fundamental aspect of a whole network is centrality or popularity. Then there is the density of the whole network: the number of direct connections or ties that exist, divided by the number of possible direct ties. Size is always important. Small groups tend to have high density, whereas large networks, though connected, tend to have low density. The email network of a university may connect all the students and faculty, but most of these are not directly connected so the email network is relatively sparse and has low density. This is typical of large networks. The distribution of reciprocated or unreciprocated dyads, centrality, and overall network density may account for most of the variance in the distribution of triads in human sociability networks (Faust 2007). This brings us directly to a more detailed discussion of whole networks in the next chapter.

3 Basic Network Concepts, Part II
WHOLE SOCIAL NETWORKS

IN THE PREVIOUS section, some basic concepts were introduced about nodes and the relations between pairs and triads. Key concepts that informed the discussion were homophily (the tendency of pairs of nodes to share the same characteristics) and balance (the tendency of the third in a triad to share or have a characteristic that complements the other two). Important as these ideas are, the essence of social network theory and analysis lies in a consideration of an entire network, to which we now turn.

A sociogram, the graph or diagram of a whole network, examples of which were shown in the first chapter, is one way to understand an entire network. As Yogi Berra reputedly said, "You can observe a lot by watching." However, sociograms that contain more than ten nodes are hard to grasp and subject to different interpretations depending on who is "watching." Analytic concepts and methods that account for the entire network and describe and summarize various aspects of it are necessary. *Distributions* of network properties are the first set of key descriptors and include the number of dyads and triads in the network. Other distributions discussed in this chapter include: *Density*, the number of connections contained within the network, and its opposite, *Structural Holes*, a category concerned with the lack of connections. A related concept, *Strength of Weak Ties*, hypothesizes that important things flow from people with whom one has limited connections. *Popularity and Centrality* demonstrate that some nodes have more connections than others and those connections serve as links to other nodes. Other distributions describe the *Distance* across the network between nodes. The radius of distances from any given node is an important descriptor. In terms of people, those nodes directly connected with a focal node comprise the *Interpersonal Environment*. The number of nodes in an interpersonal environment is related to the key concept of *Small World*, which describes the relatively small distances that link a given node to all the nodes in a given network. *Multiplexity* recognizes that there may be many networks that connect, in different ways, the same nodes. Finally, *Position or Role* is a concept that is not distributional but invokes how nodes relate to other nodes in the network. As will be seen, position is the most traditionally "sociological" of the concepts I will be presenting and serves as a link to the next chapter that takes up how whole networks can be partitioned into coherent segments.

Distributional concepts help illuminate the sociogram that follows. In a much-analyzed example of a small group, anthropologist Wayne Zachary (1977) carefully observed a karate club comprised of 34 members for more than two years. In this example, we are not concerned with how the network came into being but rather the consequences of its structure. The sociogram was drawn by a computer program, Pajek (Nooy, Mrvar, and Batagelj 2005) and presented by White and Harary (2001). It depicts the network of friendships among the club members (figure 3.1).[1]

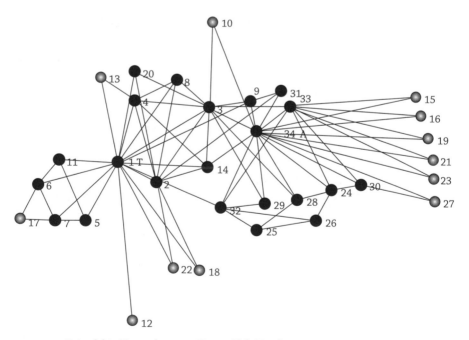

FIGURE 3.1 Friendship Network among Karate Club Members

White, Douglas R., and Frank Harary. 2001. The cohesiveness of blocks in social networks: Node connectivity and conditional density. *Sociological Methodology* 31:305–359, figure 14. Copyright © 2001 John Wiley and Sons, reprinted by permission.

Distributions

DYADS AND TRIADS

In this case, because the graph concerns friendship, it is symmetric: the assumption is that if you are my friend, I am your friend. The connections are based on the observations of the anthropologist and not on the self reports of the members. There are 1,575 symmetric dyads in the network (triad type 3-102 in chapter 2, figure 2). A computer program randomly shuffled the network of 34 people and the 156 symmetric connections between them, called "edges" in graph theory. In each shuffle, the program counted the number of symmetric dyads. The number of dyads was much greater than would have been found by chance. In terms of full triads, club member number 17 on the far left is directly connected with 6 and 7; they constitute a symmetric triad. Another is 6, 7, and 1. Also, 11, 5, and 1 is a symmetric triad. There are 45 such triads in the entire network (triad type 16-300 in chapter 2, figure 2), also far more than expected by chance. The dyads and triads calculations were not made by hand, an effort that would have been tedious and likely to have resulted in many mistakes. Rather, these and later calculations that illustrate distribution concepts in this sociogram, were accomplished by me with a widely used computer program, UCINET 6 (Borgatti, Everett, and Freeman 2004).

DENSITY

Density is defined as the number of *direct* actual connections divided by the number of *possible* direct connections in a network. The karate club network is obviously densely connected. The overall density is 0.139 with 156 connections out of 1,112 possible connections. There seem to be at least two parts to the network—the right side and left side—and within each part the density is obviously greater than the average. We will discuss partitioning a network into "natural" groups in chapter 4.

Density is at the heart of community, social support, and high visibility (when people in a network can see what others are doing and monitor and sanction their behavior). Density facilitates the transmission of ideas, rumors, and diseases. Other things being equal, the greater the density, the more likely is a network to be considered a cohesive community, a source of social support, and an effective transmitter. Classic agricultural communities or villages have greater density than modern cities, and people tend to know one another in many contexts—as relatives, coworkers, church attendees, and so forth. Given the human limitation on the number of sustainable connections, smaller networks will have greater density. It is easier to know everyone in a small group than in a large community. In comparing different networks in terms of density, one therefore has to take into account their size.

STRUCTURAL HOLES

Density is based on the idea of connection. But one can turn the idea on its head and focus on the *lack of a connection* (Burt 1992).

Consider the following network (figure 3.2), which I created to illustrate this point:

There are two obvious clusters: 5, 6, 7 and 2, 3, 4. Each cluster is totally connected, that is, each of their members is said to be structurally equivalent to each other. However, the members' only link to one another is "Ego." Ronald Burt calls the situation in which Ego connects individuals who are themselves connected but who, without the presence of Ego would have no connection with one another, a "structural hole." In the karate club sociogram, nodes 1 and 34 are the key linkers, and their actions are the least constrained by others in the network. The important implications of structural holes and the role of Ego as a "broker" will be considered in greater detail in chapter 5.

WEAK TIES

"The strength of weak ties" is the title of an article by Mark Granovetter (1973) that has achieved almost as much fame and certainly more citations than the more popularly known "small world" described by Stanley Milgram in his *Psychology Today* article (Milgram 1967).[2] Like structural holes, "weak ties" also focuses on holes in the network. The most authoritative statement of the idea is Granovetter's 1982 reprise:

> [O]ur acquaintances ("weak ties') are less likely to be socially involved with one another than are our close friends ("strong ties"). Thus the set of people made up of any individual and his or her acquaintances will constitute a low-density network (one in which many of the possible ties are absent), whereas the set consisting of the same individual and his or her *close* friends will be densely knit (many of the possible lines present).

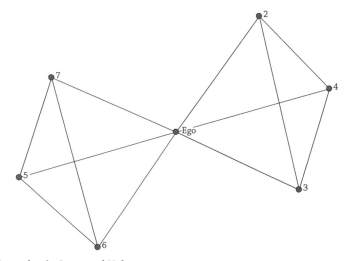

FIGURE 3.2 Example of a Structural Hole

...Ego will have a collection of close friends, most of whom are in touch with one another—a dense "clump" of social structure. Ego will [also] have a collection of acquaintances, few of whom know one another. Each of these acquaintances, however, is likely to have close friends in his or her own right and therefore to be enmeshed in a closely knit clump of social structure, but one different from Ego's... These clumps would not... be connected with one another at all were it not for the existence of weak ties. (Granovetter 1982, 105–106 [italics in original])

Weak ties have several interesting consequences (Granovetter 1982, 106). First, weak ties facilitate the flow of information from otherwise-distant parts of a network. Individuals with few weak ties will be deprived of information from distant parts of the social system and will be confined to the provincial news and views of their close friends.

Second, weak ties help to integrate social systems. The macroscopic side of this communication argument is that social systems lacking in weak ties will be fragmented and incoherent. New ideas will spread slowly, scientific endeavors will be handicapped, and subgroups that are separated by race, ethnicity, geography, or other characteristics will have difficulty reaching a modus vivendi.

There are various complications to the analysis of weak ties. First, the definition of what constitutes a weak tie or relationship can be somewhat slippery. Is it the length of time one knows someone else, the frequency of interaction, the subjective "closeness" one feels, or whether the others one is connected with are defined as relatives, friends, or acquaintances? Second, it is important to understand that the critical function of weak ties is one of bridges between network segments. As Granovetter puts it, "The importance of weak ties is asserted to be that they are disproportionately likely to be bridges as compared to strong ties, which should be underrepresented in that role. This does not preclude the possibility that most weak ties have no such function" (Granovetter 1982, 130). Third, it must be the case that "(1) something flows through these bridges—they actually serve as conduits bearing information and influence to groups they otherwise would not get, and (2) whatever it is that flows actually plays some important role in the social life of individuals, groups, and societies" (ibid.). A flow can occur only under some circumstances. Passing along information or exercising influence should not be too costly to the weak tie that constitutes the bridge; otherwise, strong ties that are willing to bear the cost will be more effective in making the bridge. For example, if a mere acquaintance knows about a job (the original context of Granovetter's study), and the acquaintance does not need the job himself or herself, then there is little cost in passing along the information. It would take a strong tie to pass along information that might cause a loss to the person passing it along.

"POPULARITY" OR CENTRALITY

Popularity can be broken down into several different ideas—all under the general rubric of "centrality" (Freeman 1979). It is obvious in the karate club that persons 1 and 34 have great centrality. Many lines radiate from them (or go to them, because friendship is reciprocal). The sheer number of connections is called "degree." Person 1 has a degree of 16 and person 34 a degree of 17. When the network is directed (not reciprocal), there is an indegree, number of "votes" received, and an outdegree, number of choices made. Almost all networks have nodes or persons with higher degrees than other members of the networks, whether the topic is friendship or corporate connections to banks.

An interesting variation on the focus on the number of votes is the source of the votes. A node is more popular or powerful if it receives nominations, or indegrees, from nodes that themselves have high degree. The individual or entity is popular among the popular. There are various measures of power or prominence that take this factor into account. In the karate club, while nodes 1 and 34 have the highest degree and the most power, nodes 3 and 33, because they receive nominations from 1 and 34 and others with high degree, also score fairly high on power.

An inspection of the network shows that 1 and 34 are in the middle of things. One can get to other members via these leaders. This is called "betweenness" (Freeman 1979). There are various methods for measuring betweenness, but all are based on the idea of a switching point. The person or organization that serves as a connector or a switching point can be very important, above and beyond their "popularity." In the structural hole diagram, Ego has high betweenness. In the karate club, although 16 and 34 each have almost the same degree, 1 has a higher betweenness score. Node 1 connects the cluster on the extreme left with the rest of the club, making node 1 a bridger or broker.

Centrality has many substantive implications. A classic series of experiments with networks of various shapes showed that "where centrality and hence, independence are evenly distributed, there will be no leader, many errors, high activity, slow organization, and high satisfaction" (Leavitt 1951, 50). On the other hand, when a network was shaped in a "wheel" pattern—so called because individual persons, the spokes, were coordinated by a central person—the organization was efficient, but only the person E in the center of figure 3.3 below had high satisfaction.

DISTANCE

Not only are there many direct connections in the karate club network, but also many indirect ones. For example, 17 is directly connected with 7 and indirectly connected through 7 and 6 to 1 in a second step. While the symmetric dyads and triads are by definition transitive (see chapter 2), it is not assumed that indirect connections, such as between 17 to 1, are transitive. That is, 17 is not necessarily a friend of 1 or 1 a friend of 17. That two-step connection is the shortest connection of 17 with 1. But also, because this is a dense network, 17 can get to 1 in three steps via 5 or via 11. All the nodes are eventually connected with one another through paths of various lengths. The longest path with direct connections is of length 5, and there are 16 of those. For example, 17 to 15: $17 \rightarrow 7 \rightarrow 1 \rightarrow 9 \rightarrow 33 \rightarrow 15$. This is a compact network whose average distance is 2.4 paths. Not so incidentally, the computer program that drew the network placed 17 and 15 at opposite sides of the diagram.

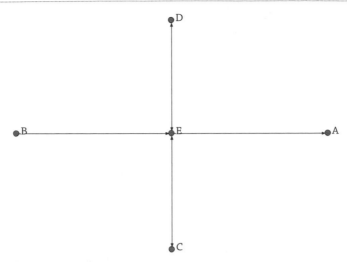

FIGURE 3.3 Example of a Wheel Pattern

Formally, the distance between two nodes is defined as the length of the shortest path via the edges or binary connections between nodes. This is called geodesic distance. Shortest paths are efficient, but there are also consequences to inefficient or redundant paths in which there are many ways to get from one node to another. Redundancy, as noted in connection with density, makes sense in the diffusion of norms, attitudes, or values. One might have to hear the same thing from several different sources until it takes root. Then too, in terms of diffusion, we might want to discount a source that is several steps removed because messages might get garbled as they pass from one node to another that is not transitive. So one might count the first step as important, the next step as less important, and so on. On the other hand, some things, such as computer viruses (not "social" in the human sense), spread unadulterated through many steps.

The set of nodes directly linked to any given node is called the first-order zone (Barnes 1972; Mitchell 1969). The nodes two steps removed from a focal node are called the second-order zone, and so on. When the first-order zone is about individual persons, the term "interpersonal environment" is often used (Rossi 1966; Wallace 1966). In graph theory, this is called the "neighborhood." As will be seen shortly, these interpersonal environments can vary considerably in their size. The friends of the friends in the first-order zone are reached in only two steps. If the first-order zone is large, then many friends of friends can be reached (one of the principles of Facebook). If the friends in the second-order zone are not the same ones as in the first-order zone, then Ego has a large reach indeed. Reach or connectedness (the famous "six degrees of separation") was studied by Milgram in his "small world" experiments (Milgram 1967).

Larger whole networks such as cities or communities would be ideal subjects for the study of distance, popularity, and density. However, we have not been successful in collecting large-scale network data that would make such an examination feasible. A possible alternative means of getting information about networks is to study members of the first-order zone of a sample of respondents through the use of "name generators" (Wellman 1993). This system produces ego-networks, that is, networks centered about a particular individual. In a widely utilized data set, the General Social Survey in 1985 asked respondents to name up to five others with whom they "discussed important matters." In these types of surveys, information about each of these "others" is sought from the survey respondent on such topics as how they came to know the other, for how long, some of the social attributes of the other, and the extent to which each of the others knew each of those named in the first-order zone (Marsden 2005, 1990). The study might include a number of different name generators, and more than five individuals might be pursued. Although this ego network might seem to be a limited application of network ideas, the data so generated has been extremely powerful and the source of a number of insights into social networks that will be referred to throughout this book. One can measure the density and the social characteristics of the ego's interpersonal environment, that is, the dyadic relationships between ego and each of the persons mentioned. One can also try separately to survey the persons mentioned in a "snowball" technique, thereby moving out a number of steps from ego.

Size of the Interpersonal Environment

The number of individuals in the interpersonal environment or the first-order zone varies from about 100 to 5,000 persons, depending on how it is measured (for example, people you know by name) and the type of society in which the focal person is embedded (Bernard et al. 1989; Killworth et al. 2006; Killworth et al. 1990; Pool and Kochen 1978; Zheng, Salganik, and Gelman 2006).

In general, as we will see, in classic village societies "everyone knows everyone else," so the number of steps from one person to any other is minimal. Village societies are also relatively small and confined so that the first-order zone may be no more than about 500 local persons (Boissevain 1974), thus limiting the number of persons who can be directly reached. In contemporary urban societies, professionals and middle-class people have a larger first-order zone than blue-collar and lower class people (Kadushin and Jones 1992). On the other hand, in these societies there may be serious barriers across class and ethnic lines, making for greater distances between persons in different classes and ethnicities (Wellman 1999a). The issue is a complex one and will be taken up later.

Organizations too have first-order, second-order, and tertiary zones, as suggested by the concept of external economy described in the previous chapter—those aspects of an organization that it relies upon to survive and thrive but which are not formally a part of the organization. The network of part suppliers for automobile manufacturers is part of their external economy, but so is the absorption of the costs of carbon emissions by the rest of society. These matters will be discussed when we come to organizations and overlapping circles.

The "Small World"

If there were no overlap in people's personal networks, then as we suggested in the Introduction, one could reach the entire population of the United States in two or three steps (Pool and Kochen 1978). Suppose everyone in the United States knew 500 other people and that each set of 500 was unique—none of the people you know are known by, say, your brother or sister. Then, each of the 500 people you know in turn knows 500 unique others, and they each know 500 others, and so on (Pool and Kochen 1978, 33). Five hundred people raised to the power of three is 12,500,000, much greater than the size of the U.S. adult population age 18 and over in 1977 (154,776,287).[3]

However, to the extent that the same people are encountered in the interpersonal environment of different nodes, that is, to the extent that personal networks overlap, more steps will be needed to reach the entire population of the United States. Under such circumstances, getting out of one's immediate circle becomes more difficult. Social structure, as Pool and Kochen demonstrated, reduces the number of unique individuals in the iteration of steps; and therefore, the expansion to a large population takes more steps or links. For example, it is more difficult for whites to reach African Americans. This topic will be analyzed when we discuss social circles of individuals.

Despite the theoretical number of two to three steps between any two persons in the United States, experiments done by Stanley Milgram and his students in the 1960s estimated the actual number of steps to be six, reached through five intervening persons (Milgram 1969, 1967; Travers and Milgram 1969), hence the popular phrase, "six degrees of separation."

The alleged "six degrees of separation" does not, however, take account of variation in people's skills at making connections. In Milgram's original experiments, most people were not able or were unwilling to make the requested connections. A recent experiment using the internet found that few of the chains were actually completed and concluded that, although in principle people were connected, the actual successes depended on their motivations and incentives (Dodds, Muhamad, and Watts 2003).

In Milgram's experiments, people were asked to reach a target person in a distant city by means of a person most likely to know the target person on a first-name basis. The experiment worked like a chain letter. The number of steps was higher than the theoretical number because there were social structural barriers to network linkages. In the first experiment, Milgram reported that links between men and women were much less frequent than same-sex linkages, a finding repeated in the recent experiment. Similarly, there were barriers between social classes. Hence, personal agency or motivation became a factor in establishing linkages. Organizations, too, vary in the extent to which they actively seek to relate to other organizations and are skilled in this endeavor.

Multiplexity

Thus far, only single-stranded ties have been formally considered, though we have given some examples of multiple connections. The members of the karate club had more than one kind of relationship with one another. That is, their relationships were multiplex. The members could relate to one another in eight different contexts such as going to the same classes or hanging out together in a bar across the street from the campus (Zachary 1977, 461). The karate club network depicted earlier reported any relationship originating in any one of the eight settings. The density of the network based on any one relationship would obviously be less than shown above.

In most situations, there are multiple connections between nodes. Multiplexity is related to the concept of homophily discussed in chapter 2, for the bundling of particular kinds of ties is hardly random and follows the laws of homophily of position that we have already discussed. Multiplexity has been used in the network literature in two related senses: one, sometimes called role multiplexity (Beggs, Haines, and Hurlbert 1996), refers to the possibility that two nodes occupy more than one position that ties them together, typically, the situation described earlier in which two nodes have an organizational relationship, say "supervisor" and "assistant" (to the supervisor), but are also friends. Classically, this occurs in village societies in which people are simultaneously kin, workers on the same farm, members of the same religious cult, and the host of shifting roles common to village economies in which tasks are largely filled by part-time specialists in which the blacksmith may also be the head of a clan, the godfather to a number of persons, and a local intellectual sage. Boissevain offers this proposition: "Because the activity fields in this small community overlap and the same actors play different roles to the same audience, we may also expect high multiplexity" (Boissevain 1974, 72). In complex non-village societies, roles may become bundled in a somewhat different way. Merton calls attention to "role sets," the set of relationships that ensue because one occupies a given role (what he calls status), an idea that Rose Coser further elaborates (Coser 1975; Merton 1968b). A school teacher relates to students, parents, a school administrator, the Board of Education, and so on. This is the role set that goes with the status of teacher. This role set can of course be analyzed using the formal tools of network analysis, especially those that work with "ego networks." They may or may not also be multiplexed networks.

The second sense refers to the possibility that, as a result of having a given role relationship, say "coworker," there are a number of different flows between a pair of persons, for example, advice, friendship, and work on common tasks (Lazega and Pattison 1999). This has been called "content multiplexity" (Beggs, Haines, and Hurlbert 1996). Further, the same tie, for example advice, can have a number of different kinds of ideas flowing through it: a solution to a problem, a reformulation of the problem, information about solutions to the problem, reaffirmation of an already identified solution, and the credibility of a proposed solution (Cross, Borgatti, and Parker 2001). Attention here is directed to the different consequences of these multiple flows and how they link or conflict under different circumstances.

The concept of multiplexity has an important place in sociological theory. First, as we have alluded to, other things being equal, multiplexity is arguably an important indicator of the presence of folk or village society forms of organization and even rural-urban difference in modern America.[4] Whether intimate ties can be sustained despite the decline of multiplexity is at the heart of network research that inquires into the relational health of people that live in modern urban settings (See, for example, Wellman and Haythornthwaite 2002; Wellman et al. 2001; Wellman 1999a, 1979).

Second, given the multiple bases upon which relationships can be formed within a community, multiplexity has an important role in theorizing about economic forms. Padgett shows that over two centuries (1300 to 1500) in Florence, the birthplace of financial capitalism, commercial banking firms were formed on four distinct bases: first on the basis of family and patrilineage, next on the basis of guilds, then on the basis of social class, and in the last period, on the basis of patronage (Padgett 2001; Padgett and Ansell 1993). The extent that access and trust are available to bolster economic relations is a consequence of multiplex relationships of different types. For example, ethnic enclaves have been shown to be advantageous to certain kinds of ethnic businesses in part because of the multiplexity of relationships (Portes and Sensenbrenner 1993). Trust, so established by virtue of the ethnic tie, also has global aspects (Tilly 2007). The effect of ethnic enclaves on labor market outcomes, however, is greater for less skilled workers than for professionals (Edin, Fredriksson, and Åslund 2003). Trust among the French financial elite was bolstered by multiplex relations of party, neighborhood, and friendship (Kadushin 1995).

Third, a very substantial proportion of the literature on organizations is concerned with the relationship between ties based on formal positions in the organization and those based on informal relationships discussed earlier. The consequences of formal and informal modes of relations within organizations hinges on the how these multiplex relations are construed in different settings. Informal relations were first identified as loyalties that impeded production (Homans 1950). Others have found informal relations augment formal relations by facilitating the accomplishment of various tasks (Lazega and Pattison 1999). There can be complex relations between formal and informal relations that encourage mentoring or prevent the acquisition of values appropriate to a given organizational role (Podolny and Baron 1997).

While multiplex relations can be described qualitatively and discursively, and one can often get an intuitive sense of what is involved in multiple relations, more precise characterizations of the consequences and causes of different permutations of ties has proven to be a difficult task. The possible combinations of ties can be quite daunting, and the factors that lead to one sort of tie may not have the same force on another type of tie.[5]

In theory there can be two opposite consequences of multiplexity. Multiple flows between positions as well as multiple simultaneous positions can enhance a relationship and build trust, for example, friendship between supervisor and assistant or between political leaders. On the other hand, depending on the circumstances, the same friendship can create a conflict of interest or even the possibility of fraud (Baker and Falkner 1993). Obviously, much depends on the context, and the context can be structural or cultural or both. Merton's role set theory concentrates on the possible negative consequences of multiple role relations and suggests various ways conflict can be managed or alleviated. But the difficulty of quantitatively testing hypotheses on multiplexity has limited formal theorizing in this extremely interesting field.

Roles and Positions

Thus far, we have developed concepts that involve a distribution of network attributes, such as density or distance, and some of the consequences of these distributions. There is another aspect of whole networks: the type of relationship between nodes. Let us call this relationship a role or a position. There is a classic literature in sociology and anthropology about positions and roles (for example, Linton 1936; Parsons 1951; Merton 1968b), and there are network analogues and equivalents.

In interpersonal environments, there are basically two kinds of relationships. First, there are those that are ordained by the social system with very specific names, typically kinship names such as mother, father, children, aunts, uncles, and cousins, or organizational positions such as boss-worker. These relationships are typically asymmetric. Second, there are those relationships that are more loosely and generically named friend, neighbor, acquaintance, or coworker and are more typically symmetric. The network properties of each named relationship, as opposed to generic relationships, are quite dissimilar and have been studied in very different ways. But both types of relationships lead to puzzles and surprises.

NAMED POSITIONS AND RELATIONSHIPS

As we know, networks always involve at minimum two nodes or positions and a relationship between them. Although this may be confusing, the concept of "role" is often used both for the position as well as for the relationship between positions.[6] Named roles, especially kinship relationships such as "father," generally specify not only the meaning of the position but also the content of the relationship, that is, the mutual obligations and expected behaviors of "father" to other named positions such as "son." Not only do named roles indicate the expected relations with other roles, but also the patterning of other relationships—the expected network past the first-order zone: "Primary roles can be cumulated into chains defining compound roles; for example, the sister of my father's father and the subordinate of my boss' protégée" (White 1963, 1). The logical complications of kin relationships can be quite complex, and formal network mathematics can help to specify the implications of such matters as bilateral cross-cousin marriages in which "one's wife is also both Mother's Brother's and Father's Sister's Daughter" (White 1963, 17). Anthropologists have tended to gather networks of named relationships in almost all of their fieldwork, in part because they can do so with only a limited knowledge of the local language. It is one matter to gather the data about the relationships, and another to understand their implications, as controversies in the literature about the causes and consequences of cross-cousin marriage suggest (Homans and Schneider 1955; Lévi-Strauss 1969; Needham 1962). Named relations are of course far from being the whole story, for anthropologists have gathered massive data about the official names of the positions, but not necessarily systematic data about the actual relationships between the positions.

INFORMAL POSITIONS AND RELATIONSHIPS

We will not enter into the details of kinship analysis and the predictions that can be developed from using network analysis to describe kinship structures mathematically. But the principle illustrated by kinship is the association, or lack of it, between formal named and instituted relationships and those that are "informal" or unanticipated. More generally, almost all network analysis involves at some point comparing the network mandated by culture and the social system to networks created and negotiated by people in the process of trying to manage and work the "system." The so-called "formal system" is contrasted and compared with the "informal system." There are those social scientists who feel this distinction is unwarranted, that everything is negotiated and the relationships and mapping between relationships are entirely created through the process of living. To take this extreme point of view is to deny the weight of tradition and habit, but most of all, to deny that concepts and names have consequences with which people daily struggle.

In *Crime and Custom in Savage Society*, Malinowski (1959 [1926], 70–84) gives a poignant example of the problems of a young man who wanted to marry a woman who was, according to kinship rules, forbidden to him. Because Malinowski spent all of World War I in the Trobriand Islands, and therefore had considerable time to observe the local population, he was able to compare the rules to the way they were actually carried out. "...I found the breach of exogamy—as regards intercourse not marriage—is by no means a rare occurrence, and public opinion is lenient, though decidedly hypocritical" (ibid., 80). While Malinowski observed many examples of the breach of exogamy and "[m]ost of my informants would not only admit but actually did boast about having committed this offence or that of adultery..." this was true only of intercourse not marriage. He was aware of "only two or three cases of marriage within the clan." Nonetheless, these violations did exist.

Informal relations are thus not independent of formally defined or culturally named positions. The informal exists in reference to, or even in opposition to, the formal relationships. It is as if the non-prescribed paths or relationships or exchanges are "draped" upon a scaffolding of the formal relationships. The instituted or prescribed relations are always in some way, even negatively, "taken into account." A good example is formal hierarchy, a feature endemic to organized society.

Informal Relations and Hierarchies

There are network equivalents to power or status positions. Hierarchy in networks can be seen as a transitive tree or pyramid structure as in figure 3.4 below.

The relationships are transitive in a power structure because A can command or instruct B who can command F. A's command of B is binding on F. They are asymmetric because B cannot command or instruct A. The inequality of the three levels in the pyramid—A, B, C, D; and F, E, H, I, J—is exogenous or external to the network (Martin 2009, chapter 6). The inequality may stem from the organization's rules or structure, from a social class system or some other system of ranking. The tree structure as depicted has no horizontal connections—B, C, and D, for example, are not connected,

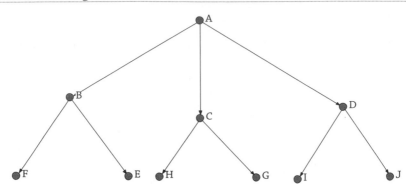

FIGURE 3.4 Example of a Pyramid Structure

and we have shown no other networks in which B, C, and D might also participate. In real-world networks, there are often horizontal connections so that rank or status can "leak" or flow by the principle of homophily—a node can acquire the prestige of those she or he hangs out with, as any social climber knows (Podolny 2005, chapter 2).

Further, in real-world trees there may not be symmetry of command, but there may be symmetry of information because information may flow up and down the levels. Figure 3.4 would look different if information flowed up and down: we would draw arrows at both ends of the lines connecting the nodes.

But formal hierarchy is often not the whole story. In a large manufacturing organization I observed, there were formal hierarchical relationships that defined the positions in the organization—the "organizational chart" similar to the stylized hierarchical chart shown above. When critical decisions were made, individuals often "skipped levels" and enlisted support above the level of their immediate superior. True, this is an "informal system" for making decisions. But the person chosen as the one higher in rank than the one supposedly entrusted with the decision was hardly picked at random. The choice could be predicted from the organizational structure—it did not follow directly from the "rule book" but was surely related to it. Which brings us to the issue of embeddedness.

EMBEDDEDNESS OF THE INFORMAL WITHIN INSTITUTED OR NAMED NETWORKS

All enacted relationships or networks are embedded within formal arrangements. Embeddedness means a number of different things to different students of networks. All agree, however, that networks are influenced by and related to cultural and social structural frameworks. And the converse holds true as well. Information and ideas are affected not only by relations between pairs, but are also responsive to being part of dense networks that amplify and transmit the ideas and the information.

A good example of embeddedness is the constant struggle to determine how power in America actually works. In American national politics, channels for creating legislation are prescribed by law. But certain committee members and lobbyists count for more than others and are the ones who critically determine what a new law is likely to look like. One needs to study all these systems carefully—the kinship, the organizational, and the national legislature—to uncover the informal connections. Nonetheless, these connections are related to the mandates and functions of the formal institutional structure that the informal one elaborates. This is an obvious point, but one which is often neglected when we become entranced by the continuous reenactment and creation of structures.

OBSERVED ROLES

Anthropologists distinguish "emic" and "etic" concepts. Emic ideas are those that "insiders" to a culture use, and "etic" ideas or concepts are those that observers impute to the culture or find useful in describing it.[7] Unnamed positions or roles are those that observers ascribe to a structure which may or may not be so described and noted by the "natives." A "leader" found through network analysis may or may not be recognized as such by the members of the network. The relationships between the individuals and the central role played by the coordinating figure in the "wheel" communications structure described earlier were imposed by the design of the experiment. Yet in the wheel configuration, most experimental subjects, when asked about "the organization of your group," were able to describe it. On the other hand, subjects in other configurations were not able to do so (Leavitt 1951). There is an important literature in the network field that refers to "roles," as discovered through network analysis methods that create partitions of whole networks (White, Boorman, and Breiger 1976). But these partitions are not necessarily defined as normative named roles by the participants in the network. Positions that have "structural similarity," as discovered through network analysis, can be described as occupying a role or a status, though this may not be so noticed or conceptualized by participants in the structure.[8] Partitioning whole networks is a complex topic with many ramifications that will be presented in the next chapter.

Whether or not the roles are emic or etic does, however, have important consequences.

Roles, statuses, or positions that have names are much more likely to have a longer life than roles or positions that have been ascribed to a structure as a result of network analyses. Persons in an organization who occupy a position discovered through network analysis that allows them "structural autonomy"—that is, the ability to act as brokers between persons who otherwise would not be linked (see the karate club example, above)—are not very likely to hold that position a year later (Burt 2002). In contrast, a person who holds a named position is more likely to continue in that position.

To summarize the matter of positions and roles. Network relations can be prescribed by values, organization, and institutions. Often, when relations are prescribed, they are given a name. Relational names are very important in predicting the forms that networks take. But the prescribed relations are only part of the story, since relationships are further elaborated on the base of the prescribed. Under many conditions, the elaborations become instituted and so become prescribed, and another round of elaboration begins. Since most people know the prescriptions, one "charm" of network analysis occurs when the additional elaborated relationships are revealed. But these revelations are only part of the story. Even the prescribed relationships are sufficiently complex so that participants in society see only the relationships that immediately surround them in the first-order zone and are rarely aware of the implications of second-order zones. Participants are unable to visualize, much less model, the entire system. Networks have been compared with traffic jams—you can see the cars that surround you, but it takes a helicopter to get above the mess and see the entire picture.

Summary

This was our first systematic encounter with the essential subject matter of the book—complete social networks. We began with a small network taken from real life observations—a karate club. We first analyzed it with the help of concepts from the previous chapter: dyads and triads. Besides those concepts, we needed the help of computer programs to draw the sociogram and to carry out the analyses. As one would expect, the club was more "social," cohesive, and clustered than a random network. We knew this because the computer program showed that there were more symmetric dyads and triads (the 300 type in figure 2 in chapter 2) than would have occurred by chance. This was a compact network; the average distance traced from one member to another was only 2.4. And it was a dense network, especially in the two segments of the network. Some members were clearly more popular and better connected than others. The concept of centrality captured the notion of "popularity." Who is "fairest of them all" can be indicated by degree (the number of "votes" a person obtains); power (the number of votes from those who are popular); and betweenness (acting as a switching point between members of the network). The network was dense because it was based on multiplex relations—members encountered one another in a number of different settings because they were part of a community, and communities are characterized by multi-stranded relationships. In fact, multiplex relationships may be one of the hallmarks of traditional communities. Modern societies and large networks in general are less dense and have structural holes, more dense parts of a network that are hardly connected at all; if connected, then it is by nodes that serve as brokers between the otherwise barely connected regions. Large modern world networks are held together by weak ties—relationships that are infrequent, less close and less intimate, but for that very reason very important. Flows through networks are critical and can take place through redundant dense ties or through weak ties.

We considered the number of steps or zones that radiate out of the first-order zone, the area that directly surrounds an individual. This concept leads to the small world idea in which everyone is somehow connected. The number of steps it takes to reach everyone depends on the number of persons in the first-order zone, and the extent to which persons past the first-order zone overlap with others. If there were no overlap, the entire population of the United States could be reached somewhere between two and three steps. As it is, social structure creates barriers so that the number of steps can be far greater.

Positions are a key idea in whole networks. Positions can be socially defined statuses, such as father, son, president, or positions can be defined by the observer through network analysis. Both are often called "roles." Instituted or socially defined statuses themselves form networks; they are generally elaborated upon by informal networks. Positions are sometimes arranged in a hierarchy or a tree. The rules for these hierarchies are generally created by the social system in which they are embedded, though further informal interaction can alter the hierarchies and the rules.

We now turn to the issue of network segmentation, a topic that surfaced earlier in our karate club example.

4 Basic Network Concepts, Part III
NETWORK SEGMENTATION

Introduction

Until this point, we have discussed whole networks in terms of their relationship to key network concepts such as density, centrality, and position. We learned that whole networks are held together as much by weak ties as they are by strong connections. One key idea is flow through networks. But we have thus far assumed that networks are in principle unbounded—that at least potentially, everything is connected with everything else. If the small world hypothesis has any validity, then in principle the entire world is connected as a network. True enough, but not practical. We cannot really understand social networks by looking at the entire world. Nations, communities, organizations, classrooms, even if connected with one another, have boundaries. What is true about one entity may not be true of another. We can look at institutional-sector networks such as the networks of banks and see that there are different clusters of banks and that they have clustered relationships with corporations (Eccles and Crane 1988; Mizruchi and Schwartz 1987). If we examine systems of government, the networks that compose them are clearly segmented and clustered (Higley et al. 1991; Laumann and Knoke 1987). In short, people, organizations, institutions, countries—any social unit one can imagine—are not uniformly related to one another but tend to come clustered into groups or sets. Furthermore, networks such as trade, diplomatic relations, and airline connections cross national boundaries. Every organization has relations with other organizations. Classrooms have relations that extend beyond the particular class (Moody 2001). One of the major tasks of network theory and analysis therefore is to develop ways of describing and analyzing these clusters or groups and to separate whole networks into smaller meaningful segments. An influential article even claimed "that the presently existing, largely categorical descriptions of social structure have no solid theoretical grounding; furthermore, network concepts may provide the only way to construct a theory of social structure" (White, Boorman, and Breiger 1976, 732).

We begin by noting that there are networks that correspond to names given by the participants in the network, the "emic" networks. A club with a name, a bank, and a trade association are emic networks. The folk concept of a clique is another example of a network named by participants. High school students, for example, will talk about a set of girls that constitutes a clique, though the clique may not have a formal name. It will turn out, however, that cliques as mathematically understood have serious limitations as useful ways of partitioning networks.

We will discuss formal network methods for partitioning networks. This is an ongoing topic that has attracted physicists, mathematicians, computer scientists, as well as social scientists. Testifying that this remains a frontier of network analysis, there are at least ten different methods and algorithms[1] that have been advanced in just the last five years or so, and each has strong advocates. Not surprisingly, we favor methods that have more intuitive social science resonance and have proved useful in the analysis of social network data. We will reproduce the karate club example from the last chapter to illustrate two of the partitioning methods.

We will complete this introduction to network partitioning with the most straightforward type of partition—"core and periphery." All are familiar from our school days with the idea of the "leading crowd," or core, and the periphery, the rest of us. There are other patterns for core and periphery as well.

Named and Unnamed Network Segments

As with network position, there are emic and etic clusters or groups. It will be recalled that emic positions are those that are named by participants in the culture and social system, for example, teacher, president, and father are examples, whereas etic positions are those that are found by network analysts and observers, for example, "high centrality." Emic groups are named and recognized by the "natives." These can range from a club or gang with a name such as "Hell's Angels," to a corporation such as "General Electric," or a legal government entity such as "New York State." A group or cluster has "members." That is, there are individuals who are members of Hell's Angels or General Electric, and organizations or groups who are members of "GE," such as "GE Capital." First, with respect to named groups, members know that they are members of the group; and second, others know that they are members of the group and can identify them as such. There is a third attribute to membership in an emic group that is generally but not always true: members interact with one another more than they interact with non-members. In contrast with emic groups, etic segments of a network are those that are identified by observers. Examples are the "C's"[2]: clusters, cliques, clacks, circles, cabals, (but not clubs—they are emic), coalitions, and also some non-"C's" such as "group" and "block."

Generally, the boundaries of these structures are not firmly established and are the product of the observer's analysis. Even cliques, in popular language, are often fluid entities whose membership may be a matter of disagreement. The interplay between the formally named entities and the observed unnamed clusters is the subject of much network analysis demonstrating how informal groups within formal organizations either grease the wheels of the organization, act as impediments to the organization achieving its goals, or both. We will have much more on this topic in the chapters that follow. In the meantime, we introduce the problem of network segmentation and partitioning through a brief discussion of "primary groups" and cliques.

PRIMARY GROUPS, CLIQUES, AND CLUSTERS

The concept of primary group was introduced by Charles Cooley in 1909:

> By primary groups I mean those characterized by intimate face-to-face association and cooperation. They are primary in several senses, but chiefly in that they are fundamental in forming the social nature and ideals of the individual. The result of intimate association, psychologically, is a certain fusion of individualities in a common whole, so that one's very self, for many purposes at least, is the common life and purpose of the group. Perhaps the simplest way of describing this wholeness is by saying that it is a "we"; it involves the sort of sympathy and mutual identification for which "we" is the natural expression. One lives in the feeling of the whole and finds the chief aims of his will in that feeling. (Cooley 1909, 23)

Cooley notes that members of a primary group identify themselves with it. Nonetheless, the concept is a construct of the observer and not of people themselves.

Clusters, a formal term, have some of the structured characteristics of named groups or organizations, and there may be a clear hierarchy of positions within the cluster. In most formal analyses, clusters do not overlap. That is, a node cannot simultaneously be a member of two clusters, though we will consider overlapping clusters below.

Large-scale social network patterns and clusters are inherently messy matters unless there is a formal intervention that prescribes patterns of relationships and hierarchies, as found in the typical formal organization or corporate structure. Even these are "ideal" patterns best described on organizational charts that few within the organization actually pay attention to. More often than not, when members of an organization are queried about the formal organizational chart, they respond by saying, "What chart?" We will take up some of these complexities in the chapter on organizations.

Segmenting Networks from the Point of View of the Observer

Most of the work on partitioning and segmenting networks has been done from the point of view of the observer or network analyst. The aim is to take what appear to be continuous networks and break them down into more meaningful units for analysis. There are two "master ideas" or principles about social relations in networks. One is the principle of cohesiveness or "closure" and the other is that of reaching out to others or "structural similarity." We will have more to say about these ideas in the next chapter on psychological foundations, but here we will use them to partition networks.

SEGMENTING NETWORKS ON THE BASIS OF COHESION

Cohesiveness defines "cliques." Although clique is a term of everyday language, it also has a mathematical definition—a maximal complete subgraph of three or more nodes (Luce and Perry 1949). In a maximal complete subgraph all members of the graph "choose" or are linked to one another (Wasserman and Faust 1997, 254). In clique interaction, since all persons interact with one another, the persons can not be distinguished from one another (Martin 2009, 29). They are mathematically equivalent to one another. While a neat and clear definition, this imposes too high a standard. The volume of mutuality in relationships is simply too great to sustain in real life. This designation also means that a person can be a member of only one clique: membership in two cliques would require that all the relationships be mutual and result in the collapse of the two into a single clique. The idea is obvious in the following graph (figure 4.1).

Each of these five-person cliques is totally connected and mutual. But no one can be a member of the other clique without all ten being connected and mutual.

Originally defined as total direct connectivity, the maximal complete subgraph can be relaxed to include indirect connections with one or more steps or links between nodes (Alba 1973; Mokken 1979), but these methods have not been entirely satisfactory. The large number of maximal complete subgraphs generated leaves one with the problem of how further to cluster them. Oddly, satisfying both criteria simultaneously—more internal connections and fewer external ones—is not easy to accomplish. Identifying cliques in this sense is difficult or impossible to achieve with a network algorithm that works under all circumstances (Kleinberg 2003), though there have been several interesting attempts to do so (Frank and Yasumoto 1998).

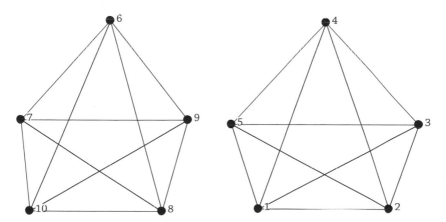

FIGURE 4.1 Two Totally Connected and Mutual Five Person Cliques

Recently, mathematicians and physicists have developed algorithms for creating clusters in large graphs based on "modularity." The idea is to compare the number of within "community" or group connections (edges, in graph theory terminology) with the number in some equivalent randomized network which has no community structure (Newman 2006a, 2006b; Newman and Girvan 2004; Girvan and Newman 2002). Newman successively splits networks into two separate "communities" using statistical criteria, such that the number of edges or connections between nodes in a community is greater than the number expected by chance alone. Since the network is successively split, the clusters or communities so created are hierarchical, that is, located in a nested tree or divisional structure. Other than a smaller community also being a part of a larger one in a tree structure (as Chevrolet is a part of General Motors), there is no overlap between communities. A member can be a member of one community only. If the statistical conditions cannot be met, this approach will "refuse" to further split a network.[3]

The lack of overlap creates a problem. Overlap of groups or communities is a common-sense sociological view but antithetical to most algorithms that attempt modularity. In real life, social circles (Kadushin 1966) tend to overlap, forming an essential aspect of urban social systems, as Simmel observed long before there were formal algorithms to define circles and cliques (Simmel 1955 [1922]). On the other hand, since almost all statistics are based on the idea that a unit of analysis is independent of other units, cutting up large networks into separate non-overlapping pieces for analysis is very useful for statistical analysis.

RESISTANCE TO DISRUPTION

White and Harary (2001) utilize the sociological concept of group cohesion. In a further elaboration (Moody and White 2003, 106) observe, "A collectivity is structurally cohesive to the extent that the social relations of its members hold it together." Furthermore, "A group is structurally cohesive to the extent that multiple independent relational paths among all pairs of members hold it together . . . The strongest cohesive groups are those in which every person is directly connected to every other person (cliques), though this level of cohesion is rarely observed except in small primary groups." The cohesiveness of a group can be gauged by looking at two processes that are the obverse of one another. First, a group is cohesive to the extent that the members are pulled together when confronted with disruptive forces. On the other hand, cohesiveness can be estimated by seeing what happens to the disconnectedness of a group when one or more members (nodes) are removed or, keeping the same number of nodes, when one or more paths or connections between the members or nodes are removed. The former is called cohesion and the latter adhesion. These two measures are equivalent. It is obvious to the naked eye that in the karate club example, the removal of "T" or "A" or the connections to them would disrupt the group. Other disruptions may be more subtle and require a computer algorithm to find them. Interestingly, a group may have low density of relations between its members and be relatively resistant to disruption, while an equally dense group may be less resistant to disruption, less cohesive in these terms. Especially interesting is the possibility that there are groups with sparse connectedness that can actually be quite cohesive in terms of their resistance to forces that would break them up. The method creates nested hierarchical trees but also allows for overlaps between groups within those trees.

The karate club introduced in the previous chapter on whole networks is an example of the method applied to some familiar data. The case illustrates how groups can be disrupted and helps to explain why and how the club fell apart. I reproduce that graph here (figure 4.2). The clusters are indicated by nodes colored black or grey.

When the club split, those closest to leader T (the karate teacher, node 1) followed him, and those closest to A (the administrator, node 34) followed him. Detailed analysis shows that a few members were on the fence, and one could not predict which faction they might join. It is evident that in a real situation such as this one, there are overlapping cohesive groups that have some degree of ties to one another but are nevertheless more aligned with one faction than the other. Individuals aligned themselves with the leaders with whom they had the most cohesion. Members 1–8, 11–14, 18, 20, and 22 followed T; members 9, 15, 16, 21, and 23–34 followed A; and 17, 10, and 19 belonged to neither faction (White and Harary 2001, table 4.6). The Girvan-Newman algorithm described above produces a very similar picture, but does not allow for overlap.

STRUCTURAL SIMILARITY AND STRUCTURAL EQUIVALENCE

The other way of partitioning or segmenting networks utilizes the master idea of reaching out to other nodes and examining the pattern of a node's relations with the *other*

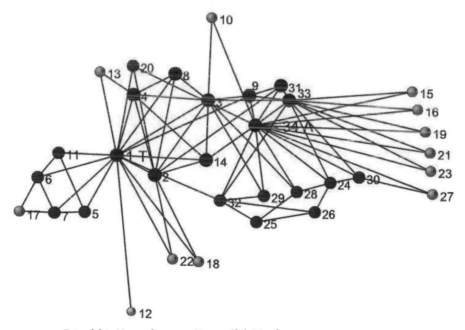

FIGURE 4.2 Friendship Network among Karate Club Members

White, Douglas R., and Frank Harary. 2001. The cohesiveness of blocks in social networks: Node connectivity and conditional density. *Sociological Methodology* 31:305–359, figure 14. Copyright © 2001 John Wiley and Sons, reprinted by permission.

nodes in the network, rather than looking for cohesion in terms of relations *between* the nodes. Nodes that have similar patterns of relationships with other nodes are grouped together. This idea is called structural similarity (Burt 1992; Borgatti and Everett 1992). Managers may have similar patterns in their relations to employees in their units. Structural equivalence, a more strict formulation, is defined as nodes that are connected to the *same* other nodes in *identical* ways. To be structurally equivalent, two managers would have to have the same relationships to the same employees, an unlikely situation. Since identical relations are relatively infrequent, there are ways of modeling "ideal" patterns and then assessing how well these patterns fit the data (Doreian, Batagelj, and Ferligoj 2005) or how similar they are (Breiger, Boorman, and Arabie 1975). The method was first developed by White, Boorman, and Breiger (1976) and was called "blockmodeling." Blockmodels partition networks into non-overlapping segments—an advantage or a disadvantage depending on what one is trying to do. The modeling aspect comes from the fact that blocks so constructed are abstractions from the data and can be algebraically manipulated.[4] Clusters or blocks can be represented by a matrix of 1's and 0's. In the following example (table4.1), there are two blocks, A and B, each consisting of a number of nodes. The 1's represent the presence of a relationship; the 0's the absence of a relationship. The tables are read in terms of the rows relating to the columns. In the first row, block A relates to block A and to block B. In the second row, B relates to A but not to itself. Remember, these are not individual nodes, but clusters of nodes.[5]

This core/periphery model to which we now turn has wide applications in social science. Relationships can be read by moving across the rows. The nodes within block A relate to one another and to block B. The nodes within block B do not relate to one another but do relate to block A.

Core/Periphery Structures

Core/periphery structures are the simplest forms of network segmentation. The reason core/periphery structures are so familiar to us is that we have all experienced them, starting from our days in a playground. There were kids who were on the inside while others were on the outside. This patterning continues through grade school, high school, and, dare I say, throughout life.[6] However, even in this apparently simple structure, there are different patterns to explore.

Consider the following example of a symmetrical network (figure 4.3), adapted from Borgatti and Everett (1999)

TABLE 4.1

Example of a Blockmodel

	A	B
A	1	1
B	1	0

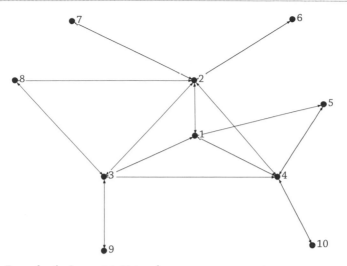

FIGURE 4.3 Example of a Symmetric Network

The adjacency matrix, table 4.2 below (an adjacency matrix shows which node relates to which other nodes, hence "adjacency"; see chapter 2), also adapted from Borgatti and Everett (1999) is exactly equivalent to figure 4.3 above. If the intersection of the row and the column depict a relationship, the adjacency matrix (table 4.2) has a "1"; the matrix has a "0" if there is none. In the matrix below, 1 is related to nodes 2 through 5 but not to nodes 6 through 10. This matrix, like the figure above, is symmetric. One could get the same information from either the upper or lower half of the matrix, when it is split along the main diagonal. In this matrix, nodes are not related to themselves, so the diagonal is blank. It is possible, however, to define a relationship with oneself, though at present we are not considering this possibility.

In terms of blockmodels (table 4.3, below), nodes 1, 2, 3, 4 can be abstracted as block A, and nodes 5, 6, 7, 8, 9, 10 abstracted as block B. The blocks' abstract relationship to one another is depicted as the core/periphery model encountered above.

Not every B is related to every A, though none of the B's are related to one another. This particular core/elite model assumes that the core and the periphery have some mutual relationship, but generally on terms dictated by the core. The core obviously has the most to offer, since we see that the periphery does not relate to itself. Along with studies of national and community elites (Laumann and Pappi 1976; Laumann and Knoke 1987; Higley et al. 1991), there are studies of interlocking directorates that show a core (Mintz and Schwartz 1985), studies of world systems that utilize a network approach to show an economic core (Snyder and Kick 1979), and organization studies that show a core leadership (Faulkner 1980). The concept of core/periphery has an important place in studies of rates of currency exchange between countries, as well as studies of migration and the diffusion of ideas and knowledge. While the general idea is clear, Borgatti and Everett note: "Given its wide currency, it comes as a bit of a surprise that the notion of a core/periphery structure has never been formally defined. The lack of definition means that different

TABLE 4.2

Blocked Adjacency Matrix

	1	2	3	4		5	6	7	8	9	10	
1			1	1	1		1	0	0	0	0	0	
2		1		1	1		0	1	1	1	0	0	
3		1	1		1		0	0	0	1	1	0	
4		1	1	1			1	0	0	0	0	1	
5		1	0	0	1			0	0	0	0	0	
6		0	1	0	0		0		0	0	0	0	
7		0	1	0	0		0	0		0	0	0	
8		0	1	1	0		0	0	0		0	0	
9		0	0	1	0		0	0	0	0		0	
10		0	0	0	1		0	0	0	0	0		

TABLE 4.3

Core/Periphery

	A	B
A	1	1
B	1	0

authors can use the term in wildly different ways, making it difficult to compare otherwise comparable studies" (Borgatti and Everett 1999, 375).

But even this simple idea can be elaborated. There are several other kinds of elite cores.[7] There is a "caucus" type of core. Breiger (1979) suggests that this type of cluster can be applied to the community power literature. Those active in block A "run" the community and do not pay much attention to the others who do not have political relationships (though they might have other kinds of relationships) with each other or with the core. The core does not take account of the periphery, and the periphery has no relationship with the core or with others. The block model, table 4.4 below depicts a caucus.

If we consider directed graphs, those that are not necessarily symmetrical, then we can have the Groucho Marx situation as in his famous line, "I sent the club [the Friars Club] a wire stating, 'Please accept my resignation. I don't want to belong to any club that will accept me as a member'" (Marx 1959, 321). Block A relates to A, B relates to A, but A does not relate to B nor does B relate to itself (table 4.5).

TABLE 4.4

	Caucus	
	A	B
A	1	0
B	0	0

TABLE 4.5

	Groucho Marx Core	
	A	B
A	1	0
B	1	0

More generally, this is a diffusion model from a core: The core has what other nodes want, so they look to it. Unlike a trading situation, the core does not want anything from the periphery. The relation is not symmetric.

There can be a situation, shown in table 4.6 in which A remains the elite in that A relates only to other A's, but B also has some density of relating to other B's, and also to A. Breiger calls this situation one of "deference." A wants nothing from B, but the B's have something to offer to one another.

To complete the logic of core/periphery, there can be the following kind of relationships (table 4.7), in which the last come first and "the meek inherit the earth."

This simply turns the caucus or the elite core blockmodel on its head, assuming that the B block has fewer power attributes. We suspect that in reality this model is largely empirically absent.

TABLE 4.6

	Deference	
	A	B
A	1	0
B	1	1

TABLE 4.7

	The Meek	
	A	B
A	0	0
B	0	1

The "meek" blockmodel (table 4.7), however, suggests a proposition about core/periphery networks.Cores possess whatever attributes are most valued by the network. While this seems like a simple tautology, it is not and may be the result of extremely complex processes. The network is about relationships and flows, not about the attributes of the nodes. This proposition says that in core/periphery structures, the valuation of the attributes is related to the structure.[8] The proposition does not state which comes first, however one must ask, do the nodes that have the most of what is valued come to be the core, or do the nodes that already have the most of what is valued impose their values on others who have less and confine them to the periphery? This proposition was first formally noted in terms of leadership and norms by George Homans in his reinterpretation of the "Norton Street Gang" in *The Human Group* (Homans 1950). Leaders were said to embody more of the norms of the group than the followers. Similarly, the core in world/systems theory has the more advanced economy; political core elites have more power; the core in overlapping corporate boards of governors have more control; and the core in cultural diffusion has cultural hegemony. This proposition will be elaborated upon in the chapters that follow.

Thus far it seems that network analysis is a scheme that merely enforces the status quo. That is, the network embodies the values of the system, and the core/periphery model allows for no change. Yet there is one logical possibility that has not yet been examined. In terms of the network relations in the political arena, there could be a situation of two clusters or caucuses polarizing the community (table 4.8). They relate to themselves but not to one another.

This polarizing situation occurs in a modern community in which there is some overlap of circles in an unstable situation. Coleman describes this kind of structure as the second stage in community conflict after an issue is introduced (Coleman 1957). This blockmodel implies the following idea: network polarization is central to social change. Social transformation leads to polarization of networks, or, the reverse, polarization of networks leads to social change in terms of norms, values, and other social structures. The karate club, above, was an example of polarization. The ramifications of this model for social change will be discussed in the chapters that follow.

In the real world there are rarely two choices, and blockmodels can be complicated by incorporating additional blocks, C, D, . . . N. The models above that depict just two blocks are intended to present the basic idea of core/periphery models—the most simple of networks. Even they can be complex.

TABLE 4.8

	Polarization	
	A	B
A	1	0
B	0	1

How best to partition networks, especially large ones, remains one of the frontiers of network analysis, though much progress has been made recently (see chapter 8). Whole large networks are messy matters, but the network field has gone a long way from talking about social relations and networks as metaphors to analyzing them and building testable models. The following chapters will review and expand upon some of the things we have learned.

Where We Are Now

The first of the three chapters discussing basic network concepts began by considering the nature of sociological connections—propinquity and homophily in dyads. The basic sociological unit of a triad was then introduced along with the idea of balance and the census of triads in a network. In discussing whole networks, we introduced a key principle of network structure: position. There were positions in networks that were discovered by observers of the network and those that resulted from names that network participants gave to them. There were multiple relations between nodes and positions, and the paradoxical effects of weak relations on whole network integration. Finally, in the third chapter we moved from a characterization of the positions of individual nodes in a network to partitioning whole networks. We reviewed two basic ways of chopping up or partitioning networks that stem from the two basic principles of networks—looking within relations or looking outward to other relations. The most elementary of network patterns, belonging or not belonging to a central core, lies at the heart of many kinds of social structures, and that very fact suggests more complications that one might have at first imagined. The basic concepts and ideas presented in the first three chapters will emerge in various ways in the chapters that follow. First, we will return to the idea that nodes can be people, not only abstractions and organizations, and introduce some basic psychological principles that underlie the formation of networks of people.

5 The Psychological Foundations of Social Networks

IN KEEPING WITH our goal to understand social networks "as if people mattered," we begin our exploration of network theory with the psychological foundations of human social network behavior, a topic surprisingly ignored by many social network analysts. The foundations are both motivational and cognitive. They explain the urge to "network" and the limitations of human abilities to manage networks. Two kinds of basic human motivations respond to primary needs: first, to feel safe and second, to reach out. These correspond to two basic and complementary aspects of social networks: the connections between some of the elements of a network and the holes or non-connections between other elements. One motivation is to stay within one's social cocoon, for the connections between people and social units lead to feelings of safety, comfort, and support. Another motivation is to reach out and make connections where there were none. In addition to these primary motivations, there is one created by the network itself. It goes by various names such as envy, "status seeking," or "keeping up with the Joneses." Ego compares him/herself with others in comparable positions in the network and finds him/herself wanting. The dynamic is as old as Cain's envy of his brother Abel (Genesis 4:4–5). As we have observed before, a process such as motivation is constrained by a network of others in an ever-recurring feedback cycle. Motivations for safety and for reaching out tend to shape networks as well as be dependent upon them. Status seeking, while having an effect on networks, especially depends on the shape of social networks, as the networks provide targets for envy.

An additional cognitive psychological process is critical. One's network size, either in terms of outreach or making connections within one's immediate social environment, is bounded by human cognitive abilities. The average person historically has had a maximum effective network size of about 150, but that size appears to have doubled in current Western countries such as the United States. To be sure, both motivations and cognitive abilities are affected by social structure and culture, and note will be taken of those factors. We begin with a discussion of two features of networks: getting things done and community.

Getting Things Done

An influential early work in the field of social networks, *Friends of Friends* (Boissevain 1974), begins with an account of how a Sicilian academic solved a problem about the education of his eldest son. The professor feared that one of his enemies was blocking his son from graduating from high school, thereby foreclosing the son's chance for a university education. An elaborate network of relatives and friends was mobilized, first to verify that there indeed was a problem, and second to ensure that the son was actually admitted to the university. At one point he enlisted the help of a reputed Mafioso. He now owed a favor to someone to whom he might not otherwise wish to be beholden. Boissevain observes that most of us do not use such elaborate or extreme means:

> All of us have problems which we at least attempt to resolve via friends and friends-of-friends with whom we may even form temporary alliances ... My discussion thus concentrates on the way in which interpersonal relations are structured and influenced, on the way individuals seen as social entrepreneurs seek to manipulate these to attain goals and solve problems, and in the organization and dynamism of the coalitions they construct to achieve these ends. (Boissevain 1974, 3)

Thus we see that while the social system structures the patterns of relationships between people, the social network does not necessarily determine the outcomes of that structure. Within structured patterns, people have agency. They can use existing connections in various ways, activate old disused connections, or make new ones. The "system" does not automatically rule. Boissevain calls attention to individuals who become "highly expert network specialists" (148) or brokers: "A broker is a professional manipulator of people and information who brings about communication for profit" (ibid.). Of course, the "profit" is not in terms of cash delivered but in the collection of favors that can be "cashed in" when needed, in the fashion made famous by the *Godfather*, Puzo's account of the Italian mafia (1969). In his famous "small world" experiment, Milgram (1967, 1969; Travers and Milgram 1969) asked subjects to find brokers who would lead them to a particular targeted person. The median length of the chains linking the starting point to the target (the wife of a student living in Cambridge) was five, but the length varied from one to eleven intermediaries. Of 160 chains that were started in Nebraska, only 42 were completed.[1] People thus vary in their motivation to play the broker role, as well as in the skills required to perform the position efficiently.

Community and Support

Networks are not only about getting things done but about "community" (Craven and Wellman 1973; Wellman, Carrington, and Hall 1988), "social circles" (Kadushin 1966; Simmel 1955 [1922]), and the "social support" (Cohen and Syme 1985) one receives from these communities. When examining community and support, one first checks for the presence of ties embedded in the social system. One looks in particular for co-hesion, dense relations, and contagion rather than holes or the absence of ties. De-spite, or perhaps because of, the seeming disconnectedness of modern society, cohesion, support, and diffusion have strong effects on people; ties and connections are found in communities that do not necessarily have geographic proximity (Wellman 1999a; Wellman and Haythornthwaite 2002). In this literature, what Burt calls "clo-sure" (mutual connectedness) seems more important than agency. However, both bro-kerage and social density are matters of fundamental necessity in any network situation. The apparently neat distinction between feeling safe and reaching out be-comes muddled in modern society. Cohesion and support become even more impor-tant in modern society than in traditional systems because community and propinquity are often the consequences of particular actions rather than the passive results of the social environment.

One of the major interests of the founders of modern sociology, perhaps a major factor in the creation of sociology as a discipline, was to explain the shift from tradi-tional to modern societies that seemed to come to a head in the nineteenth and early twentieth century societies. For example, Durkheim in his *The Division of Labor in Soci-ety* (1947 [1902]), identified density and cohesion with the "mechanical solidarity" of traditional societies, and "organic solidarity," a situation replete with holes, as a modern condition requiring additional efforts to create cohesive situations. Simmel's cross-cutting circles (1955 [1922]) can be viewed as an argument that individuals in a metropolis create their own mix of communities. In some of these cases, the sole point of contact may be the person who created that mix. Since communities are created through the agency of talented individuals making connections across hitherto-unconnected nodes, modern societies require talents conventionally associated with brokerage and structural holes. On the other hand, the "structurally autonomous" broker who manipulates structural holes depends in part on her/his own base of support, a situation conventionally associated with cohesion.

In order better to understand the fundamental duality of cohesion and brokerage, we need to understand theories of motivation within networks. These motivations are "hard wired" into the original human network of an infant and her mother and father or other household members, or what George Homans (1950) called "The Human Group." And the original human group, as told in the Bible story, was responsible for Cain's envy of Abel.

Beginning with the Enlightenment, most social theorists include in their analysis of social structure some account of the psychology of motivation. Here we will utilize contemporary theoretical strands in psychology: relational psychoanalytic theory as expounded by Greenberg (1991) and eclectic academic psychological theory as synthesized by Haidt and Rodin (1999). The former deals with safety and effectiveness (which requires reaching out), and the latter mainly with effectiveness, though individual effectiveness also requires systemic support or feelings of safety. Status seeking or "keeping up with the Joneses" is generally discussed in relation to economic theory and the desire for material resources and gaining rank through networked resources (Lin and Erickson 2008a). However, psychologists find evidence that status (or what we call rank) is also a valued resource in itself in addition to its material value (Huberman, Loch, and Onculer 2004).

Safety and Affiliation

In general, modern object relations and self-psychology theory have assumed that since other people are necessary to satisfy basic human needs, the seeking out of others is a primary human activity. The mother is frequently described as the initial target or object of the infant. Thus, network activity is the natural, necessary, and original human condition. The problem for Greenberg is not that seeking out others is a fundamental human motivation, but the related question regarding what needs others satisfy. For example, he writes, "In my [Greenberg's] view, Fairbairn's[2] drive theory is based on a rather simple notion of what the child wants: it is a one drive model based on self-preservative needs manifested in the child's (and later in the adult's) dependency" (Greenberg 1991, 73).

But dependency, while a lifelong condition, is surely not all there is to life, since with dependency, agency all but disappears. Greenberg concludes, as did Freud, that there are two basic human forces: the safety drive and the effectiveness drive. Safety is fundamental because "people will not risk either new kinds of behavior nor new kinds of experience unless they feel safe enough to do so...[T]he importance of feelings of safety is one of the strongest findings that has emerged from a century of psychoanalytic investigation" (Greenberg 1991, 132–133). Further, safety is an affiliative drive: "The workings of the safety drive invariably move people closer to their objects" (133). Greenberg goes on to emphasize, "[T]he safety drive...is inherently and from the beginning directed at a human object.... [B]ecause it aims at feelings of physical, intellectual, and psychological relaxation, the safety drive moves us closer to other people" (134, 137).

Effectiveness and Structural Holes

In contrast, efficacy "drives the child's urgent, exuberant activity...what Hendrick (1942, 40) has succinctly called the need 'to do and to learn how to do'...[E]ffectance is characterized by a sense of self-sufficiency, autonomy and individuation" (Greenberg 1991, 137). Effective needs pull one away from other people: "Culture [read, society], as a broad reverberation of human needs for relatedness, is indispensable because it serves our need for safety, for being embedded in a secure structure (Fromm 1941). But it is stifling because it can thwart effectance strivings, which often push against the norms of social living" (139). The drive for effectance is as innate as the drive for safety:

> It is a sensation that begins in the body, probably in the muscles, and is initially experienced as pleasure in movement for movement's sake alone. Soon after, it expands to include the early sense of agency that Stern (Stern 1985) believes the infant feels when he first experiences volitional acts, such as deliberate movement. Later in the course of development it is extended outward, becoming inextricably involved with feelings of competence and mastery over the environment. (Greenberg 1991, 136)

This is an urge for independence from others, particularly one's mother. Greenberg relates that "[t]he effectance drive is, therefore, a construct well suited to account for what are, unquestionably, aversive elements inherent in all object relations. Freud used aggression (and even the death instinct) to explain wishes to move away from the object" (137). Relational theory as expounded by Greenberg, however, presupposes neither a primary drive to destructiveness nor a reaction to the object's inevitable failures.

Similarly, academic psychologists Haidt and Rodin describe motivational aspects of control: "[E]ffectance is an intrinsic motivation of striving for competence or mastery. The satisfaction of effectance leads to a pleasurable feeling of efficacy" (Haidt and Rodin 1999, 329). Effectance may be divided into a need for competence and a need for autonomy, though the latter "may be a particularly Western need" (ibid.). That is, whether or not effectance strivings work to overcome a "stifling" environment may depend on the culture. There is a universal social condition for effectance, however, that Haidt and Rodin call "systemic supportiveness": "A supportive system is a system that provides the affordances that an individual needs to take on and master new challenges" (332). While there are many aspects to supportive systems, a key underlying assumption is safety, in Greenberg's terms, a feeling that stems from satisfactory primary relationships.

Safety and Social Networks

In network terms, safety or supportive systems are usually equivalent to density in networks, a condition that has been generally associated with "social support," "cohesion," and "embeddedness." Dense social networks are characterized by the sense of "trust." That is, it is assumed that if you act in a certain way toward the other, the other will in turn satisfy your needs. Note that the relationship takes place in time. The self moves toward the other, and then the other reacts, that is, you build up "credit" with the other (who may have to return the favor with "interest" or with something of greater value). In the perfect case of trust, there is no need for long-term credit. What self gives is what self gets back in return, often because the time lapse is negligible. In the simplest case, in a dyadic relationship, it is assumed, for example, that if you give the bus driver the money for a fare, he will accept that money and not throw you off the bus.[3]

In general, trust takes place in a situation of relatively high density and visibility, and over a short time span. This situation is frequently described as one of "cohesion" and "social support." Of course, cohesion and support can be varied. There is a large literature on exchange situations in which the visibility of the network and/or its shape as well as the discounted value of the exchange to the dyad (typically, by altering the "payoff" matrix in the experiment) are experimentally altered so that, among other things, the extent of cohesion and support are also altered (see Molm, Takahashi, and Peterson 2000 and references cited). In addition, experimenters can alter the balance of power in the exchange so that one or both sides of a transaction are less motivated to trust one another.

In more complex situations, there can be an elaborate chain of interactions in a network, and there may be a certain degree of discounting. That is, because there is a time delay, self expects to get a bit more in return than self originally invested. Perhaps the most interesting form of trust occurs when the trust is placed not in the partner to a dyadic transaction but in the system as a whole, and there is a significant time delay. This occurs when it is apparent to nodes that they will get a return not necessarily from their direct partner, but from some other node(s) in the system at a later date. Anthropologist Malinowski described this type of network trust in the Trobriand Islands. The "kula ring" was an exchange in which shell necklaces were traded clockwise around the ring of the Trobriand Islands, and shell armbands were traded in the opposite direction. Trades took place a year or more apart (Malinowski 1922). The American Western frontier "barn raising" is another example of "net generalized exchange," Claude Lévi-Strauss's term explicated so convincingly by Ekeh (1974). Net generalized exchange—reciprocity not with specified others but with an entire social system—is not merely an attribute of frontier society or isolated Pacific Islanders but is very much alive in modern society. As an academic, when someone asks me for a reference to an article I comply, knowing that if I ask some other academic for a reference, I am likely to get one. This "cast thy bread upon the waters" principle is dependent in turn on the "discount rate" of future returns, the visibility of the system, the tightness of the system network structure, the cost of present support efforts, and one's place in the system hierarchy. Those in higher places in the hierarchy have more investment in the system and hence demonstrate "noblesse oblige." In the example of giving a reference that I mentioned, the mere act of giving establishes me in a superior position, and besides, it costs me nothing because even though I "gave away" the reference, I still have it. (For details, see Kadushin 1981; Uehara 1990). Trust is not merely an attribute of face-to-face dense relationships, but is affected by third party relations, "friends of friends," (Burt 2006) and leads to the stability of one's reputation in the community.

To be sure, as Greenberg points out, and as is evident in Durkheim's "mechanical solidarity," density and cohesion exact the price of conformity and can be stifling. There is a large sociological literature on trust. Social networks play an important part in the establishment of trust in society (Cook 2001) but there are obviously additional elements.

Finally, as we shall see when we discuss effectiveness, trust and safety are very much a matter of insiders versus outsiders. Relationships with insiders are more dense, supportive, and trusting, while relationships with outsiders are less dense and therefore open to the manipulation afforded by "structural holes."

Effectiveness and Social Networks

We can turn the concept of density in social networks on its head, as it were, and look to the holes in the network, the lack of connectedness, rather than to cohesion. As I noted earlier, this idea was developed by Burt in his influential *Structural Holes: The Social Structure of Competition* (1992). By focusing on the holes rather than the connections, we concern ourselves more with efficacy than safety. In competitive situations, other people's cohesion can be a disadvantage. Persons embedded in a dense cohesive network have the same information. Each is constrained by the other but, at the same time, cannot be played off against the other. In this dense system of mutual relationships, no one can gain an advantage. On the other hand, if a person is a bridge between more dense parts of a network not directly connected with one another and thus characterized by structural holes, the person gains information from diverse clusters without direct access to one another, and one node can be played against the other. Burt explains that "[p]layers with relationships free of structural holes at their own end and rich in structural holes at the other end are structurally autonomous. These players are best positioned for the information and control benefits that a network can provide" (Burt 2000, 45). Support at the player's end (free of structural holes) and a lack of density at the other end make the player effective. Note the very language has changed from self and actor to "player." This individual is best described as an entrepreneur who gains advantage by mediating between others and "making an offer that can't be refused" because the other has no alternatives. Mediation is not without advantage to the mediator. Burt shows that persons active in "building relations between dissimilar people," gain many valuable resources such as early promotion in organizations because they "know about, have a hand in, and exercise control over, more rewarding opportunities" (ibid.).

Motivation, according to Burt, is created by the network itself: "[T]he network is its own explanation of motive. As the volume of structural holes in a player's network increases—regardless of the process that created them—the entrepreneurial behavior of making and negotiating relations between others becomes a way of life... If all you know is entrepreneurial relationships, the motivation question is a nonissue" (Burt 2000, 36). This is an extreme structural position that denies the independent contribution of other factors, especially the content of network flow. In later work, as discussed below, Burt modifies this extreme position and investigates personality attributes characteristic of brokers (Burt, Jannotta, and Mahoney 1998). As to the content of the motivation, Burt quotes Schumpeter (1934, 93) in describing the entrepreneurial motivation as "the will to conquer; the impulse to fight, to prove oneself superior to others, to succeed for the sake...of the success itself." In short, to be effective. The motives in this situation would be described by Greenberg as being quite different from those associated with safety. The effective person does not want to be close to everyone, but only to some; other persons are pushed away or ignored. The effective person is not necessarily "nice." She seeks control and profit rather than affiliation and equal exchange. Competition is a network aspect of effectiveness.[4] Not everyone can win. Network theory further suggests that one competes with or tries to beat or at least keep up with those who are structurally isomorphic. Persons are structurally isomorphic if they have the same pattern of relations with other nodes—though not necessarily the same nodes (Borgatti and Everett 1992). Note that they do not have to be in connection with one another. It is easiest to see this structural pattern with culturally named role relations. Within a given kinship system, all "fathers" are structurally isomorphic. The drive for effectiveness then becomes a motive: "Keeping up with the Joneses" because each father keeps an eye on the other fathers. Little League baseball competition is as much about the fathers as the children. Finally, lest we associate effectance with sheer manipulation, we note that there is a less Machiavellian side to brokerage that will be further explored in the chapter on diffusion: the person who has connections with a variety of others in different clusters also has access to information and ideas that are not present in her own cluster. Reaching out leads to more ideas than are available in the cocoon.

Both Safety and Effectiveness?

Since both safety affiliation-trust-density and effectiveness-competition-structural holes situations are inherent human motivations and present in all social networks, when does the one or the other become more salient? "Keeping up with the (equivalent) Joneses" as a status-seeking correlate of efficacy motives is an attribute of situations with many structural holes rather than situations of high cohesion. These motivations are necessary when the costs of acting as well as the return on investment are high, when the visibility is low, when the discount rate on future returns is high and when one may not be in moral command—in short, in situations in which the modern market is predominant. In such situations, actors attempt at least to keep up with, and at best surpass, others with whom they are structurally similar. Note that in the formulation just given, the actors can be organizations, nation-states, or other kinds of collective actors.

The main difference between effectiveness networks and safety networks as ideal types is the location of trust. In safety networks, trust tends to be an attribute of the entire network, not just of the "player's" side. In effectiveness networks, trust is present only to a limited degree between the player and the other who is the object of play. Furthermore, since total visibility in effectiveness networks can be low, one of the startling and perhaps magical findings of network research is that actors need not be consciously aware of these structurally similar others to behave as if they were trying to keep up with them. Nevertheless, both Greenberg and Haidt and Rodin assert that although effectiveness and control are both basic human motivational needs or drives, effectiveness is dependent on prior conditions of safety and systemic support. As Greenberg points out, "The safety and effectance drives operate continuously and *both* pulls are *always* present, although one or another is likely to dominate conscious experience at any particular moment" (Greenberg 1991, 138; italics in original). To be autonomous, which is an early, deep-seated drive, one must also feel safe and supported. This is an ultimate paradox of human existence.

There is also a practical paradox. Suppose there were no costs involved in making a new contact that bridged a structural hole and dropping a contact that was redundant. Then if *everyone* in a network decided to adopt a strategy that maximized structural holes, a simulation shows that the end result would be total equality in the network with no one able to be a broker, and further, no closure or support either (Buskens and van de Rijt 2008). Of course, in "real life," making connections, as we saw in the example with which we began this chapter, does have costs, and not everyone has the personality or the desire to act aggressively in reaching out. Furthermore, we saw that there are institutional aspects that spur the motivation toward effectiveness and reaching out. "Keeping up with the Joneses" as a driver for effectance is most often found in market situations.

Given that safety and efficacy are deep-seated drives tied to early development, it seems plausible that there might be personality attributes tied to these drives. Burt found that an aggressive entrepreneurial personality was related to the formation of networks with more structural holes (Burt, Jannotta, and Mahoney 1998; also reported in Burt 2005). But this personality also must have some underpinning of trust or feelings of safety to be effective. Recent research using a triad census (see chapter 2) provides an interesting theory regarding the relationship between closure, structural holes, and personality:

> While network closure and structural holes co-occur, the likelihood of one structure reduces the likelihood of the other. Furthermore, the two structures are associated with different psychological profiles, with our regression model explaining 15% of the variance in this component. People who opt for network closure are more social, energetic and skilled in handling social situations. They enjoy social situations more and are more at ease with themselves. They hold allocentric values, such as obedience, security and duty. More importantly, they view the world as "us versus them," and their social identity is important to the way they see themselves and the world. These findings may explain the tendency for network closure; after all, these people may sever relationships with people who are not part of "us." (Kalish and Robins 2006, 79)

They also found that people with strong structural holes are more neurotic, suggesting that "there is something stressful in keeping your close friends separated, exactly as

(Granovetter 1973) would have predicted. It might also be that neurotic people, who trust other people less, would opt for a 'divide and rule' strategy in constructing their network" (Kalish and Robins 2006, 79).

Driving for Status or Rank

There is a special case of effectance and reaching out that has been mentioned, "Keeping up with the Joneses." This is the Cain-Abel problem. It too is a fundamental motivation of childhood induced in the family of origin, as described in the biblical story.[5] As long as there is a network containing at least one dyad, and that is true by definition of all networks, the other in the dyad is a referent. Am I equally regarded or do I have as much of whatever is valued as the other? I need not murder the other to set things equal, but motive to equal or surpass the other is always there. There are two aspects to this motive, one set by the network and the other by the social and cultural system within which the network is embedded. The network creates two situations. One situation is the similarity created by structural isomorphism referred to above. Here one "keeps up with the Joneses" because they occupy a similar position in a network. The interesting thing about this kind of need to emulate or keep ahead of is that it is not a conscious process in which one knows directly whom one has to keep up with. One need not have a clear picture of the network—and participants rarely do—for the emulation of others to occur. A person need not even be directly aware of the Joneses or that he or she is competing with them or trying to emulate them. This would seem unreasonable, yet there is a great deal of consistent data that suggests that this is true (Burt 1987; Burt 2005). We will see examples of this phenomenon when we discuss diffusion and the spread of ideas.

A more visible network structure that creates the motivation to keep up with or exceed the other is the authority pyramid (Martin 2009, chapters 6 and 7). The occupational- or economic- class pyramid also generates motivations to get ahead (Lin 2001). Less politely, these situations generate the conditions for deferring to authority and for social climbing. As we will see in the next chapter on small group leadership, the motive to associate with those of higher rank and gain their resources is not unbounded. As will be explained, there is no motivation to associate with or be envious of those who "won't return your phone calls." There is no point for me to envy Bill Gate's or George Soros's fortunes. They are entirely out of reach. One is more likely to compare oneself and to try to associate with those others who are not too far removed from one's own rank. Authority and rank pyramids therefore create the situation for envy and emulation and, at the same time, limit the targets for both.

In the previous chapter, we described core/periphery structures and observed that the core has more of whatever is valued. These valuations depend on the cultural and social definition of what is valued: for example, money, power, family connections, or learning (Weber 1946). While the network establishes *who* the referent is, the social system generally establishes *what* one strives for. Unless, of course, it is rank itself.

A desire for rank or status may be a strong motive regardless of the content of the rank (Huberman, Loch, and Onculer 2004).

Cultural Differences in Safety, Effectance, and Rank

Some cultures emphasize safety, others effectance, and still others status or rank. Markus and Kitayama (1998) have engaged in a series of studies that suggest that in European and American cultural contexts, "a person is an autonomous entity defined by a somewhat distinctive set of attributes, qualities, or processes." In contrast, "the interdependent model of the person gives priority to social structural and interpersonal frameworks such as families, work, work groups, social roles, positions, or relationships defining the person." Asian cultures tend to elaborate this interdependent model of personality. The interdependent model is more consistent with density and support, whereas the autonomous model is more consistent with structural holes and effectance. In later work, Markus and Kitayama specifically invoke two models of agency: the "disjoint" (people follow their own goals, are independent of others, and the emphasis is on "efficacy"); and "conjoint" (relationship focused and agentic feelings may include solidarity and relatedness; Markus and Kitayama 2003). These models correspond to what we have called efficacy and brokerage on the one hand, and closure and support on the other. By and large, we can assume that persons and collectivities that are congruent with the dominant culture/personality mode will be more valued. Going "outside the box," however, as we saw with the Sicilian academic, can be dramatically effective if there is also a cultural prescription that allows for such relatively unusual behavior.

Motivation for rank may also follow cultural modes, though this may not directly follow as a consequence of an interdependent or autonomous personality. A cross-cultural experiment suggested the following order in sensitivity to rank: Hong Kong, Turkey, the United States, Sweden/Finland (Huberman, Loch, and Onculer 2004, 110). These are results from one experiment. It might be that cultures that emphasize honor generate stronger sensitivities about rank. Further, the motivation to "keep up with the Joneses" may be more prevalent in advanced market economies. The idea that status or striving for rank varies by society or culture seems plausible, but further investigation is required.

Motivations and Practical Networks

To summarize on the matter of network agency: what are the benefits of cohesion on the one hand and structural holes? Cohesion, as the vast literature on social support[6] shows, provides access to needed resources, emotional or otherwise. The motivation for support satisfies basic needs and sustains the status quo. Structural holes are not for satisfying present needs but for creating change and movement. The more autonomous node, in the sense that it is in contact with other nodes not densely related to one another, plays one node against the other and reaps the advantage. As was suggested, this can result in personal strain. The manipulator lacks the immediate and effortless access to resources enjoyed by those embedded in total cohesive networks. Although the broker must rely on at least some trusted partners, trust cannot be the sole motivator because it is not present throughout the network, only in parts of it. Note how difficult it is to gain trust in a bargaining situation in which the players have limited contacts with the "other side" but relatively dense contacts with those on "their side." The literature on conflict resolution is replete with examples of the need to gain the trust of the other side, typically, through greater personal contact. On the other hand, the support literature by and large shows that support is rendered when the costs are low or the chance of direct reciprocity is very high (or there are special kinship norms), which is typical of situations in which safety is the motivator.

In real social life as opposed to social theory, it need not be an either/or situation. Podolny and Baron (1997) suggest that in corporate settings in which the focus is on individual executive mobility, situations with structural holes make it easier to assimilate diverse sources and play people off against one another, but equally important for the manager is the distinct social identity that is associated with smaller, more cohesive networks. When people compete for jobs, having a coherent, well-defined organizational identity, with precise and consistent role expectations, is as important as having access to information and resources. There is a paradox: Network structures most conducive to information and resources and brokerage are NOT conducive to clear social identity and vice versa. There are, therefore, two kinds of effective mentors who help persons advance through organizations. The first is described as a source of social resources and information and characterized by not being tied to the close networks that surround a particular candidate. This mentor, who classically is able to take advantage of structural holes, is tied to varied and less mutually connected social structures which, because of their lack of tight connections in the world of the protégé, do not support a consistent organizational identity for him or her. This very spread is what makes these mentors so valuable to the more constricted protégé who does not have such a scope. The other kind of mentor is embedded in a more dense support network shared by the protégé that allows for acceptance of the organization norms and consistent identities. Candidates have to straddle both worlds. In his latest book, Burt finds closure (density) and brokerage to be complementary, each having certain advantages. Closure makes one's life easier, but perhaps complacent, while brokerage seeks out the advantages, however temporary, of moving beyond one's closed circle and leads to the development of new ideas (Burt 2005). These two facets encapsulate the essence of basic human motivations. Burt further offers a model of the simultaneous effects of brokerage and closure on effectiveness (when each is considered simultaneously as a continuous variable rather than as an attribute).

In this graph (figure 5.1), closure is given half the weight of brokerage because Burt finds it less important, though a factor. But because of personality factors, it may be that while both closure and brokerage may coexist, one structure tends to drive out the other (Kalish and Robins 2006). The relative importance of brokerage and density or closure, and hence of the corresponding motivations of effectance and safety, further depend on both cultural and social structural contexts.

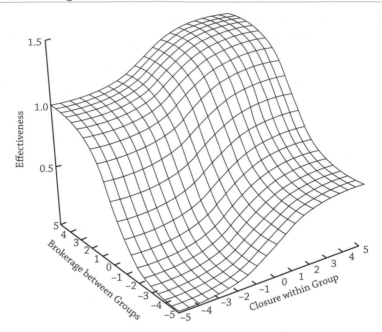

FIGURE 5.1 Burt Closure versus Brokerage Model[7]

Motivations of Corporate Actors

Thus far we have been considering motivations and networks as if they were properties of individuals. There can be networks of inanimate objects such as transportation networks, citation networks, international economic exchanges, Web crawling and, combining abstract with the personal, organizations. What is true for individuals is also true for organizations. Talmud and Mesch (1997) show how both safety-support through embeddedness and effectiveness-brokerage through structural holes are important in predicting corporate stability in Israel. Uzzi, in analyzing New York City's garment industry, shows that "some firms transact using principally arm's length ties; other firms, in keeping with embeddedness, appear to form tangible networks of production linked by embedded ties" (1996, 690). He goes on to state that "embeddedness is a logic of exchange that shapes motives and expectations and promotes coordinated adaptation...actors do not selfishly pursue immediate gains, but concentrate on cultivating long-term cooperative relationships...These actions and motives are themselves not assumed to be due to the hard-wired orientation of economic actors or conformity to abstract norms, but to the emergent properties of concrete network relationships" (693). Uzzi warns, "Embeddedness, however, yields positive returns only up to a threshold point. Once the threshold is crossed, returns from embeddedness become negative...Optimal networks are not composed of either all embedded ties or all arm's-length ties, but integrate the two" (694). In a study of lending patterns between banks and small businesses, Uzzi amplifies and extends this point:

In economic sociology, there are two general theories for understanding how social relations and networks create economic and social benefits. The weak-tie approach argues that a large, nonredundant network of arm's-length ties is most advantageous; the strong tie approach argues that a closed, tightly knit network of embedded ties is most advantageous (Sandfleur and Laumann 1998). How can these opposing approaches to tie quality (weak versus strong) and network structure ('"holey' versus dense) be reconciled? My analysis of arm's-length ties supports the weak-tie thesis, demonstrating that weak ties are superior at "shopping" the market for publicly available information. Similarly, my analysis of embedded ties supports the strong-tie approach by showing that embedded ties are superior at "plugging" actors into the unique collective resources of dense network clusters. Thus I suggest that embedded ties and arm's-length ties are complementary rather than cannibalistic when they are combined within the same network, because one type of ties helps overcome the limitations of the other type while enlarging information and governances benefits. (Uzzi 1999, 500)

In general, both safety (embedded "dense" ties) and effectiveness (arm's-length "holey" ties) are necessarily found to some degree in all networks that somehow involve people, because people are always motivated to act in terms of both safety and effectiveness.

As further evidence for the advantages of both safety and effectiveness, consider what people do when they are in a position of choice.[8] It is assumed that persons of higher rank or social class have more choices. In work-based networks, the higher one's rank, the more numerous one's strong and weak ties in the work context. Erickson observes that weak-tie network diversity grows steadily from employees to supervisors to managers to owners (Erickson 1996), but there is the same progression in the proportion of people who say they feel close to people at work (shown in Erickson's unpublished report). In general, persons of higher social class have more diverse social networks as well as cohesive ones, whereas persons lower in social class have more geographically local cohesive networks but fewer weak-tie diverse networks that convey a competitive advantage (Kadushin and Jones 1992). In general, then, persons who have greater resources in life also have more useful network ties. This is not a surprising finding since, "to those who hath shall be given," a scriptural truth hallowed in science, in deference to the Gospel, as "The Matthew Effect" (Merton 1968a).

"The more the more," is a proposition that is generally true for much of life. But this may be begging the question. What is the optimal balance between safety and effectiveness for different structures and for different situations? For individuals who are attempting to navigate their way within groups and organizations, and for organizations seeking to survive and prosper in mixed economies, there is usually a delicate balance between safety and effectiveness or between density and structural holes.

Safety/density/support and effectiveness/structural holes can vary simultaneously such that one can have relative amounts of one and the other as shown in the diagram above. That is, they are vectors that define a space. At one extreme there is the "buccaneer," who is low on support but high on effectance, and at the other extreme there is the "conservative," who is high on support but low on effectance. But how long can a person be effective as a pure buccaneer or "operator"? There may be a price to be paid in personal strain. Is it possible that having both support and effectance is in the long run a better alternative? Is the person who is high on both, typical of politicians, more generally effective? Those who are low on both, true isolates who strictly cultivate their garden, can be happy under some circumstances but are not likely to have much social impact. The question of balance can be translated into asking what the contextual effects are. A person or collectivity high on density but low on structural holes might be effective in one context but not in another. The example with which we began, the Sicilian academic whose foiled ambitions for his son were resolved by mobilizing an elaborate skein of friends and relatives, lived in a society fundamentally high on density that valued mutual support. Arguably, his hole-bridging efforts were successful precisely because the normal state of that system tended more toward traditional society and the support pole rather than toward the relatively rare entrepreneurial buccaneer, who when invoked, however, can be quite powerful.

Then there is the matter of striving for rank or status. Ambition fuels social systems and makes for innovation and progress. "Keeping up with the Joneses" is the subtext of much modern advertising. In both cases, a social network sets the targets. Scientists and entrepreneurs are driven by the need to achieve, though in one case is the motivation is professional honor and in the other increased wealth. Consequences for ambitious individuals in terms of happiness and satisfaction, however, are the subject matter for novels and psychotherapy.

Cognitive Limits on Individual Networks

The infant's horizon for potential networks is constantly expanding as he or she matures and begins to move in circles and activities beyond the immediate family. In traditional societies, the infant becomes aware of the extended family as a network and begins to absorb the meaning and relationships implied by terms that have always confounded this student of kinship. In contemporary industrial societies, children go to schools and acquire a network of persons outside their nuclear families. This acquisition of an ever larger network continues to develop, even as aided by internet devices such as Facebook. Nevertheless, there is a limit to the size of the safety and effectance networks than any individual can manage or remember, though of course there is considerable variation in this ability. In addition to their motivations to engage in network behavior, the size of the network that humans can cognitively manage is the other important psychological underpinning of social network theory. The size of this network and the sources of variation in size produce one of the fundamental building blocks of social network theory.

Network behavior is in the first place subject to limitations on the extent of human actions. But specifying this limit is not so simple, because it depends on both biological and cultural mobilization and tends to be cyclical. "All humans have a limit or ceiling of actions. Below this ceiling, an accustomed level of mobilization is established. Periods of mobilization above par of the accustomed level tend to be followed by mobilization below par, and vice versa" (Zetterberg 2011, 139). The quality of the actions can vary, not to mention the physical stamina of the actors including sleep patterns and the ability to multitask (the teenager who listens to music while doing her homework), all of which have some cultural components. Nonetheless, there is a limit, and this limit may be related to the limits on the size of the networks humans can manage and remember. The size of this personal circle or network is a critical social and cultural phenomenon. First, as Bernard and Killworth (1979) pointed out, this size is a major determinate of social and cultural evolution. They assume that with a given technology, a hunting and gathering group's population size steadily increases until it has to split so that it can continue to exploit its environment. Thus far this is the conventional view of human evolution as seen from the point of view of Julian Steward's school of cultural evolution. But there is an additional factor: Bernard and Killworth maintain that if groups are constructed randomly, then the upper limit to their size is about 140; beyond that they have to split so that individuals can comprehend their position in the group and function effectively without a formal system of coordination. In addition, they show that the limits of informal networks of networks or groups is probably around 2,500 after which some formal institutions must be developed.

Hill and Dunbar argue that "[i]n primates, social networks are more easy to define . . . and are often delimited by the size of the social group" (Hill and Dunbar 2003, 54). Primate relationships involve intense social grooming. The grooming group size is relative to neocortical volume. "Since the size of the human neocortex is known, the relationship between group size and neocortex size in primates can be used to predict the cognitive group size for humans" (ibid.). Dunbar therefore predicts that preliterate humans should live in groups of about 150 in size (Dunbar 1993).

To what extent does this biological limit apply to historical and contemporary human society?

> 150 is the usual unit size of armies in the Roman Empire. It was also the size of infantry companies fighting World War II. It also seems to be around that number that rural village compounds and zadrugas divide. My impression is that artistic and scientific coteries also tend to break up into fractions when they reach this limit. (Zetterberg 2011, 115)

Using samples of convenience in Britain and Belgium and such techniques as inquiring about Christmas card sending, and administering tests of cognitive ability, Dunbar and associates confirm the size of about 150, but with a large standard deviation (about 85) for close personal relationships (Roberts et al. 2009; Stiller and Dunbar 2007; Hill and Dunbar 2003). The results, however, are based on small data sets of white Europeans whose sampling characteristics are unknown.

In a series of interesting studies, Killworth, Bernard and members of their research team have attempted empirically to find the number of persons known to an average contemporary American. Their latest finding is that the number is larger than the historical 150: somewhere around 280. But there is a very wide standard deviation, meaning that some people have a much larger effective circle and some a much smaller one (Killworth et al. 2006). We will further discuss the size, distribution, and extent to which the circle is highly skewed in a later chapter on the "small world." Recent analyses discussed in that chapter, using data from the Killworth et al. studies, but applying a different statistical technique, suggest that the mean size of one's circle of acquaintances may be as high as 650 for men and 590 for women, again with a highly skewed distribution in which a few people have very large circles (Zheng, Salganik, and Gelman 2006).

Some of the variations are related to social location. For example, in an urban setting, persons of higher social class have a wider circle than persons lower in class (Kadushin and Jones 1992). One of the early students of this variation notes differences between village and urban society (Boissevain 1974), something Simmel (1950 [1903]) commented on earlier. Whether the internet is responsible for the high figures obtained by Zheng, Salganik, and Gelman is not clear. Variation in size is related to talent, cognitive abilities, and motivation. Some politicians such as Bill Clinton seem to have a mental electronic database capable of instantly retrieving at least 5,000, if not more, individuals by name and face. We do not as yet have a theory or a systematic study of the causes of these variations. There are even some training programs that claim to enlarge one's ability to recall and manage personal networks. Whatever the limits, the size of one's directly reachable and knowable network is finite and has a strong biological component. This limit, along with the motivations for safety and effectiveness, will prove to have very important consequences in the development of theories about social networks.

Where We Are Now

We have shown that three basic, deep-seated motivations to make contact and network, rooted in early human network experiences, are always present in social networks. *Safety* is the motivation to derive support from one's social environment. Safety corresponds to dense, cohesive networks. *Effectance* is the motivation to reach out beyond one's current situation and comfort zone. Effectance corresponds to networks with structural holes. Making connections, or acting as a broker to networks that otherwise would not be much connected, is a priority. An important difference between safety networks and effectiveness networks is the location of trust: in safety networks trust is an attribute of the entire network; in effectiveness networks trust is more likely on the player's side. *Status* or rank seeking and, in its minimal form, keeping up with the Joneses, is generated by network pyramid structures, occupational or socioeconomic pyramids, and by market-driven situations. While the pyramid structures are generally visible to network participants, similar location in complex networks may not be. Nonetheless, similar location can still motivate the desire to keep up with the Joneses. As with any network process, network motivations are both responsive to network structure and at the same time serve to alter networks or generate new ones. Motivations are also not a situation of "either, or." An effective broker needs some sort of support on her side, and may often be additionally motivated by status seeking.

Those surrounded by a cocoon of relations do need to reach out. Finally, the strength of these motivations seem affected by the cultural and social context.

In addition to motivational factors, there are cognitive limits to the *size* of networks that humans can easily process. Researchers have discovered that the average maximum size of networks that an individual person in the United States can effectively manage is around 300. Recent work, however, suggests it may be double that, but vary considerably according to social location and personal ability.

We will encounter these psychological foundations in all the analyses that follow. In the next chapter, chapter 6, "Small Groups, Leadership, and Social Networks," motivations for safety and effectance as well as motivation for achieving rank are crucial in the formation of small-group leadership. In chapter 7, "Organizations and Networks," we will find that pyramids and rank are especially important in managing organizations; brokers make a difference in large organizations. The size of the networks one can easily manage is relevant to the design of efficient organizations. Chapter 8 demonstrates that small worlds, circles and communities all depend on safety and effectance, but most of all on the size of the networks in people's immediate circles. Diffusion, chapter 9, depends on the mechanisms of brokerage and structural holes, though diffusion occurs most rapidly in dense connected networks. Chapter 10, "Social Capital," is mainly about accessing resources through social networks in which both dense networks and socioeconomic pyramids have important roles.

The motivations to engage in the types of social networks described are thus crucial to network analysis, and yet, network theorists have by and large been uninterested in psychological foundations, believing that networks themselves produce motivation. While that is true, motivations also produce and sustain networks. Cultural and social differences in these motivations are under-researched. The role of motivations in sustaining and creating networks and the human cognitive limitations in handling networks, even in the era of Facebook and Twitter, are areas where much more research is needed

6 Small Groups, Leadership, and Social Networks
THE BASIC BUILDING BLOCKS

Introduction

All networks are comprised of smaller units. This chapter explores small networks in which everyone knows each other, and the actions of the members of the networks are visible to all. The members of the small networks considered here are individual people rather than collective actors. These kinds of networks are generally called "small groups." They are the "primitives" of social network analysis. These small groups are important because much analysis of more complex networks in organizations, to be taken up in the next chapter, focuses on the difference between networks produced by formal systems of the organization and small group networks created informally by office friendships and politics.

There is a long history of analysis of small groups, often called "primary groups" (see chapter 3), but propositions about how and why they develop have only been recently formulated. In the analysis of how and why small groups are formed, we will draw upon work in the previous chapters. Motivations for safety, effectance, and status are critical in establishing rankings within small groups; balance theory and triads are central to defining the boundaries of small groups. The observed characteristics of networks in small groups will be derived from a small set of simple assumptions. While previous work on small groups is important, the present formulation puts together ideas about small groups that may not heretofore have been seen as related to one to another.

Primary Groups and Informal Systems: Propositions

A primary group is an interactive unit that is observed as such by an outsider, whether or not people identify themselves in these terms. In analyzing primary groups, it is helpful to consider "pure" groups or situations which Leifer calls "interaction preludes." In the first, there are no formal positions and, in the second, roles have not yet emerged and actors are jockeying for status (Leifer and Rajah 2000; Leifer 1988).[1] In family or kinship small groups, roles are in part defined by the formally prescribed kinship terms and culturally expected relationships. There are also small groups created by experimenters in which the experimenter manipulates the roles and positions to see what effects different roles and positions have on individual behaviors. In formal organizations, there are also primary or face-to-face groups in which most of the relationships are prescribed by the organization. George Homans in his path-breaking book, *The Human Group* (1950), observed that some interactions in human groups are prescribed by the formal system, that is kinship, the experimenter, or the formal organization. These interactions he called the "external system." Other interactions develop from processes within the groups themselves. Some interactions are based on "sentiments" or feelings that people have for one another; some interactions stem from participation in common activities, whether or not dictated by the external system. Interaction generally leads to positive sentiments; these sentiments in turn lead to further interaction. Moreover, the activities and interactions called for by the external system are always elaborated. The ties and common sentiments generated by this elaboration produce cliques.[2] These cliques and the resulting social solidarity are Homans's "internal system" (what I refer to as the informal system) and become embedded within the external system.

Informal groups, through interaction, develop or reinforce certain common ideas or styles of relating to one another. These become the "norms" of the group or clique and are further reinforced by mutual interaction. Informal leaders adhere more to these norms than do non-leaders, in part because, through leadership, they enforce the norms, and in part because groups choose leaders who exemplify the norms of the group. These are the core ideas of informal systems that are pegged to formal ones but that influence the way formal systems operate. Each of these ideas is found in Homans (1950) who, along with Bavelas (1948), was one of the originators of social network analysis for small groups and organizations.

Over time, all informal small group systems develop clusters or cliques. Inevitably, and related to the clusters, a ranking system develops in which some persons are preferred over others. Related to the ranking system, and perhaps both a cause and consequence of it, people in informal systems tend to develop feelings or sentiments about one another. Those who rank higher in the system are the leaders. People tend to defer to them; members choose them more often (the very definition of rank in this system). Paradoxically, leaders tend more often to *initiate* interaction with members either directly or through others. These characteristics will be found within work groups in any formal organization. Homans insisted that they are true of all human groups, including families.[3]

These statements can be formalized as propositions. Homans's propositions refer to small primary or face-to-face groups, where "small" for the moment remains undefined. All are understood to include a statement "other conditions being equal." What are these "other conditions" remains at the moment unclear.

1. Interaction and activities that require interaction lead to sentiments or attitudes that group members have for one another.

2. The sentiments can be positive or negative. Positive sentiments lead to further interaction, and negative sentiments lead to less interaction.

3. Thus 1 and 2 are in a feedback loop, the limits of which are unclear but generally determined by the requirements of the formal system (one needs to get work done) or by the inherent limits on individual action in the internal system (there is some limit on the number of interactions or activities any person can sustain within a given period of time).

4. Since (a) the formal system requires certain differentiated activities, (b) these activities lead to interaction and interaction leads to sentiments, and (c) all of this is in a feedback loop, it follows that in any small group there will develop clusters or cliques of individuals who have more dense patterns of interaction and sets of feelings about one another. These clusters will generally follow the interactions dictated by the formal system. In this sense, an informal network is "draped upon" or embedded within the formal (external) system.

5. Similarly, and the source of this is not clear at the moment, individuals will be evaluated differentially by the internal system (according to the criteria important to the internal system), and these differences in evaluation will lead to differences in interaction. Through the feedback process, these differences will lead to some clusters or cliques of individuals having more dense patterns of interaction and feelings for one another. These clusters are dictated by processes in the internal system.

6. The two kinds of clusters or cliques, those created by the external system and those by the internal system, will be related to one another. The form and nature of this overlap is not clear at the moment.

7. "Leaders" are those who are chosen more often by others as a result of the activity, interaction, and sentiment feedback loops. Since the differential evaluation of persons in the system is based on something, leaders tend to have more of that "something" than others. This something is said to be a better match with the tacit standards or "norms" of the group than others in the group possess.

8. Because they are at the fulcrum of choice by members of the group (or by members of subgroups or cliques), leaders tend to initiate interaction more than others, reinforcing their leadership. In some respects, initiating interaction is the essence of leadership.

I would like to unpack this set of ideas. Homans himself did not reduce them to the propositions just stated. The propositions may be shown, however, to be the result of the playing out of a smaller set of ideas. It is also obvious that at least analytically, the two systems, the internal and the external, need to be differentiated. It will be useful therefore to try to find informal (internal) systems that are "pure" or relatively so. It may then be possible to systematically isolate the influence of external systems on small groups.

Pure Informal Systems

A pure informal system is of course an abstraction, but the parameters that define its variants can be specified. On the one hand, among the informal systems, the simplest cases to specify through observations are the "networks in a box." That is, networks such as those within the four walls of a classroom or, more generally, in which the boundaries are very clear (see chapter 2). These networks are characterized by total visibility; everyone within the network can "see" everyone else or be aware each other exists. Informal political influence networks, on the other hand, do not meet these criteria, though the interactions and sentiments that emerge are not prescribed by the formal political system. Visibility in political and organizational influence systems is limited.[4]

Within organizations, there are informal systems that cross "chimneys," where a chimney is defined as a chain of command of a division, say a parts department, an engineering development department, and a production department. The informal system enables communication across hierarchical systems without the communication having to pass up to the top of a department, across to the other department and then down again. Within work groups, there may be visibility, but much communication is formally prescribed in reaction to either the formal or external system. I follow Freeman's insight that a pure informal system "permits observation of interaction that is voluntary and informal and ranges over a broad spectrum of activities, [and] there is no reason to suspect that the individuals are interacting in terms of external constraints" (Freeman 1992, 163). Hybrid systems are those in which interaction is constrained by virtue of the needs of production, as for example in the Bank Wiring Room discussed by Homans,[5] or are systems in an office where there is a "boss," or in which there other prescribed roles. In hybrid systems, an informal system is embedded within and partly constrained by the formally named statuses or, in Homans' terms, by the external system. The karate club analyzed in the previous chapters also had an external system: a leader teaching karate. These hybrid systems are the most frequent, but a theory of what interaction patterns look like informally needs to be developed under the relatively rare situation in which there are no or few formal system constraints. Once such a theory is available, it will be possible to understand the relations between the formal and informal systems that constitute the heart of network analyses of organizations.

There is a further and important consideration in delineating pure informal internal systems from those that are influenced by the external system. A pure informal system is most easily observed and described when the activity is merely interacting or hanging around. If we observe interaction, we can say who is interacting with whom without specifying who initiated the interaction. We simply note that two members of a group were seen together. In formal terms, the relationship is symmetric: if I interact with you, then you also interact with me. If we are friends, then I am your friend and you are mine. In terms of process, one might examine how the interaction came to be. Often, one individual might have been the first to initiate the interaction, but that is not the present concern in defining pure informal systems.[6] In contrast, external systems tend to impose qualities and criteria on the interaction, and then it is easy to explain how the interaction came about.[7] It might be possible in pure informal systems to observe who initiated the interaction, or for that matter, ask people whom they choose as partners or want to be with (as in the Moreno study of girls' cottages).[8] These choices may or may not be reciprocated. By definition, the more popular persons will not choose the less popular, but the less popular are more likely to choose the more popular than each other. These choices by the less popular are equivalent to social climbing. These asymmetric situations are more likely when the external system intrudes on the internal system, as in most real-life situations.

How to Find Informal Systems

A pure informal system is one in which relationships are likely to be symmetrical and there are few or no named statuses and roles.[9] Though sociograms, as a depiction of social networks, are most easily constructed on the basis of dichotomous ties (either a pair is related or not), in real life people are closer to some than others. Even when relationships are symmetric and depicted as dichotomous, a type of hierarchy exists, with those who interact most often with one another dominating those who are less frequent partners.

Freeman (1992) evaluates two empirical tests of the sociological concept of group. One, proposed by Winship (1977), formalizes a definition of a group that is based only on observed closeness of ties, combining Rapoport's (1954) hypothesis that "the likely contacts of two individuals who are closely acquainted tend to be more overlapping than those of two arbitrarily selected individuals" with Heider's triadic balance theory (Freeman 1992, 155). In a triad, "a balanced state exists if all three...relations are positive in all respects, or if two are negative and one is positive" (Heider 1946, 110). For positive relations, this situation is equivalent to that of transitivity for directed ties. That is, if A affiliates with B, and B affiliates with C, then C affiliates with A (see chapter 2). Winship's definition of a group requires that within the group only transitive ties are present, a condition that also describes a strict hierarchy in a group (Freeman 1992, 154). For symmetric ties, groups defined in this way also have the mathematically neat, if not always empirically useful, characteristic of being non-overlapping. Most observed networks are messy, however, and have overlapping circles, and many intransitive triples.

To decide, in a situation in which a symmetric relationship is observed, whether or not a relatively pure informal system is present, the second of Freeman's (1992) empirical tests of the sociological concept of group is useful. Here, he uses a different adaptation of Rapoport's idea: Granovetter's (1973) concept of weak and strong ties. Weak ties are those between people who are not very well connected, as described in chapter 3. But what do we mean by "not well connected"? Freeman proposes a formal definition built from the very interaction matrix itself. First, consider a matrix of relationships such that the relationship is a matter of degree (people meet more often, have known one another for a longer time, or any such reasonable candidate for strength of tie). Freeman suggests that we define the highest level of attachment X, in such a network, that will divide between weak and strong ties so that the latter produce no intransitive triads, that is, where a path of strong ties connect A to B to C but A and C have no tie whatever.

Granovetter's transitivity would allow a triple to be termed transitive if it has two people who are strongly connected but a third one who is weakly connected to the other two. Freeman called these triples "G transitive," and triples that do not meet at least this condition, "G intransitive." But how does one know the right level below which relations are weak and above which they are strong? This ambiguity has continued to plague the otherwise neat concept of strong and weak ties. Freeman developed an algorithm[10] in which, by starting with the most closely linked nodes in a network and moving down to the less strongly connected, he keeps dropping the level of X that defines strong ties in the network until a statistically significant number of G intransitive triples are encountered. The lowest level of intensity of tie that retains G transitivity with very few exceptions defines X. Everything above that level is termed "strong," and everything below it is "weak."

Freeman applied this algorithm to seven data sets that had observed (not self-reported) counts of interactions. Strength or degree of tie was defined simply as the number of interactions, or for persons interacting at events, the number of common events attended. Strictly transitive relationships were very rare in all of them but the number of G transitive triples in four of them was far greater than would have been observed by chance alone. These were all situations in which "no evident constraints on interaction" (Freeman 1992, 164) were imposed by the external or formal system. This suggests a roundabout way of ascertaining whether or not a situation is one involving a relatively pure informal system: a pure informal system is one in which there are more G transitive triads than one would expect by chance. That is, using the relaxed definition of transitivity proposed by Granovetter, there are more such triads (which include the purely transitive ones) than would be expected by chance. The inner core of a system, the "clique" of insiders, is often comprised of people who are connected by strong ties; they are surrounded by hangers-on who are linked only by weak ties. Because pure informal groups are rarely found or documented, the idea of G transitivity has rarely been used, though it does give a formal way, based on the useful idea of weak ties, to locate pure informal groups.

Freeman provides a useful illustration with a famous dataset, "Old South," collected in the 1930s (Davis, Gardner, and Gardner 1941, 148) and reintroduced to students of small groups by Homans (1950). Based on observation by an ethnographer, "it provides records of women's coattendance at a series of small, informal social events" (see table 6.1).[11] A matrix such as table 6.1 that combines two kinds of data, in this case people and events, is called a hypergraph. Events can be linked in terms of people who attended them, and people can be linked in terms of whether they attended the same events. It is called the "duality of persons and groups" and is a very important idea in network analysis because it allows us to link social structures at one level to social relations at another level (Breiger 1974).

The strength of the ties between the women is defined as the number of these social events they co-attended. While there are many G intransitive triples among those who co-attended three events, there are very few (Freeman mistakenly says none) among those who attended four events, and these differences are statistically significant. Hence, Freeman sets X at level 4: Those who attended four or more events were defined as having strong ties, and the other ties were therefore said to be weak. Figure 6.1 shows the strong ties between the women according to X = 4.[12] It identifies cliques that are very similar to those in the ethnographic report.[13]

Figure 6.2 shows the weak ties between the women according to X = 4 and includes another four women and the majority of the ties in the network. The weak ties shown as lighter lines are those between women who are connected because they mutually attended three, two, or one event(s). It is evident that there are many weak ties in the sense defined by Freeman, and some of these ties serve as extensive bridges between the two cliques. Moreover, if one counts these weak ties, one can see that members of a clique may interact as much or more with outsiders, in number of ties through shared events, "than they do with some of their fellow

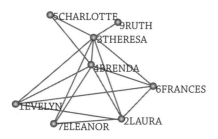

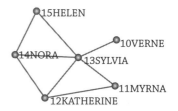

FIGURE 6.1 Strong Ties in the Old South Data Set

DEEP SOUTH

TABLE 6.1

Frequency of interparticipation of a group of women in Old City, 1936—Group I

NAMES OR PARTICIPANTS OF GROUP I	Code Numbers and Dates of Social Events Reported in *Old City Herald*													
	(1) 6/27	(2) 3/2	(3) 4/12	(4) 9/25	(5) 2/25	(6) 5/19	(7) 3/15	(8) 9/16	(9) 4/8	(10) 6/10	(11) 1/23	(12) 4/7	(13) 11/21	(14) 8/3
1. Mrs. Evelyn Jefferson	X	X	X	X	X	X		X	X					
2. Miss Laura Mandeville	X	X	X		X	X	X	X						
3. Miss Theresa Anderson		X	X	X	X	X	X	X	X					
4. Miss Brenda Rogers	X		X	X	X	X	X	X						
5. Miss Charlotte McDowd			X	X	X		X							
6. Miss Frances Anderson			X		X	X		X						
7. Miss Eleanor Nye					X	X	X	X						
8. Miss Pearl Oglethorpe						X		X	X					
9. Miss Ruth DeSand					X		X	X	X					
10. Miss Verne Sanderson							X	X	X			X		
11. Miss Verne Sanderson								X	X	X		X		
12. Miss Katherine Rogers									X	X	X	X	X	X
13. Mrs. Sylvia Avondale							X	X	X	X	X	X	X	X
14. Mrs. Nora Fayette						X	X			X	X	X	X	X
15. Mrs. Helen Lloyd							X	X		X	X	X		
16. Mrs. Dorothy Murchison								X	X					
17. Mrs. Olivia Carleton									X		X			
18. Mrs. Flora Price									X		X			

Davis, Allison, Burleigh B. Gardner, and Mary R. Gardner. 1941. *Deep South: A social anthropological study of caste and class.* Chicago, Ill.: University of Chicago Press. Figure 4. p. 148. Copyright © 1941 The University of Chicago. Reprinted by permission.

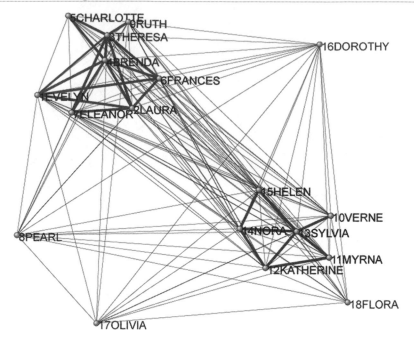

FIGURE 6.2 Strong and Weak Ties in the Old South Data Set

group members" (Freeman 1992, 164). This is important to observe because we have asserted that pure informal systems can link people or groups in different organizational chimneys or even different organizations. The bridge or link is likely to be some form of weak tie.

Still unanswered is why some persons in an informal system hang out together to such a degree that their ties with one another are in balance in terms of G transitivity, while others are less systematically tied and remain on the periphery? The answer will be related to asymmetric ties and the way these ties develop in the absence of, and as a result of, external systems.

Asymmetric Ties and the Influence of the External System

Some people are more popular than others. We noted that groups in which ties are not symmetric are closer to real-life groups, and that therefore there is generally some embedding of the informal system within the formal one. It was observed in the previous modeling of pure informal systems that, despite the symmetric nature of the ties as observed, a ranking system could nonetheless be discerned in which at the very least there are strong and weak ties. By considering asymmetric ties, we can advance to an understanding of what might determine the interaction patterns in the first place. How does a ranking system develop if interaction is not determined by the demands of an external system? And further, what happens when external system values are introduced into an informal system? To answer these questions, we need to review the topic of motivations in networks.

When we look at basic human interaction, without considering the effects of the demands of an external system, we see that even without external demands, some persons are more motivated to interact with others. These individuals' interactions and their motivations are components of Homans' "sentiments." We learned in chapter 5 that there is a fundamental motivation of "safety" or affiliation. That is, people are motivated to interact with one another because they can meet each other's needs in this way. This goes all the way back to an infant's interaction with its mother as the source of its needs and is therefore a very primitive motivation. Safety or affiliation, a motive that leads to cohesive networks, is not all, however. Nothing would happen in life if that were the case. One can also observe in very early childhood the tendency to reach out, to take risks, and move out of the zone of comfort. This tendency, present in all human beings, is called the "effectance" motivation. This motivation has its counterpart in network structure as well and leads, as we saw, to the exploitation of "structural holes" (Burt 1992). Finally, the third motivation is to seek status or rank. We can apply these motivations to small group development. To fully develop the analysis, however, an additional idea is required: the extent to which a person pays attention to others and is influenced by them. There may be a theory of how susceptibility to influence might be related to more primitive motivations and to early child development patterns, but that is beyond the scope of the present analysis. A full practical theory that explains what happens in a concrete situation might observe that certain kinds of systems recruit persons with different mixes of motivations. For example, some systems might prefer persons with stronger affiliative tendencies while others might tend to recruit persons with stronger motives for effectiveness. But for the present theory, consider that the incidence of these motivations is random.

In Gould's theory (2002), it is assumed that in any group there is some distribution of judgments about the attractiveness or quality of the members of the group. The bases for these judgments lie in the external system and cultural values that are brought to the group. Gould assumes, therefore, that in a small group there is no inherently correct set of values or evaluations. Rather, judgments in a group are a "self-fulfilling prophecy" in which the "Matthew effect" (Merton 1968a) holds—"to he that hath shall be given"—meaning that judgments of those who have greater rank in a group are given more weight than those with lesser rank and so the hierarchy is preserved. This matches the assumptions of a Nash equilibrium (made famous for non-game-theory experts by the book and movie *A Beautiful Mind*) that states, "If there is a set of strategies with the property that no player can benefit by changing her strategy while the other players keep their strategies unchanged, then that set of strategies and the corresponding payoffs constitute the Nash Equilibrium" (McCain 2002). This does not mean that the current state is the best possible, but rather that, given the constraints imposed by others, no better position is possible. The current distribution of social goods is the "right" one simply because it is socially confirmed. Note that this result is similar to Homans' feedback loops in which interaction leads to sentiment, and in turn to interaction, and in turn to a ranking system with leaders. The source of the evaluation of members is outside of this feedback loop and is located in either cultural norms or the requirements of the external system. On the face of it, this is a rather uncomfortable assumption in that the source of the evaluation is outside the small group system. This is a conservative assumption because it assumes that the basic values upon which evaluations rest never emerge directly from a small group but rather are culturally or organizationally determined. There may be group norms, as for example, group "standard operating procedures," but these specify the way that values are implemented, not the values themselves.

In building a model of a small group, we begin with safety, because we first have to have people who want to interact. Recall that in all groups there is some evaluation or feelings by members about the other members—Homans's "sentiments." These evaluations lead to a differential ranking of each member. As noted, it is not necessary for the model that we know the basis of these sentiments, just that there is some distribution of them. We also add Homans's now-familiar observation that sentiment leads to interaction and vice versa. Now introduce two corollaries of a basic motivation for interaction, safety and effectance, as discussed in chapter 5. First, in terms of sentiments towards the other, Gould observes that people have positive sentiments preferentially toward those who return those sentiments. I like those who like me and interact with them. I prefer not to interact with those who do not like me. This is a version of safety. In short, as Gould wryly observes, people like to have their phone calls returned. A second corollary takes account of the ranking in a group: it is sweeter to receive positive sentiments from those for whom you have positive sentiment yourself than from others you value less. Gould observes, "Consider how much more pleasant it is to be sought after by people you like than by people you do not" (Gould 2002, 1153).

We next introduce the motive of striving for rank or social climbing, which is related to effectance. People enjoy the fruits of rank. "[I]ndividuals like to receive attachments that they do not repay, inasmuch as such attachments signify (and contribute to) their status" (Gould 2002, 1152). This is a result of the desire to direct positive sentiments to others of higher rank, mitigated, of course, by the pain of not having these sentiments returned. This is the risk factor in social climbing. One wants to do better, even though this may lead to less positive sentiments from some. But effectance is limited by safety. There is therefore a trade-off between people attaching themselves to the most desirable others and to the most available ones. If asymmetry were totally painful, then people would "remain unattached, sort themselves into cliques in which everyone was tied equally to everyone else, or forge collections of symmetric dyads" (ibid., 1150). On the other hand, if no one cared about the asymmetry, then everyone would attach him or herself to the most desirable person. Real life lies somewhere between these extremes, so although total fragmentation and winner take all do fit the requirements of a Nash equilibrium, this situation is rarely if ever encountered. In the more likely case, individuals who do not receive positive sentiments from the most desirable others will tend to direct their sentiments to others who are less attractive than the "best" but who are likely to return the favor. This produces a ranking system like the ones described by Freeman for symmetric ties. In addition, the dynamic is likely to form a Nash equilibrium because no one has an incentive to change his or her pattern of sentiments given everyone else's pattern of sentiments. This definitely does not mean that the equilibria maximize social welfare but merely that they result in a state of affairs with which everyone is willing to live.

Note, too, that although the model finds the basis for evaluations to be outside the interaction system, the way effectance, safety, and desire for rank play out is a function of the mix of persons in the interaction system, and this mix is also not part of the model. Since the motives of effectance, safety, and rank are basic personality traits developed at an early age, people will differ in the strength of these motivations. Thus the shape of the system is not entirely dependent either on the external system or the dynamics of interaction; in part, the basic character of those in the system also has an effect. Gould further assumes that people differ in the extent to which they allow the opinions of others to influence them.

The equilibria operate in a closed system in which those producing the attributions of attractiveness are also those who are on the receiving end of these attributions.[14] There is, however, a further important aspect of these closed systems that has already been noted. The perceived quality of another is not only a function of some objective value external to the system, but is also influenced by the evaluations that the individuals in the closed system have made of the other. This is Merton's "Matthew effect" that we have earlier discussed. Those favored by the group tend further to receive favorable evaluations just because they are already popular. A similar observation about the strategies of interaction is made by Leifer and Rajah: "Once this inequality in being targeted starts to appear, it grows into what is commonly called a Matthew effect. Addresses are cast increasingly in the general direction of those who are addressed the most, as a directed address from them is worth the most" (Leifer and Rajah 2000, 261).[15] Further, the opinions of some individuals in some social systems are more susceptible to the influence of others, and some are less susceptible. For those less susceptible to influence, the external or "objective" factors will be more important; for those more susceptible, the opinions of others in the group will be more important. Whichever the case, both external and internal system factors have to be taken into account.

Formalizing the System

Gould offered a mathematical formulation that includes these axioms and ideas. The advantage of formalization is that one can draw a number of less-than-obvious conclusions from working out the algebra. In our terms, the model predicts that the subjective judgment of the quality of another by a group member is influenced by three factors: (1) the intrinsic quality of the other—judgments which may partially derive from the external system; (2) the interaction patterns of the internal system that develop from the safety and effectance motives; and (3) the weight of social influence in the internal system that affects this subjective evaluation of the quality of the other. Since this is summed over all the members of the group, the number of persons in the group also enters as a factor. The system becomes weaker and has less effect the larger the group.

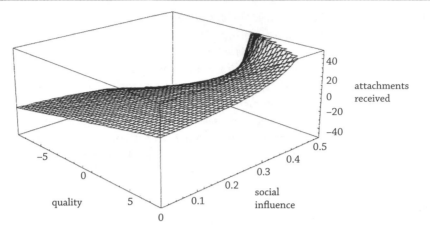

FIGURE 6.3 Attachments received (choice status) as a function of actor quality and level of social influence (n = 10, s = 2.5; reproduced with permission from Gould 2002, 1158).

As Gould himself observes, his equation for the choices received for any individual actor (see Gould's original article for details) is difficult to interpret. It also may fall apart as the number in the group gets large. He offered us a graphical representation assuming a modest group size (n) and a moderate degree of symmetry (s). In the figure 6.3, Q, quality, is centered on 0, as are the attachments received by an actor (otherwise known as social rank). Social influence, measured by w, is allowed to vary from 0 to 1. A small group of size 10 is shown in the graph, and the extent to which reciprocity in evaluations is valued is also moderate, meaning that a person is willing to tolerate some imbalance or some negative consequences for choosing persons of higher rank than him or herself. Since the size of the group is a factor, working this equation through over time will also show that low-ranked actors can give high deference to higher ranked actors without losing much rank themselves in another round. Basically, this occurs because the larger numbers dilute the overall reduction in their individual rank that would occur because of their giving deference to others (recall that group size is in the denominator). This is less true of smaller systems, which means that smaller groups find a more egalitarian system easier to sustain than do larger systems, something that agrees with common intuition about groups.

Notice that inequality in rank increases sharply as social influence increases, showing that social influence or the Matthew effect exacerbates whatever quality differences there are in the system. If there are no quality differences, then social influence has no effects except for the cascade of choices focusing on a single actor. Gould quips, "Ironically…the only status hierarchy that is stable when quality differences do not exist is the most extreme version of hierarchy—that of hereditary monarchs, for instance, or film celebrities" (Gould 2002, 1158).

The formal propositions regarding small groups that follow elaborate Homans's own.[16] Only four basic assumptions or axioms and two corollaries are required: (1) the safety motive and its two corollaries; (2) the effectance motive as constrained by safety; (3) the susceptibility to influence; and (4) the assumption that interaction leads to sentiment and vice versa. A large set of non-obvious propositions is derived. Some of the key propositions are summarized here:

1. Asymmetry: The more popular actor receives a greater "vote" from the less popular actor than he or she receives in return. The asymmetry is in proportion to the differences in their ranks as determined by the choices or "votes" each receives.
2. But, similar to the point noted above, this asymmetry declines with group size.
3. Actors who are similar with respect to quality get similar choices from similar others and, consequently, direct similar choices to these others. This fact results in the familiar observation of structural similarity partitioning of groups (see chapter 4). These consequences derive from the logical consequences of asymmetry (effectance and rank motive) coupled with the safety motive of preferring to choose those who are like oneself. Once again, however, the effects of asymmetry decline with group size.
4. Since actors direct choices to others in proportion to those received, actors with the highest number of choices received are also those with the highest degree of interaction directed toward others. But the cumulative distribution of popularity is more skewed or unequal than the distribution of the choices of individuals. Interestingly, given any two actors, it can be shown from Gould's equations that the one who is higher in choice rank directs *more* interaction or choices to any third actor, even if that third actor is very low in rank. This is none other than Homans's leadership paradox. Leaders direct more interaction to others even though the leaders have higher choice rank. No semi-mystical attribution of qualities or adherence to norms that Homans has attributed to leaders is necessary for this result. Leaders are those who enjoy and tolerate greater asymmetry in their choices than others, and, as a result of group processes, regardless of differences in qualities they possess or whether these qualities are derived from the external system or not, their rank is magnified by social influence processes within the group. And, as we have generally seen, these processes are mitigated by group size. That is, the propositions about leadership apply to the "small group."[17]

We can say a bit more about leadership. In this theory, it is a mix of three factors. First, there is indeed a "personality" factor, but it is quite different than the one usually attributed to leaders, such as character or charisma. Rather, leaders are those who can tolerate greater "unrequited love," but who are also interested in the less popular members of the group; they can tolerate greater asymmetry of choice. In terms of the strategy of interaction, Leifer and Rajah observe that in the milling-around stage, "It is strategically better to receive directed actions than to send them" (Leifer and Rajah 2000, 264). Good leaders are good listeners. Established leaders are, as a result of the processes described here, past the undifferentiated role phase. Nonetheless, adroit managers try to mask emotion so as not overly to tip their hand, thereby giving some advantage to those of lesser rank in the group. Second, leaders do possess more of the attributes of value to the group: beauty, brains, brawn, and the like. But, third, this differential distribution of attributes may be quite small; the differences are amplified by small group process so that the attribution of valued qualities by members of the group exceeds the objective differences.[18]

Where We Are Now

A limited set of simple assumptions can generate the major features of informal systems and networks in small groups. The first assumptions are the safety and effectance motivations. Humans, from birth, desire to interact with others in order to feel secure and satisfy their needs. These assumptions were added as a corollary to Homans's proposition that interaction with others leads to feelings, sentiments, or evaluations about these others, and these sentiments, positive or negative, in turn have consequences for future interaction. Obviously, if the sentiments are positive, a person engages in more activities (interactions) with the other; if the sentiments are negative, interactions are reduced. A second corollary is Gould's symmetry assumption coupled with the motivation to achieve rank. In interaction motivated by safety concerns, people prefer to extend choices or interaction with others who will return the favor. In symmetric interaction, for example, hanging out together, these assumptions lead to homophily of rank: pairs who hang out together or otherwise interact tend to have the same rank or share the same number of common activities. But networks are more than a collection of pairs of individuals. At least three are required to make the network non-trivial. A second assumption, based on Heider's balance theory, is required. As we quoted above, "A balanced state exists if all three relations are positive in all respects, or if two are negative and one is positive" (Heider 1946, 110). That is, if A is affiliated with B, and B is affiliated with C, then C is affiliated with A. We now have all the conditions that produce the interaction hierarchy modeled by Freeman. People are sorted into sets of mutual interest or regard. Above a certain number of common interactions, and this number differs according the group, the interactions are balanced and are said to be strong ties. Below that number, not all the interactions are transitive, and these ranks are said to form weak ties. The motivation for safety, accompanied by a desire for symmetry in interaction and the sentiment that flows from the interaction, accounts for the development of strong and weak ties in a small group. The safety motivation and symmetry in interaction also lead to grouping people together according to the amount of interaction or activities that they have in common.

In potentially asymmetric situations in which choices or attractions to others are considered rather than merely whether people hang out together, effectance and rank or status achievement become more salient. The effectance motive leads to the desire to control or make a difference in one's interaction environment and a need for rank directs the interaction. In this situation, some people are chosen more than others because rank homophily is not the only consideration. Social climbing or achieving rank is a factor. People like to choose others who are more attractive than they are, subject to the safety condition that too much unrequited love is painful. Attractiveness is of course not necessarily physical, but the possession of any attribute valued by the group. A third motivational factor in asymmetric systems is the tendency to be influenced by the opinions of others. That factor leads to the amplification of choices beyond the original differences in the possession of valued attributes. This leads to the ranking system Gould described and to the interesting consequences that ensue logically from this situation. Leaders, those with more rank, have more of what is valued by the system, and they tend to direct interaction towards others of less rank, that is, they lead. We also observe that the logic of rank dictates that the group becomes segmented by structural similarity. That is, layers are formed in terms of people who have similar ties or relationships with others. Thus, an opportunity for further effectance or manipulation is possible because persons can bridge relationships between people whose ties are weak and reap the advantage of being brokers.

Given the basic character of unformed or elementary small groups as depicted here, it is rather surprising that so little theoretical network analyses have been done with them. In part this is because they are hard to find. Laboratory-formed groups do not fall into this category because the demands of the experimental design and of the experimenter form a clear external system that impacts the group. The useful data all seem to come from careful field observations. And that practice has fallen out of fashion among network analysts. There is a line of theorizing from Goffman (1967) to Garfinkel (1967) and to the investigators of conversation patterns such as Schegloff (1999) that involves face-to-face interaction but is not necessarily group oriented, yet is very much concerned with the strategies of pure interaction. These theories seem to have gone out of fashion. The work on which this chapter is based is ten years old. A new work (Martin 2009) does address these issues but finds that horizontal structure and clique formation rather than a hierarchy of status or leadership is typical of gangs and other such informal groups. Clearly, there is room for more work in this field.

Whatever the research status on small face-to-face small groups, these entities are nonetheless endemic to social life. Understanding how rank and leadership in a group develops when there are no external requirements is useful because these processes underlie leadership and group activity in more complex situations as well. Organizations are an arena in which there has been much focus on small groups and leadership, but of course there are important demands from the "external system." The interplay between these demands, authority systems, small groups, and leadership will be a major focus of the next chapter.

7 Organizations and Networks

ORGANIZATIONS ARE SOCIAL structures designed to get things done through the cooperation of individuals. Organizations face four related challenges: first, motivating people to do what the organization wants them to do; second, deciding what should be done; third, accomplishing what needs to be done; and fourth, acquiring the needed resources. Additionally, the borders of an organization are not necessarily clear, and organizations have numerous stakeholders who must be placated and/or convinced to cooperate. All of these challenges involve utilizing a chain of authority or command to force people to perform—in other words, networks. While deciding what to do may involve individual creativity, most ideas are not original and come from others and the cultural milieu. Organizations use internal and external networks to develop ideas that help them decide what to make and/or what services to provide and how to do it. Networks help raise capital to provide organizations with resources. While the emphasis in this chapter is on for profit organizations, the issues of authority, clients, capital, and outcomes are common to public sector and governmental organizations as well, though they are often cast in different terms.

A formal organization consists of a designed chain of authority. A number of books describe the process for creating organizational structures (Mintzberg 1979).[1] But as we learned from the previous chapter on small groups, all formal or external systems breed informal networks that are grafted onto them. By way of the motivations of safety, effectance, and status achievement, the informal networks develop leaders that match the norms and culture of the informal network, and these may or may not match the norms and culture of the host organization. Further, modern organizations originated in Western democratic societies in which coercion as a motivating force is available only under special circumstances, for example in jails and in the armed forces. Even in these situations, pure coercion is rarely if ever successful, as (Sykes 1958) demonstrated for jails and Etzioni (1961, 56–59) reviewed for combat organizations.

The official leaders of formal organizations are appointed and not elected. In modern publically held corporations, executives are beholden not to the employees and their informal networks but to the quarterly report, government agencies, or nonprofit boards. Nonetheless, cooperation in formal organizations is gained essentially through the consent or at least the indifference of the governed. Our first task therefore is to review some classic propositions about authority in formal organizations. Then we will show how formal authority systems are changed or subverted by the informal networks that inevitably and necessarily emerge. We will assume that organizations have known boundaries within which authority networks and emergent informal networks hold sway. This assumption will then be relaxed when we examine organizations whose networks extend beyond the box or the walls of the organization. Throughout, we will show how the development of what to do and how to do it is tied to the informal structure as much as it is to the formal official structure.

The Contradictions of Authority

Modern organizations are rational-legal systems, based on universalistic principles and are supposed to be "fair" (Weber 1946, 78–79). In contrast, emergent social networks are based on particularistic principles. To the extent that friendship, homophily, and propinquity play roles, these networks are fundamentally "unfair." In a rational-legal system, the position, not the person, is obeyed because the subordinate believes the system is legitimate; consent is given by the subordinate rather than enforced by the leader. Thus, according to Chester Barnard, an important early thinker about formal organizations, authority "lies with persons to whom it [an order] is addressed, and does not reside in 'persons of authority'" (Barnard 1938, 163). The paradox is that we live in a democratic society of representative government in which leaders are elected according to the principle of one person, one vote. Yet we spend most of our lives in non-democratic organizations in which the leaders are appointed by those with financial power or other fiduciary power, and we are expected to obey them. Barnard's solution to this paradox is to insist that even these appointed leaders govern only with the consent, or more likely, the indifference of the governed.

Barnard thus laid the groundwork for a social network-based theory of management. A formal designed network does not imply blind obedience to any whim of the person in a leadership position. As Max Weber (1946, 199) pointed out, a designed network not only specifies the relations between the members of the network, but also specifies the boundaries of each position in the network, in other words the formal role relations each has with the other. It is not a personal fiefdom. This leads to Barnard's "zone of indifference": "The person affected [by an order] will accept orders lying within this zone and is relatively indifferent as to what the order is" (Barnard 1938, 169). Simon (1947, 133) characterized this phenomenon as an "area of acceptance," within which requests are accepted as fitting and legitimate but outside of which they are not. In the modern contract between a male supervisor and a female subordinate, for example, a request to find an item in a database is legitimate, but a request to fetch coffee is not.

Formally designed networks also include elements that are not strictly social authority arrangements, such as the factory production line, but nonetheless imply authority. In the continuous production system designed by Andrew Carnegie's chief engineer, railroad cars with coal and iron ore entered one side of a steel mill and rolled steel eventually emerged on railroad cars at the other end of the mill. The entire process was governed by a complex network flow that involved workers, supervisors, and blast furnaces, not to mention a railroad (Chandler 1977, 261). This system, which appeared to be entirely "technological," actually relied on a human supervisory network to ensure coordination between the various processes. "Production lines" and the organization of work through mechanical means are not confined to factories. Bureaucracies have them too. In a classic study by Peter Blau (1955, 54–55), the permanent placement of boxes with job orders on the desks of interviewers responsible for finding jobs for unemployed workers in one section of a state employment agency and the movement of boxes from one desk to another in a different section of the agency had important consequences for the flow of interaction and the extent of competition between the interviewers.[2]

Emergent Networks in Organizations

THE FACTORY FLOOR

The factory floor, assembly line, and repetitive forms of production are designed to maximize control of the workers and minimize their opportunities for informal interaction. But in the previous chapter on small groups, we saw in the seminal Western Electric studies of mechanical production situations, and their reanalysis by George Homans, that formal relations in what he called the "external system" were elaborated by the "internal system" into an emergent network of relationships. All interaction, that prescribed by management as well as any other interactions that emerged, was accompanied by "sentiment," and sentiment led to further interaction in circular fashion. Workers also brought their own cultural values and attitudes into the situation. Among those values, as we will see, was the working-class fear of unemployment. We also saw how the interaction system developed leaders that exemplified these same values. The challenge for management is to ensure that leadership and authority is granted by subordinates to leaders appointed by management and/or that the emergent leaders accept the values of management. The opposite challenge is faced by trade unions when they attempt to organize workers in the face of resistance by management. A union wants their members to take their cues from the union shop stewards, not management. These challenges have been especially cogent in factory floor situations. In the "Bank Wiring Room," an entire social system emerged from the designed network that linked wirers, solderers, and inspectors in a layout of workbenches forming an assembly line.[3]

Workers in the Bank Wiring Room frequently traded jobs (Roethlisberger and Dickson 1939, 506). However, as shown in the emergent informal network diagrammed by the researchers (figure 7.1), they also helped one another and formed friendship cliques. (In the diagram, W refers to wirers and S to solderers.)

Helping is another form of "deciding how to do it." The formal design of the system did not allow for helping. Yet, innumerable studies have shown that no assembly line works entirely as planned and that without improvisation by workers in modifying the line or improving it, production breaks down.

Besides encouraging socializing and fun (and antagonisms as well), the elaborated network also reinforced restricted output. So that even though workers were paid on a piecework basis (meaning that the more they produced, the more they got paid), they produced less than was possible. The authors of the study and the then-dominant "Human Relations School"[4] thought the worker behavior in the Bank Wiring Room was economically irrational and reflected an interest at odds with that of management (Roethlisberger and Dickson 1939, 534). Blau and Scott, however, argued that in view of the 1932 Depression, when these workers, including the researchers themselves, were laid off and the Bank Wiring Room existed no more, "restricting productivity was the most rational course open to workers to prevent layoffs" (Blau and Scott 1962, 93).

While the factory floor was the original scene of the early research on emergent networks, almost all current research takes place in organizations whose tasks are less routine or less mechanistic.[5] Part of the reason for the absence of studies is that access to factory floors is difficult. Not only is management less interested in studying these kinds of systems, but since many of these organizations continue to be unionized at this level, the permission of the union is also required. The few studies of which I am aware are proprietary and unpublished. The following is an example.

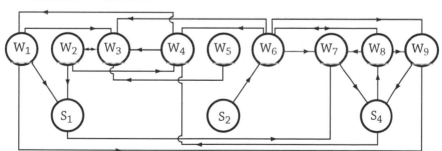

FIGURE 7.1 Helping Network in the "Bank Wiring Room"
Reprinted by permission of the publisher from *Management and the Worker: An Account of a Research Program conducted by the Western Electric Company, Hawthorne Works, Chicago* by F.J. Roethlisberger and William J. Dickson, p.506, Cambridge, Mass: Harvard University Press, Copyright © 1939 by the President and Fellows of Harvard College. Copyright renewed © 1966 by the President and Fellows of Harvard College.

I conducted a network study of a large continuous-process chemical plant in Europe that was part of a multinational firm. There was a small supervisory hierarchy, some support staff, and many workers with a high degree of technical skill who operated the plant. The plant ran 24 hours a day. It was unionized, and the only reason we were able to conduct the study was that both the management second-in-command, who was on his way up in the organization, and the plant union leader were enthusiastic about the research. The union was concerned about its shop stewards and wanted to know if members still looked up to and consulted with them. A network study showed that the management-designed hierarchy was not the main authority. Centrality scores were high for the shop stewards and the second-in-command manager. The chief executive was not central. The second-in-command who authorized the study was moved to another part of the organization.[6]

The study illustrates a frequent paradox of network centrality. The classic machine bureaucracy is a pyramid structure with a wide base culminating in the chief executive officer at the top. Information flows upward, and control or authority flows downward. While the issue of span of control—how many people should report to a single position or individual—is complex (Jaques 1976, 82–85), in general, the person at the apex of a bureaucratic structure has relatively few who directly report to him or her, as was true of the chemical plant. In contrast, a central person in a network, however this is measured (see below when we discuss the role of an executive secretary), has direct or short indirect connections with a large number of positions or persons in the network. Other persons in the network must go through the central person either directly or indirectly to reach other persons. This was true of the union shop stewards but not the CEO. Though the person at the apex has bridging properties and can link persons or positions not otherwise connected, he or she can have a low centrality score in terms of friendship and other informal relations. Bridging situations were infrequent in the organizational design of the chemical plant and were mainly confined to the second-in-command who more directly supervised several departments and who had a high centrality score. Thus, the number of persons who report to a position of higher authority involves tradeoffs. In a pyramidal mechanistic system a relatively small number of persons in authority ensure compliance, subject of course to revision on the factory floor. But to the extent that a system is modern and more complex, the ideas and inputs from a variety of positions and persons become valuable, and the emergent networks tend to undermine the carefully constructed systems of authority. If the organization emphasizes innovation and individual entrepreneurship, then having a large number of persons reporting to a position means that they cannot be directly supervised, and inevitably they must develop their own resources. Consultants to these types of organizations emphasize the construction of "flat" organizations with relatively few levels in which many people report to the next higher level (Tichy and Sherman 1993). This flat form may help to provide for entrepreneurship simply because those nominally in charge cannot micromanage so many people.

INFORMATION-DRIVEN ORGANIZATIONS

Factory assembly lines and other organization systems that involve repetitive standardized mechanistic activity continue to be important, but most organizations now focus on knowledge creation and symbol or idea manipulation rather than creating physical objects and are constantly changing (or trying to change) in the face of environmental pressures, even when they do have a mechanistic component. They are called organic systems (Tichy and Fombrun 1979; Burns and Stalker 1961). Law offices, health delivery systems, R & D, high-tech firms, financial firms, media production firms, high fashion firms, and many nonprofit organizations are all organic systems. Though automobile firms, for example, have a factory floor that fits the description of a mechanistic system, their economic health depends on the design and engineering units that are information driven.

Even though informal networks or emerging networks can change the flow of work on the factory floor, they nonetheless tend to conform to the planned network structure, especially in mechanistic systems (Tichy and Fombrun 1979; Brass et al. 2004). This is true because all social networks are draped on or embedded within instituted social systems that constrain and define the nature of the interaction; mechanistic systems constrain interaction more than organic systems that are characterized by less restricted and more flexible interaction. Some built-in constraints stem from the authority structure—superiors and subordinates obviously tend to interact. Proximity is an important factor even in the age of the internet (see chapter 2). It is much easier to interact with someone on the workbench next to you than with someone several buildings away. Proximity, as we saw in the case of the Bank Wiring Room, is governed in part by task differentiation and work flow. Nonetheless, whatever the constraints, we have seen that even in mechanistic systems with a high degree of visibility and control, informal emergent networks may counter the designed network's intentions.

Higher levels in any organization tend to be more concerned with symbol manipulation and therefore tend to have some characteristics of organic systems. In order to get a job done, communications, advice, and friendship networks in these kinds of systems, no matter what the official design, tend to skip levels and cross over into other divisions or units. There are also politics: departmental interests that may conflict with the overall aims of the organization. These concerns also create informal networks.[7] So typically, in my experience, when an outsider asks about an organization chart, executives say, "What organization chart?" implying that of course they generally work outside of the formal channels. The extent to which they do this, whether they skip levels in the organization or skip across to another unit or division, depends on the situation and the history of the organization. Indeed, it has been suggested that formal organizational structures are a ritualized form of behavior to be distinguished from what actually goes on within the organization (Meyer and Rowan 1991).

From a theoretical point of view, two network concepts are involved: the density of interaction within the basic work unit and the brokerage or structural holes bridged by the interaction, that is, the connections that are made between positions and individuals who would not otherwise be directly connected. The extent of making connections can be measured by the concept of betweeness (see chapter 3).

Betweenness is perhaps the most familiar situation in which a particular position serves as a gatekeeper for flows of information and power, vertically as well as laterally. A reminder here of how betweenness relates to power: our view of power emphasizes two-way communications, consistent with Barnard's zone of indifference. A "power score" can be constructed using this idea. The score has two aspects. Betweenness calculates the extent that the position falls on the shortest paths (the geodesic) between other pairs of actors in the network; that is, to get from one part of the organization to another, one has to go through that position. Next, and similar to betweeness, is closeness or distance of each position or node; that is, how near or far a given node or position is from all the other nodes in the figure. The Krebs Centrality Power Score (Krebs 2004) is a function of both these measures, and in this case we simply use the average of the two. While there are other measures of power or prestige in a network, the Krebs measure is easy to grasp and captures the idea of the extent to which a position is linked to others and the extent to which others have to go through this position to communicate with the rest of network. Note that at this point we are talking about communication and information. Power is of course also giving orders, though as noted, the recipient has to be willing to obey. But in keeping with organic organizations, for the moment we focus on communication as power.

People often note that the executive secretary to the CEO is a gatekeeper and that he or she has more power than the position officially warrants. Figure 7.2 illustrates the way that the position might be drawn on a chart of a multidivisional organization. The lettered boxes represent divisional leaders; the numbered boxes are units in the divisions. The secretary is drawn to the side of the CEO, as conventional for support staff rather than line executives. The CEO has the highest Krebs Power Centrality Score (0.192) and the divisions heads lower ones. B has more units reporting, and so is higher in Power than A and C. The units 1 through 8 have the lowest scores, but those units reporting to B have higher scores because they also interact with one another. The scores are normalized so that for each chart they add up to 1.0 with the lowest score being 0.

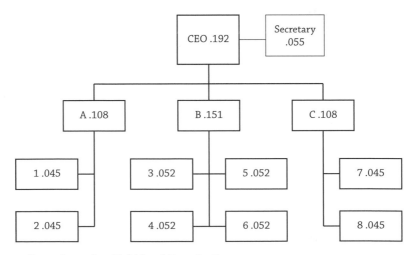

FIGURE 7.2 Power Scores in a Multi-Level Organization

But figure 7.3 in this hypothetical example is the way communications actually function between the divisions and the CEO. The figures in the position box are the Krebs power scores of the position. The score shows what is intuitively obvious. The secretary has a key gatekeeping position and the CEO, the nominal leader, has a lower Krebs power score because to get to the CEO one has to go through the secretary. The scores of the other positions have not changed because their pattern is the same as in the figure 7.3.

There is another critical aspect to life in complex organizations, and that is the "chimney" or "silo" problem. To manage complexity, to develop expertise in a given field, and to decrease the span of control, as well as to preserve organizational secrets (Oliver and Liebeskind 1997),[8] most large organizations develop separate divisions or units that specialize in particular areas. Designing engines requires a different talent and expertise than styling cars, though to be sure, one does affect the other. In the classic organizational multidivisional structure shown in stylized form earlier, units (3, 4) reporting to B have to go up the chain of command and then down again through A if they wished to note, say, a design change that will affect the work in 1 and 2. In my observations of design engineering in a major U.S. automobile company, even within the general category of engines, unit 2 that might be involved in designing engine-hose layouts would have to redo their work if say, the engine-block designers in 3 and 4 relocated the carburetor. The efficient way of working was for someone in 4 to contact a friend in unit 2 and directly work out the problem, as shown in figure 7.4.

Figure 7.5 shows the effect of this interaction on power centrality.

One can see why management may have mixed feelings about informal networks, even though a major design bottleneck has been removed: the CEO and the division managers have had their power reduced while units 2, 3, and 4 have seen it increased.

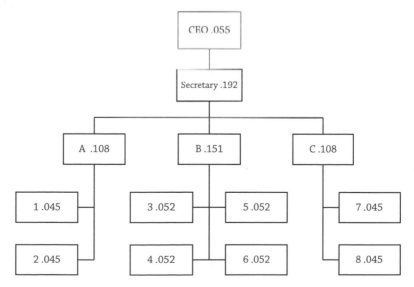

FIGURE 7.3 Power Scores in a Multi-Level Organization II

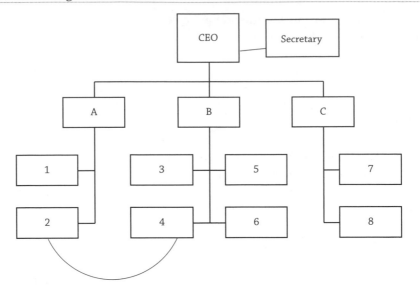

FIGURE 7.4 Example of Working Across a "Silo"

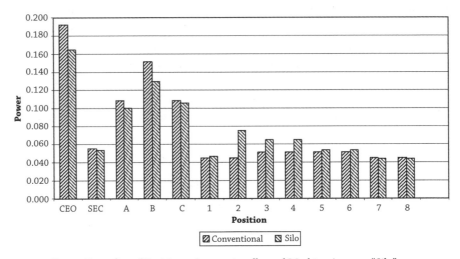

FIGURE 7.5 Power Centrality of Positions: Conventionally, and Working Across a "Silo"

And this through only one informal connection. Now suppose in this stylized example, position 2 does not like a particular decision made in the unit and bypasses her boss A to directly approach the CEO and "re-legislate" the outcome. The result is shown in figure 7.6. Supervisor A loses power while position 2 gains in power; the CEO actually experiences a slight gain since she now has direct access to position 2.

As noted, communications, though highly important in modern organizations, are but one kind of flow in organizations. Authority, and the accountability that goes with it, is still central to achieving organizational goals. "Networking" is a common buzzword in organizations that recognize that the formal structures of complex bureau-

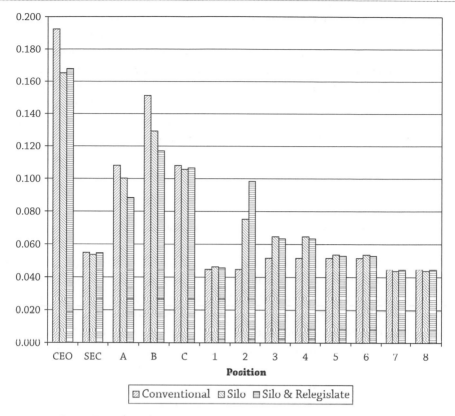

FIGURE 7.6 Power Centrality of Positions: Conventionally, Working Across a "Silo," and "Re-legislating"

cratic organizations are inherently limiting and stifle entrepreneurial initiative. Yet despite the attractiveness of using informal networks to get the job done, informal networks lack accountability. Top management has to "make their numbers" and eventually be accountable to the stockholders. Centrality communications power does not necessarily give the power to hire, fire, and be accountable. So a "double bind" (Bateson 1972) is not uncommon.[9] Simply put, a double bind is an overt imperative to do something, and at the same time, a covert imperative not to do it. The essence of a double bind in an organization is fourfold: first, there is an inherent contradiction embedded within the system or structure of an authority relationship; second, the contradiction is not apparent and therefore cannot be examined; third, the double bind transcends its origin and becomes a pattern for new situations; and fourth, none of the parties can escape from the situation. The rational responses to a recognized dilemma or contradiction would normally be: (a) "This is impossible"; (b) to try to resolve the cognitive complexity; and finally, (c) to quit. The pernicious aspect of the double bind is that none of these options can work.

Management often simultaneously sends two contradictory messages. The first is an appeal to be entrepreneurial, change, innovate, network, be flexible, and be empowered. Second, and at the same time, management insists that that it be consulted about all initiatives and maintain its prerogative to veto new ideas. Anything else is seen as an affront to its authority. This is a double bind. The mid-level executive is caught in a no-win situation because both imperatives cannot be fulfilled simultaneously. The emerging network can creatively bypass and ignore the top, making its own system. Eventually, this can lead to a modern "networked" organization with the top executive either forced to change or leave. More often than not, however, the system is mired in the status quo while its members wonder why nothing changes.

Inside the Box, Outside the Box, or Both

By examining networks within an organization, we have assumed that an organization is a "network in a box" (see chapter 2). For the moment, let us assume that the idea of a box around the organization is reasonable. Later, we will relax this idea and discuss the possibility that the conventional idea of an organization as an enclosed network is too limiting. Assuming a box, however, where are the "walls" to be placed? Networks are continuous. There is a core and a penumbra. Organizations need supplies and services. Should they be inside the organization and supervised through a hierarchy or should they be bought in the market place?

This is a classic problem addressed by Nobel prize–winning economist (Williamson 1975, 1981). In a world in which there is imperfect information and visibility, employees and outside suppliers can be opportunistic. Employees can take advantage of the employer. On the other hand, if a firm outsources, that is, buys needed products and services, the firm has to bargain with the suppliers to get the best price. Markets are not necessarily efficient, and suppliers of crucial material may hold the buyer over a barrel. The goal is to minimize these "transaction" costs. In network terms, we have encountered this before: all relationships are costly, and there is a limit to the number of relationships one can maintain (see chapter 5).

An example may clarify this predicament. Automobile manufacturing is a classic example of the "make or buy" dilemma (Walker and Weber 1984). Automobile manufacturers do not actually manufacture cars; they put them together on assembly lines. Which parts should they make themselves and which should they buy from outside suppliers? If the same sparkplug can be used by a variety of different manufacturers (low asset specificity), then a firm that specializes in making sparkplugs can produce them at lower cost than the automobile manufacturer, and therefore the manufacturer can get a better deal by buying rather than making them. A steady volume of need for the product and technological stability makes the market predictable and lowers transaction costs. Lower costs make it more efficient to buy as does competition among the suppliers. The more buyers know about the needed component, the easier it might be for them to make it themselves, but conversely, the more they know, the easier it is for them to set specifications for suppliers, thus further reducing transaction costs. In Walker and Weber's study of make-or-buy decisions in a division of a U.S. auto company, comparative production costs were the best predictors of make-or-buy decisions, and both volume uncertainty and supplier market competition had small but significant effects. Important from a network point of view, the emergent network of communications among the managers responsible for the buying was associated with the outcome of the decision. A counter example, suggesting that boundaries are fuzzier in the first place, is the Japanese system in which suppliers are related to the assembling firm in complex ways (Lincoln, Gerlach, and Takahshi 1992).

In an article that influenced much additional research, Powell (1990) argued that thinking in terms of a market or a hierarchy as a dichotomy or as continuum is unrealistic. He argued that firms with strictly defined boundaries and centralized control are historically atypical. Rather, the majority "are involved in an intricate latticework of collaborative ventures with other firms, most of whom are ostensible competitors" (ibid., 301). While strict hierarchical control may fit mass- production mechanistic organizations, modern organic organizations rely not only on internal networks, but a plethora of relations that are outside the firm's direct control. "Networks are lighter on their feet," he observed, though to be sure, networks engender conflict and limitation as well as cooperation. Automobile manufacturers not only buy parts as in the example above, but engage in complex networked relations with one another and with suppliers that go far beyond simply buying. Powell has in mind a specific kind of "network" since hierarchical organizations are also networks, as are markets.[10] More specifically, Podolny and Page define a network form of organization as "any collection of actors . . . that pursue repeated, enduring exchange relations with one another and, at the same time, lack a legitimate organizational authority to arbitrate and resolve disputes that may arise during the exchange" (Podolny and Page 1998, 59). These networks depend on the establishment of trust, obligations, and sanctions that are typical of emergent networks (Rousseau et al. 1998). A network organization draws on the resources available through the networks of its members. Put another way, they make use of the social capital of network members.

Powell suggests that these kinds of organizational networks are contingent on the setting and are likely to form under several conditions:

1. Project-based work, such as building construction (Stinchcombe 1959), book publication (Coser, Kadushin, and Powell 1982), women's clothing creation and manufacturing (Uzzi 1996), and most famously, Hollywood film production (Baker and Faulkner 1991). These diverse businesses all require flexibility, short-term often "one off" products, and rely on the trust, friendship, and reputation of workers, producers, and financiers.[11]

2. Information access "in fast-paced fields, where knowledge is developing rapidly, the sources of expertise are widely dispersed, and there is uncertainty about the best approach to a problem, organizations forge connections to other parties to access relevant expertise" (Powell and Smith-Doerr 2005). These are fields in which much knowledge is tacit and experience based. Word of mouth is important because by the time a publication is issued, it may be too late to take advantage of the knowledge. The biotech field is typical (Powell

et al. 2005). These are networked connections, to be sure, but they are based on the mutual need to stay informed rather than on friendship, per se, and are often backed by contracts and agreements.

3. Regional propinquity. Geographical co-location fosters networked organizational relationships as explained in chapter 2. There are two key concepts: one is homophily—not of individual persons but of organizations that "flock together." The other is external economy—the economies firms can achieve by using facilities and structures that are not formally part of a firm's organizational structure (Hoover and Vernon 1962).[12] There are many examples, all signified by the name of a geographical location. Most currently, "Silicon Valley" has fostered the development of computers and software through an interchange of ideas, people, capital, and facilities (Saxenian 2006, 1994). The biotech industry also had startup geographic centers in California, Boston, and San Diego (Owen-Smith and Powell 2004) but eventually, with more financing, extended much further (Powell et al. 2005). The most famous ones are now somewhat diminished as the work in these centers of activity have become more globalized: "Hollywood"—the center of film making; "Wall Street"—the center of finance and a symbol of capitalism; "Madison Avenue"—the center of advertising; and "Seventh Avenue"—the center of fashion. All these depend on the circulation of ideas, personnel, and technical resources ranging from special-effects studios and button suppliers to venture capitalists. The external economy and commodity homophily thrives outside the United States. In Europe or the Arab bazaar, all the spice stores are together; the clothing stores next to one another. In Paris, there is one quartier to go to for porcelain, and another one for linen, and so on.[13] Despite the power of the internet and email, personal contact remains important in all these arenas.

As is common with the particularistic character of social networks, there is a down side to the facilitative aspect of organizational networks. As we said, social networks are by definition particularistic and "unfair"; many of the challenges of an organization require a universalistic solution: "While networks can be beneficial, they do not always enhance performance" (Galaskiewicz, Bielefeld, and Dowell 2006). The use of social networks for information sources as well as help and advice can limit searches and lead to inbreeding or even collusion, as seen in indictments over "insider trading." The fastest and most efficient way for me to find good references to the literature for something I am writing, for example, is to ask knowledgeable friends; but use of the Web of Science gives me a wider scan. One of the benefits of having a CEO serve on the boards of other organizations is the scan of business practices that they gain (Useem 1980). But this scan has the same limitations as my use of friends to find a reference. Employers prefer hiring through referrals, but this tends toward a biased pattern of employment and possibly less effective workers (Fernandez and Sosa 2005). Corporate interlocks, that is, common board members, do not necessarily improve corporate performance. Not only are social networks "unfair" or biased, as we have often noted, they are costly in terms of maintenance. The cost can sometimes exceed the benefits gained. Social capital is not a free commodity, as will be further explored in a later chapter on social capital.

Which brings us to the complexity of social capital, consisting not only of who you know, the usual understanding of social capital, but what you know. Networks between organizations, especially in information-intensive leading industries, such as biotech or electronics, are even more complex than we have indicated. There are three levels of networks in intellectual capital exchange, including not only ideas but "how to do it" in the lab (Oliver and Liebeskind 1997): (1) interorganizational networks at the firm or organizational level, such as formal agreements about patents and their exploitation; (2) networks between scientists and engineers in different organizations that concern the latest idea, discovery, method, and pre-publication drafts of articles; and (3) networks between persons within an organization intended to bridge the silos that organizations sometimes develop as a matter of the control and ownership of ideas or simply as a device to manage complexity. The motives in each level of networks differ. Agreements between organizations are motivated by the desire to control financial payoffs and ensure that an organization's investments and joint arrangements with another organization are not harmful to the bottom line. This concern is not confined to the corporate world. In the 1920s, the University of Wisconsin reaped the benefits of discovering how to add vitamin D to milk. By patenting the process and assigning the patent to a university research foundation, researchers made millions for the university (Tatge 2004). Since then, most universities have created offices to explore the patent possibilities of their research. Scientists themselves may have different interests and may be more concerned with the prestige of a new discovery and being the first to publish their findings. They tend toward the free exchange of ideas as the way best to further this interest; they network with people in the same field, publish jointly,[14] and attend conferences together. Both corporate and university managements try to exercise some control over these exchanges. Within organizations, scientists and engineers exchange ideas across silos, partly to get the job done, partly as a result of playing out the norms of science, and partly as a result of social and political relations, as with other intra-organization networks. As Oliver and Liebskind point out, we have much to learn about how interorganizational networks actually operate. Important as they are (Borgatti and Foster 2003), there are surprisingly few empirical studies of interorganizational networks (Provan, Fish, and Sydow 2007). Theoretical studies of interorganizational networks deserve more attention than can be given at this point.

Bridging the Gaps: Tradeoffs between Network Size, Diversity, and Social Cohesion

Organizations without borders highlight the issue of bridging between different units of an organization and between organizations that are networked together. The type of bridging that links units that otherwise would not have mutual connections is associated with the concept of structural holes, discussed in chapter 5 on "Psychological

Foundations of Social Networks." To reiterate, a structural hole is a lack of connection inherent in the structure of a situation. We quoted from Burt (1992, 45), "Players with relationships free of structural holes at their own end and rich in structural holes at the other end are structurally autonomous. These players are best positioned for the information and control benefits that a network can provide." Autonomous players connect networks that would not otherwise be connected while their own base is well connected or not dependent on connections. Control and power granted by being able to play off others who are more constrained is useful, but access to information and new ideas is in many situations even more important.

Let us see how this works. The CEO in figure 7.3 is obviously unconstrained and connects Divisions A, B, and C. The secretary and those in positions at the bottom of this hierarchy are highly constrained. The CEO is in a know-it-all position. In this case, measures of constraint and power centrality essentially tell the same story because the figures do not deal with cohesiveness or density within the positions. But in figure 7.5, suppose A, B, and C, in addition to being division heads, also interacted regularly in a meeting of division heads. This could add to the organization's consistency and cohesiveness but also would increase the constraints. The division heads would no longer have exclusive connections to their subordinates, and this would also somewhat increase the CEO's constraints because he or she could not play off one division head against the other, though he or she would still be less constrained than the division heads. On the other hand, the CEO's power centrality would decrease and the division heads power centrality increase. There are obviously tradeoffs to the organization and the individuals involved between cohesion and structural holes. Is this "good" or "bad?" It obviously depends on other matters going on in the organization. This leads to a general consideration of tradeoffs between structural holes and cohesiveness in organizations.

While some studies show that persons who are less constrained and who benefit from structural holes are more likely to advance in an organization, in chapter 5 on "The Psychological Foundations of Social Networks" we cited a study that showed that two kinds of mentors were helpful in advancement (Podolny and Baron 1997). If a mentor bridged structural holes, then the mentor could help by making diverse resources available to the mentee. On the other hand, a mentor who was well embedded within a cohesive network could help a mentee gain a clear sense of organizational identity. Both resources and a clear sense of the organization and where one fits in it are important for advancement.

The issues of tradeoffs in an organization are neatly explicated in a recent study of an executive recruiting firm. Characteristic of modern organizations, networked or within a box, the key "raw material" processed by the organization is information. Compliance and power take second place to effectiveness and speed. In some ways, this is similar to Peter Blau's classic study, cited earlier, of a state employment agency charged with finding jobs for unemployed workers during the Great Depression. The setting now is a private "head hunting" "medium-sized executive recruiting firm with fourteen offices across the United States" (Aral and Van Alstyne 2008). Instead of card-index boxes on different desks, there are fourteen offices, and databases are the main source of information. But information is once again central to the organization's mission. The basic work of an executive recruiter is to match job candidates to the requirements of clients with job openings. To do so, recruiters must gain as much information as possible from a variety of sources including other members of the recruiting team, other employees of the recruiting firm, and contacts outside the firm: "Access to information enables higher quality decisions in this setting. Recruiters report being more effective when they receive rich information from their colleagues about candidate qualifications, circumventing screening barriers, handling difficult placements, and team coordination" (Aral and Van Alstyne 2008).

In this case, offices were geographically dispersed, and recruiters relied heavily on email from other recruiters to get the necessary information. The heavy use of email had two very important methodological consequences. The researchers were able to use real-time communication flow rather than retrospectively reported (and often erroneous) reports of interaction. Second, the actual content of the communication could be parsed (using modern computer-based methods) in terms of general categories as well as the richness of the information. Complex, modern, multivariate statistical models and simulations were invoked rather than Blau's elegant-but-one-person qualitative observations. A modern sociogram gave a sense of the way the firm was constructed. It was a modified multidivisional form with each "division" constituting an outlying office. The network of recruiters located at the headquarters was both highly clustered and dense compared to the firm as a whole (Aral and Van Alstyne 2008).[15] Despite the clustering and density (implying that a recruiter could simply walk over to someone else's desk and chat), email was a key mode of communication. Constraint in Burt's terms was moderate and while the partners were less constrained, hierarchy was not a major factor in the information flow.

The researchers concluded that there was a tradeoff between the network diversity that structural holes (less network constraint) offer, and the rich "bandwidth" (the volume of email averaged over the number of ties at a given time) that clustered relations offer. The explanation is complex. First, information in local networks tends to be redundant, whereas the weak ties characteristic of structural holes allow access to circles that expand beyond what one already knows. Thus network diversity is associated with more useful information in placing executives. On the other hand, the greater bandwidth associated with density is also associated with more diverse information. The reason for this is instructive. Passing on information is a discretionary not a mechanical activity. People have to be motivated to share, and this motivation is increased in socially cohesive situations. Social cohesion increases bandwidth as people discuss all sorts of things (the "office water cooler" effect), whereas weak ties decrease it. There is more than one way to achieve diversity of information.

This study reinforces some major basic propositions in the concepts of social capital, motivation, control, and diffusion of information as they apply to modern organizations. Network diversity contributed to performance even when controlling for the positive performance effects of access to novel information. The usual demographic factors such as age, gender, industry experience, and education did not predict access to diverse information; rather the network structure itself was the key factor.

Where We Are Now

Organizations formally conform to a system of rational-legal authority: there are rules, hierarchies, and appointed rather than elected leaders. The leaders are formally accountable to stockholders and owners, nonprofit organizations boards, or state organs. In turn, leaders hold subordinate members of the hierarchical network accountable to the next higher level.

However, in the 1930s, researchers and theorists began to show that organizations do not fully work that way. In the first place, the idea of legitimacy means that legitimate orders, those that fall within agreed upon boundaries, cannot be automatically enforced. Authority may be formally vested in the top of the organization network, but it is subject to the consent of the subordinate. In this sense, authority has been said to reside in the subordinate, not the superior. Second, it is always true that an informal network emerges alongside a formally designed network, for three reasons: first, the designed network can never anticipate all contingencies so that in order to get the prescribed work done, and done efficiently, additional relationships between the positions develop that facilitate information flow and help to ensure the organization's output. These emerging non-scripted relationships alter the power of some of the positions in the formally designed network. Second, members of the organization bring their own values to the organization, and informal leaders emerge from the ranks who conform to these values: these leaders may or may not be the same ones formally designated by the system and therefore may be supportive or subversive of the designed system. Third, the elements of sociability and office politics recognize that common interests, dislikes, and recreational activities will result in relationships both within and outside the organization. Sociability also affects the designed system, either enhancing or subverting it. The extent to which additional, non-prescribed networks emerge is partly contingent on the degree to which the organization is a mechanical system with rigidly prescribed tasks frequently limited by physical or mechanical means, or a modern organic organization that emphasizes information, innovation, and flexibility. Information-intensive organizations are more fertile ground for emerging networks, but even rigidly designed factory floors have informal relations that help or hinder the production process. Networked organizations that are highly embedded in an external economy system are likely to be even more dependent on emergent networks. To be sure, there is a bottom line: formal organizations can hire, promote, or fire their members. But even these processes are affected by emerging networks.

We began with three straightforward imperatives of an organization: First, participants have to be motivated to do what the organization demands of them; second, organizations have to decide what it is that they want to accomplish; and third, decisions must be made regarding how to meet the organization's goals. Social network concepts, measurements, and propositions illustrate how emerging networks dilute or enhance official power and centrality in designed networks. In other words, how emerging informal networks affect the first imperative of an organization—to get its participants to do what management wants them to do—and, at the same time, enhance the quality of the lives of participants. The embeddedness of organizations in external networks brings new ideas into an organization and affects the second organization imperative—deciding what the organization ought to be doing—but also the fourth imperative, to raise funds. Finally, the complex tradeoffs between the advantages of sheer network size, the presence of structural holes, and local, supportive, dense networks affect the ability of designed networks to get the job done.

Not to be overstressed is the important point that one size does not fit all. The consequences of formally designed networks and the resulting emergent networks in a given organization depend on the social and institutional contexts of the organization, its values, and the way it is embedded in other networks. These contexts will be explored in the following two chapters—one on small worlds and social circles and the other on the diffusion of knowledge and information. While in all organizations there are conceptual and process commonalities that network theory illuminates, there is no single textbook formula for a successful organization. If there were, all organizations would be successful, no organizations would go bankrupt, and organization consultants would be out of a job.

A final note. Despite the plethora of organization research and its increasing focus on social networks, there is a great deal that we do not know. At the heart of our ignorance is the relative lack of access to what is actually going on behind the scenes in an organization. We have studies on outcomes and structures, but by and large not on what people are saying and doing to one another. We noted problems of access to shop floors, but there are similar obstacles to studying design teams, labs, and executive leaders. A classic problem is boards of directors: what really takes place in board meetings? What is the actual effect of overlapping board membership? Answering these questions requires participant observation in group settings in addition to using traces such as email and questionnaires to map networks. We hope that there will be a gradual chipping away at the walls of organizational secrecy. Some of these issues, not easily solved, will be addressed in the chapter on ethics of network research.

8   The Small World, Circles, and Communities

Introduction

We have been building up from small groups to organizations, and it is now time to address the entire social world. As noted in the Introduction, the discovery that we are all connected in various ways has spurred the imagination of journalists, bloggers, not to mention social and physical scientists. A recent book by physicist Barabási (2002) titled, *Linked: The New Science of Networks* and with the copy on the front jacket reading, "How Everything is Connected to Everything Else and What it Means for Science, Business and Everyday Life," exemplifies the excitement. There have been claims and counterclaims and many technical articles in leading science journals including *Science* and *Nature* as well as more discipline-focused journals such as *Physical Review, Social Networks*, and the *American Sociological Review*. Putting aside the claim that the discovery of networks is something "new," there are seven straightforward fundamental ideas, most of which we have already encountered in our review of basic social network concepts, that when elaborated and joined account for "small world" phenomena.

The first idea concerns the number of others that people know in the interpersonal environment or the first order zone. The second is the fact that the distribution of this number is highly skewed: a few people know a great many people while most of us know far fewer. Third, the average or modal number is sufficiently large so that everybody ought to be connected with everyone else in a few steps. However, this is not the case, and whether the average number of steps is six as in the famous "six degrees of separation" or some different number, it is always larger than the number that would be expected through simple combinatorial arithmetic. Fourth, the reason for the larger number of steps is that social structure creates clusters of individual units (which could be people, organizations, or nations). Within these clusters, the number of steps between units is small. But because most units within a cluster have trouble reaching a unit from another cluster; a larger number of steps is required than what would be expected at random. Fifth, the clusters are explained or caused by two simultaneous conditions. The first is the structure of society—economic, organizational, and political, and so on. For example, a hunting and gathering community creates different cluster formations than occur in a modern industrial complex. The second and related cause for clusters is the actual network structure embedded within the social structure. Social circles, which are not formal groups, often account for network clusters. The circles are formed when the principle of homophily results in units associating because they have a number of different attributes in common. Sixth, the "miracle" of the small world occurs because the circles overlap—some individual units are members of several circles. It takes but a few of these overlaps for the entire world social network to be "rewired" so that connections are made between units that might otherwise not be connected. Finally, circles and clusters tend to overlap in hierarchical ways that produce the vertically stratified social world that we see around us.

The seven points need to be elaborated upon so that we can better see how small worlds, social circles, and communities are formed. This chapter will review each point and introduce some related ideas, findings, and controversies. The controversies occur because although the basic principles are not new, putting them together is, and there is much that we do not know. The reader should be assured that although this is a complex agenda, some of the basic mechanisms that we have already encountered, such as reaching out or effectance and safety, affiliation and support, and rank or status seeking, are also involved in understanding these very large systems. The "Matthew Effect" (the cumulative advantage that accrues to already advantaged nodes) and very importantly, homophily, are topics that were introduced in our previous discussions of networks. Small groups and organizations are also invoked.

The idea of a small world is not new. In Paul Goodman's novel, *The Empire City*, a character explains "The Theory of Our Friends."

[I]f two of us have one acquaintance in common we will prove to have three hundred in common, for we have these activities in common. We have gone to the same marginal schools; we have praised to the skies the dancer whom the rest of New York has not yet heard of; and if one of us steals off to a secluded coast that seems to us promising, he will meet another one of us walking naked toward him up Kings Beach. (Goodman 1959, 67)

In expounding the idea of the "small world," Goodman also noted some of the structures of interests and activities that gave rise to a small world. The networked-based idea of the small world was first developed around the same time (1958) in an informally circulated, underground paper by Pool and Kochen (eventually published in 1978), that we introduced in chapter 3.

Two fundamental ideas were at the basis of Pool and Kochen's investigations. First, the sheer number of people one knows obviously affects the number of links between two people, as the mathematics implies. Second, if the social circle shared by two people was identical, then no matter how many people each of them knew, neither could break out of that circle to make contacts elsewhere. Thus the Pool and Kochen article was an exploration of how many people one knew, and the extent to which the social structure clustered who might know whom. Given various assumptions about both, Pool and Kochen suggested how one might mathematically model the nature of the small world. Their abstract begins, "This essay raises more questions than it answers." But their work inspired an entire field!

How Many People Do You Know?

There are, as we said, two problems with which Pool and Kochen struggled. The first is determining how many people we know. The second is understanding the role of social structure in inhibiting or facilitating the small world phenomenon. In 1978, Pool and Kochen were not able to solve these issues. The Milgram small world experiment and the various replications of it noted in chapter 3 were attempts to get some more realistic evidence, but as we saw, those attempts were limited by the willingness or ability of people to complete the task of passing on a chain letter.

H. Russell Bernard, Peter Killworth, and their associates have tackled the first problem—determining the number of people the average person knows (Bernard et al. 1989; Killworth et al. 2006). This number is an essential component of what they call, following Adolphe Quételet's 1835 (1969) work, *Sur l'homme et le développement de ses facultés: Essai d'une physique sociale*, "social physics." The importance of the number is significant not only for scientific curiosity, though given the hype of "six degrees" that is significant in itself, but for social-policy purposes. Think about working backward with the number. In principle, if we know how many persons individuals are acquainted with, and if we also ask how many persons they know with particular characteristics, e.g., HIV positive or heroin users, then by combining these responses we could discover how many people in a given population are HIV positive, a number that we currently do not have. In general, we could discover the extent of many "hidden" populations as well as their social location and so begin to solve problems to which at present we have no solution.[1] Further, assessing these numbers and their distributions across various populations is not only a contribution to the solution of social problems but, as will be seen, bears strongly on the theory of the small world, that is, the nature of connections in very large social networks.

Unfortunately, there is no obvious direct way of discovering the number of people one knows, though beginning with Pool and Kochen there have been a number of ingenious attempts. The approach favored by Killworth and Bernard and their team involves asking a statistically representative set of respondents how many people they know in a variety of subpopulations (for example, people named Michael,[2] people who are diabetic, people who have a twin). "Know" is defined for respondents as having had contact within the last two years. The size of these subpopulations is available from published sources such as the census. The method, which they call the network scale-up method, assumes that a given respondent has a total network size of some value c, which is unknown. For any subpopulation that occupies a fractional size p of the entire population, the probability that any member of the network is in the subpopulation is assumed to be p. The number of people reported to be known in the subpopulation (m) has a binomial distribution with probability p and mean cp. The respondent is asked about many subpopulations. From the responses given, a maximum-likelihood estimate of the respondent's c (the size of their network) is computed. Providing that "many subpopulations" is equal to or greater than approximately 20, the statistical error of the estimates becomes small.

There are also non-statistical systematic errors in this method. One source of error is caused by a person not knowing that a person in their interpersonal environment has a given characteristic, say, is HIV positive. This is a transmission effect because of the varying likelihood that people you know actually tell you (transmit to you) every bit of information about themselves. Another source of error is that the differential location of a respondent in relation to a particular subpopulation causes the respondent to have greater or less access to that population. For example, alcoholics or drug users tend to know more alcoholics or drug users than the average person, and people in Oklahoma tend to know more Native Americans than do people in Pennsylvania. This is called a barrier effect because one's physical or social location can create barriers to knowing other kinds of people. As a social circle effect, it is part of the small world estimation problem, and there is no obvious way of mitigating these errors.

Killworth and colleagues (2006) have tried different modeling techniques. The methods tend to converge on finding an average size of about 290 but with a high standard deviation, meaning that there will be a number of persons with very large networks and others with quite small ones. Recall from chapter 5 that 150 was considered the average upper limit of manageable personal networks for the average adult. This number appears to be far too low for today's world.

The curves, derived from the several studies by Killworth and his colleagues (2006, 105), are fairly close to one another (see figure 8.1). There is obviously a long tail to the modeled distribution, as we would expect. The tail shows that there are a few people with very large networks. Figure 8.1 illustrates the distributions of network size from the Killworth and his colleagues studies, grouped or binned by 60.

But as with much sociological analysis, one person's "error" is another's finding. A recent paper by Zheng, Salganik, and Gelman (2006), takes advantage of the fact that the number of acquaintances in specific subpopulations is "overdispersed" and that the variance is greater than expected. Using a different statistical method, Zheng, Salganik, and Gelman reanalyze data from the Killworth-Bernard group and find that, as shown in figure 8.2 (2006, 415), the average number of persons known by men is 650

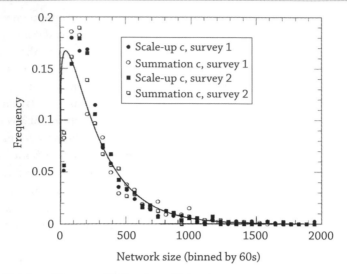

FIGURE 8.1 Number of Persons with Very Large Networks

Killworth, P. D., C. McCarty, E. C. Johnsen, H. R. Bernard, and G. A. Shelley. 2006. Investigating the variation of personal network size under unknown error conditions. *Sociological Methods & Research* 35 (1), p. 29 copyright © 2006 by SAGE Publications. Reprinted by Permission of SAGE publications.

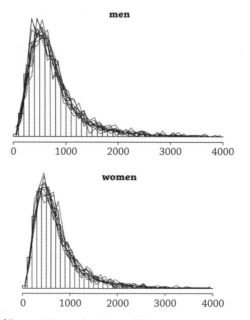

FIGURE 8.2 Number of Persons Known by Men and Women

Zheng, Tian, Matthew J. Salganik, and Andrew Gelman. 2006. How many people do you know in prison? Using overdispersion in count data to estimate social structure in networks. *Journal of the American Statistical Association* 101: Figure 2, p. 415. Reprinted with permission from *Journal of the American Statistical Association*. Copyright © 2006 by the American Statistical Association. All rights reserved.

and by women is 590, numbers more in line with some of the early Pool- Kochen experiments. The lines are blurred in figure 8.2 because of statistical smoothing.

Again the long tails.

Men and women were analyzed separately because names, such as Michael, used to defined subpopulations, were gendered, and the first substantive finding from "error" is that respondents of each sex tended to know more people in groups of their own sex. Further, women have a social network size that is 11% smaller than men, persons over 65 have a network size 14% lower than others, and in general persons with a college education, a job outside the home, and high income know more people. Non-white men and those under 30 tend to know more people in state and federal prisons. Finally, one bad thing apparently leads to another. Knowing people who are living with AIDS, who are HIV positive, who are in prison, who were victims of homicide or rape, or who committed suicide, who were homeless, or who had an auto accidents are all positively correlated. This is another circle and homophily phenomenon. There is also a geographic component: these outcomes tend to be concentrated in certain neighborhoods, along with crime and heroin use.

The circle phenomenon, which we will discuss shortly, creates the situation in which "it takes one to know one." Even controlling for a neighborhood disadvantage score, marijuana users are 22 times more likely than non-users to know another marijuana users; heroin users are 16 times more likely than non-users to know of other users (Kadushin et al. 2006).

The drug use example is one of many. Unfortunately, the epidemiology community has in the past been suspicious of these "small world" methods and has not sufficiently taken advantage of them. The methods are clearly not perfect but better than what we have for estimating hard-to-find populations.

The Skewed Distribution of the Number of People One Knows

The skewed distributions graphed above have some important formal mathematical properties that have generated a good deal of discussion. They are called power distributions (sometimes called "laws"), defined as:

> A quantity x obeys a power law if it is drawn from a probability distribution
> $p(x) \sim x^{-\alpha}$ where α is a constant parameter of the distribution known as the exponent or scaling parameter. (Clauset, Shalizi, and Newman 2009, 1)

This is called a power distribution because the distribution of the probabilities, $p(x)$, is more or less equal to x raised to the negative power of α.[3] In one of the earliest social science examples of a power distribution, Pareto showed that 80% of the wealth was owned by 20% of the population (Originally [Pareto 1896] but widely cited elsewhere). In the Pareto example, the exponent α is about 2. Unlike the familiar normal curve with which we have all grown up, shown in figure 8.3, a power distribution as shown in figure 8.4 starts high and tails off, with no cutoff.

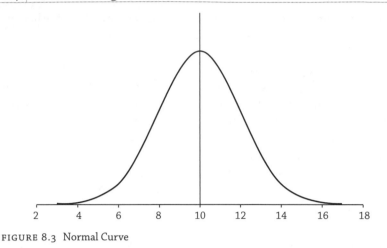

FIGURE 8.3 Normal Curve

The graph in figure 8.4 has linear scales on both axes. If those scales are transformed into logarithms, then the graph is called a log-log graph. The transformation produces a straight line, and the angle of the line to the x axis is the exponent α. A log-log graph is shown in figure 8.5. This distribution is called "scale free" because its shape does not depend on the scaling parameter. In most data fitted in social science, the curve exponents generally lie between 2 and 3.

Power distributions are said to fit many phenomena. When physicists and mathematicians first started to study networks, not necessarily social networks but those found in the natural world, it was convenient to assume that network nodes had a degree distribution that was random, that is, was the familiar normal distribution shown above (Barabási 2002; Watts 2003).

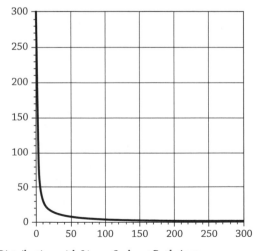

FIGURE 8.4 Power Distribution with Linear Scale on Both Axes

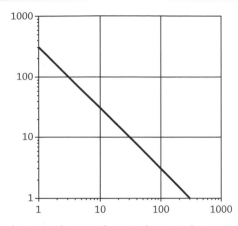

FIGURE 8.5 Power Distribution with Logarithmic Scales on Both Axes

A normal curve when plotted on a double logarithmic scale such as in figure 8.5, rather than the familiar linear scale in figure 8.4, has a well-defined cut-off above which the probabilities are essentially zero and look like figure 8.6 (Watts 2004, 251):

Since normal distributions did not produce realistic network models, Barabási and Albert (1999) suggested that internet links from one document to another, the collaboration of movie actors, and citation patterns of scientific papers did not follow random or Poisson distributions, but rather the power distribution illustrated above. They called these distributions "scale free" because, unlike the normal curve, the resulting curve stretched with no cut-off, and the shape was the same no matter what the scale of the network. The scale was governed by the exponent. The social sciences do have examples of distributions that approach looking like power distributions. But as we

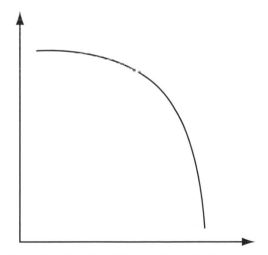

FIGURE 8.6 Normal Curve Plotted on Logarithmic Scales on Both Axes

will see, although they are highly skewed, they do not very well fit the touted power distributions.

Because they are not social scientists, Barabási and Albert did not know that they had been preceded descriptively by Pareto's depictions of income distributions mentioned earlier. They were also preceded mathematically by Price (1976), who observed that the distribution of citations followed a power distribution that he termed a "Cumulative Advantage Distribution...which models statistically the situation in which success breeds success" and identified it with the Bradford Law, the Lotka Law, and the Pareto and Zipf Distributions, all of which are forms of power distributions. Price also identified the reason for the distribution, a version of the Merton's "Matthew Effect" ("to he who hath shall be given"; Merton 1968a). In small groups, we see that "the uncertainties and subjectivity inherent in quality judgments gives rise to a self-reinforcing process in which collective adherence to socially provided assessments reproduces and thereby validates those very assessments" (Gould 2002, 1148). Scientists, presumably less subjective, are not much different. Merton observes that "cognitive material presented by an outstanding scientist may have greater stimulus value than roughly the same kind of material presented by an obscure one" (Merton 1968a, 60). Cumulative advantage is not only psychological but institutional, as Merton points out: "The rich get richer at a rate that makes the poor become relatively poorer. Thus, centers of demonstrated scientific excellence are allocated far larger resources for investigation than centers which have yet to make their mark. In turn, their prestige attracts a disproportionate share of the truly promising graduate students" (ibid., 61).

These potentially complex psychological and social structural underpinnings can be very simply modeled by assuming that each node in a network is eligible to receive, for whatever reasons, additional ties in the next time period that are in proportion to the current number of ties it has—to he who hath shall be given. As Watts explains it, "The oldest nodes in the network, therefore, have an advantage over more recent additions" (2003, 109). Over a long time period (something one can model computationally but is hard to observe in real life), the degree distribution of a network converges to become a power distribution that is similar to those observed at any single time period in empirical data.

More recent models suggest that network growth assumes that recent arrivals to a network select, at random, a member of the existing population, and that further, they are directed to a neighbor of this choice. These neighbors have a degree (nomination or choice) distribution proportional to the distribution of degrees in the network, that is, most have few degrees while a minority have very many. With this kind of skewed distribution, the average member initially chosen at random will have fewer ties than her neighbor. Feld (1991), as we have observed before, ingeniously showed that this "sad" fact of friendship networks leads to the correct sense that your friends have more friends than you do.

An intuitively pleasing extension of the idea that there are people toward the end of the tail of the distribution who know a great many others, is that these hubs or influentials—those whose rolodex minds contain thousands of names they can activate—are the brokers who link all of us and bridge separate worlds. But this principle, that the small world is created by units at the end of the tail that have many connections—including some to the less endowed such as you and me—actually runs counter to the Matthew Effect of preferential-attachment. In the preferential-attachment model, high degree nodes are linked to others with low degree. So, nodes such as 3, 11, 24, and 28 have many links, and they link small clusters (see figure 8.7).[4]

Compare figure 8.7 with the same 30-node sociogram with preferential attachments in figure 8.8 but which has been altered so that node 11 has 13 connections and node 24 has 17 connections. The connections between the clusters are now mainly made by the two nodes that have many nodes in their rolodex. In this case, high-degree nodes are linked to others with a high degree. This is called an assortative distribution or mixing (Newman and Park 2003). Put another way, the elites tend to hang out with other elites. Newman (2003) finds that a positive index of assortative mixing is characteristic of social networks. It also means that the degrees of adjacent nodes are positively correlated. On the other hand, physical networks such as electric power grids are generally characterized by adjacent nodes being negatively correlated as in the first graph: nodes with high degrees are adjacent to those of low degree. Either situation could lead to a small world model, but the mechanism is entirely different. Both are plausible, and though physical grids would hardly have a psychology of preferential-attachment, constructing a power grid that distributes energy in a hierarchical tree-like structure seems a reasonable strategy.

We need more research to understand which kinds of social networks have a preferential attachment pattern and which have more of an assortative or elite connection

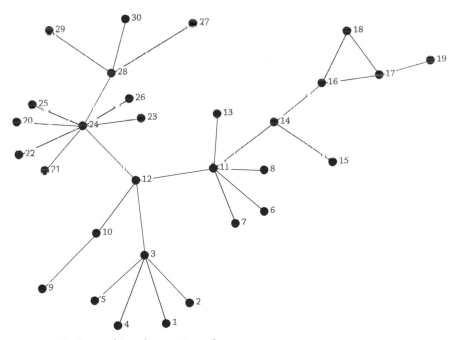

FIGURE 8.7 Preferential Attachment Network

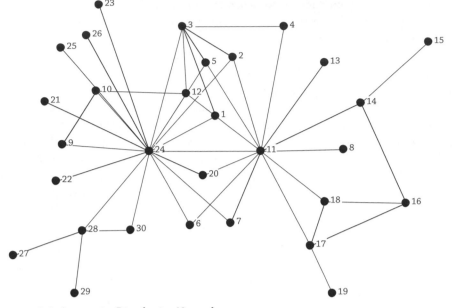

FIGURE 8.8 Assortative Distribution Network

pattern. A useful beginning is Roth and Cointet's work (2010) that examined the dynamic networks of bloggers during the U.S. presidential election of 2008. They compared the blogger networks to those formed by published papers and their authors on zebrafish from 1999 to 2006. Both social nodes (the authors) and concepts (the papers) were studied. The study of papers showed strong assortative patterns for both authors and the concepts they used: "Scientists who already had a high number of collaborations are likely to have links with similarly 'rich' scientists" (ibid., 21). This was not true of bloggers: those with many citations were just as likely to be cited by those with few as those with many, and the reverse. The dynamics of blogging and scientific research appear to be different.

In any case, we clearly need to distinguish social networks from other kinds of networks. From the point of view of social networks, Barbási's power theories postulate that the existence of hubs, or influentials, means that sooner, rather than eventually, everything is connected. But the theory does not help us much to understand real social networks, nor why the small world—that is, the ability to reach any point in a network through relatively few intermediaries—might be a reasonable hypothesis. There are a number of reasons why this breakthrough has proven less successful in understanding social networks than its proponents initially had hoped.

First, power distributions can only be fully scale free when the network is infinitely large, but real networks on this earth are finite (though the physicists found internet-based networks to be large enough to be considered infinite). Because of the limitations of human interaction (see chapter 5, "Psychological Foundations"), all networks based on human interactions have a cutoff and a starting point ("No man is an island" [Donne 1624]). Until recently, mathematicians simply plotted the observed or modeled distributions on log-log graph paper, and if the line resembled figure 8.2, they assumed that the power distribution was the correct way to describe the data.

Recently, investigators examined the distributions touted as power distributions on the basis of looking at their graphs and found the description inaccurate. Very few actually fit a power distribution. They examined 14 continuous distributions including: the numbers of sightings of bird species, the number of customers affected by blackouts, the frequency of surnames, web links, and the aggregate net worth of the richest individuals in the United States (for details, see Clauset, Shalizi, and Newman 2009, 17). Wealth, Pareto's original insight, did not fit a power distribution but did fit an exponential distribution (a similar negative-exponent distribution which is not "scale free" because a parameter that affects the shape is the time between events). Six of the 14 distributions had a "moderate" fit to a power distribution, meaning that while the power distribution was a good fit, there were other equally plausible alternative distributions. Six fit with a "cut-off," meaning that the power distribution with an exponential cut-off (a hybrid between a power and an exponential distribution) was "clearly favored over the pure power law" (ibid., 26). The power distribution with a cut-off is the one favored by Watts as more realistic for social networks. In fact, the only more or less social network distribution in Clauset Shalizi, and Newman's analysis is the size of email address books of computer users at a large university. It fits a power distribution with a cut-off but also fits an exponential distribution. The only good fit, "in the sense that it is an excellent fit to the data and none of the alternative [distributions] carries any weight," (Clauset, Shalizi, and Newman 2009, 18) is the frequency of occurrence of unique words in Moby Dick. The word occurrence distribution is the one originally proposed for a power distribution by Zipf (1949).

An obvious problem in testing the fit of social network data to any of the standard distributions is the absence of large-scale true social-interaction-network data, a deficit duly noted by most of the physicists and mathematicians drawn to the study of networks. The types of networks that have received most attention are therefore by necessity physical or biological ones. That the idea of "network" includes all these other phenomena may perhaps be a revelation to social scientists, but most of the work on non-social networks has not been very helpful to us. It is of course possible that the U.S. government in its studies of terrorism has been gathering large-scale social data, which it has been "mining" (see chapter 11 on ethics), but none of these data are publicly available.

Formal Small World Models

Small world theory requires not only that everything is eventually connected with everything else via distributions with long tails, but that there exist short paths, say less than ten steps, that serve to link nodes or vertices that might otherwise appear to be many steps away from one another. There are mathematical models that capture the small world idea; the expressions and assumptions of the model serve as a theory of why there are such things as a small world. The virtue of a model is precisely that it is simplistic; a few rules or principles can approximate a wide range of "real world" phenomena, thus performing the basic mission of theory: to link situations that might at first seem quite disparate. The first small world model that captured enormous attention was the Watts-Strogatz model (1998) published in *Nature*, a leading, widely read general science journal. The model did not assume networks based on affiliation clusters but rather, more simply, that nodes were connected on a grid to nearest neighbors (k). Although the original motivation for the model was message flow, the model was a structural model: connections were symmetric and the only "flow" was knowing someone. The connection network was neither completely ordered nor completely random. The number of nearest neighbors could vary according to a parameter (p) that specified the proportion of ties that jumped from the nearest neighbor to a further one, a condition that they called "rewiring" (see figure 8.9, taken from Watts 2004, 245). This rewiring or jumping across the network, shown in the the middle panel of figure 8.9 is what made for a small world. Observe that neither p nor k is the same thing as the distribution of the number of nodes that are directly connected with a given node (the number of persons an average persons knows)—the initial motivator for the Pool and Kochen original small world formulation. This model does not depend on the sheer number of persons known to the average individual, but rather on the *local density* of the circle known to an individual or connected to a vertex.

When p is 0, nothing is rewired, and to get to the other side of the network, one has to go through all the nodes. Everything is connected to everything else in the circle, but the world is very "large." When p is close to 1, there are connections all across the network and the world is "small" even though there are many nodes. In social terms, consider a high p as indicating extreme cosmopolitanism. The individual is connected to many others around the world. Watts and Strogatz quantified these properties with a coefficient, C, the clustering coefficient of a network. This stood for a measure of local density—the extent to which the nearest neighbors (k) were connected with one another. Another coefficient, L, is the average shortest path length. The mathematics

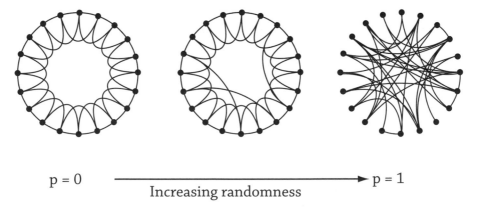

p = 0   Increasing randomness   p = 1

FIGURE 8.9 Example of "Rewiring"

Watts, Duncan J. 2004. The "new" science of networks. *Annual Review of Sociology* 30 (1): p. 245. copyright © 2004 Annual Reviews, Inc. Reprinted by permission.

that relates L and C is fairly complex but can be intuitively understood with the graph shown in figure 8.10 (Watts 2004, 245). The graph is a computation of a network with 1,000 nodes (N), and a local network (k) of size 10. The y axis is the normalized average shortest path distance. (Normalization makes the path distance vary between 0 and 1.) The x axis is the "rewiring" parameter p that runs from 0 to the maximum of 1. The top line, marked by the boxes, is the ratio of the maximum local clustering for this situation to the minimum clustering. It is logarithmic with a convex curve and appears to drop sharply after a p of 0.01. The bottom line, the dots, graphs the average shortest path distance, L, according to the size of p. It is also logarithmic but has a concave curve, that is, a curve in the opposite direction to that of the top line. It starts to rise sharply around a p of 0.01. One can see that there is a region of the graph with fairly low local clustering that is accompanied by a low average path length. That is, some degree of local ordering with a small fraction of long range, random shortcuts. This is one way of defining the small world that is consistent with the original Pool and Milgram idea but does not depend on estimating how many others the average individual might know. The connections that jump from the neighborhood or "rewire" the network are random. It is important that this model does not require hubs. However, as we will see later, extensions to the model that better fit the clustered nature of the social world involve distributions with long tails.

Figure 8.10 is of course a simulation, not a real-world example. Watts and Strogatz found three quite different networks that do fit the small world model: the affiliation network of movie actors, the power transmission grid of the western United States,

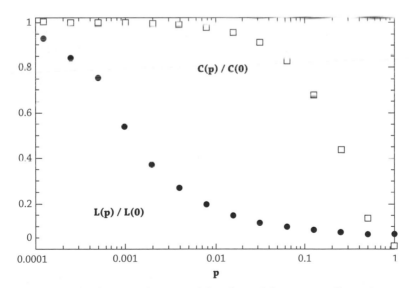

FIGURE 8.10 Normalized average shortest path length L and clustering coefficient C as a function of the random rewiring parameter p for the Watts-Strogatz model with N = 1000, and (k) = 10.

Watts, Duncan J. 2004. The "new" science of networks. *Annual Review of Sociology* 30 (1): p. 249. copyright © 2004 Annual Reviews, Inc. Reprinted by permission.

and the neural network of the nematode *Caenorhabiditis elegans* (a widely studied species of worm). Physicists have since found many other examples and added important qualifications: "small worlds will result in very large networks whenever the fraction of random shortcuts is greater than zero—that is, for any randomness at all" (Watts 2004, 247). That is, knowing just a few people outside of one's immediate surroundings will produce a small world. Further, in very large networks, the addition of only five random shortcuts halved the average path length. Finally, and this is important for social networks, if the local neighbors consist of affiliation networks, similar results ensue. As Watts points out, "the conditions required for small-world behavior to pertain are even weaker than at first thought" (ibid.). If the conditions that sustain small world phenomena are "weak" in terms of mathematical assumptions, then the ubiquitous character of small worlds is a very robust finding. Yet despite the avalanche of recent work by physicists, there are still many unanswered questions about how best to understand the small world. Just because small worlds are mathematically proven to be possible, does not mean that we understand how they actually work socially. There is less to the small world hype than is at first apparent. Watts himself points out, "Unfortunately, the Watts-Strogatz model suffers from some serious problems that render it unsuitable as a model of social networks" (ibid.).

Here are some of the problems. We need to know how embeddedness in one or another of several social structures contribute to the "rewiring" inherent in small world phenomena. That is, how do people go about using their local position to engage in searching the small world? What is the role of social structure in aiding or inhibiting path length? What role do organizations play? What kinds of key people are links in small world phenomena? What is the role of occupations and other social statuses? What is the role of social and geographic mobility? Are different networks created by different kinds of flows? We begin to answer these questions by first reviewing clustering in social networks. This will take us to a consideration of the role of social circles in the small world.

Clustering in Social Networks

Aside from the way connections are distributed in social networks, a key feature of social networks is high transitivity, meaning that if A and B are connected and there is also a connection between B and C, it is likely that there is also a connection between A and C (discussed in chapter 2). This situation does not occur in physical and biological networks (Newman 2006b; Newman and Park 2003). Transitivity leads to clustering into "communities" (chapter 3) and calls for quite different models than those that work for other kinds of networks. The clustering occurs because people belong to groups and organizations of one kind or another, or write papers together, or appear in the same movies, or belong to the same boards of directors. They also live in geographically delineated neighborhoods and, as we saw in the chapter on small groups, may attend the same events. People are said to be connected when they share membership in one of these "communities"; conversely, the "communities" are linked when

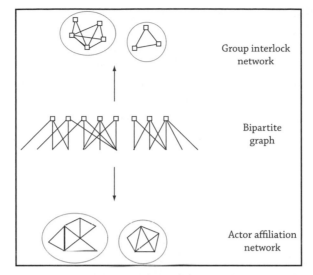

FIGURE 8.11 Bipartite (two mode) affiliation network (center), defined in terms of N actors belonging to M groups, along with unipartite (single mode) projections onto the set of groups (top) and actors (bottom).

Watts, Duncan J. 2004. The "new" science of networks. *Annual Review of Sociology* 30 (1): p. 251. Copyright © 2004 Annual Reviews, Inc. Reprinted by permission.

they share at least one person in common. This duality was first called attention to in an aptly titled paper, "The Duality of Persons and Groups" (Breiger 1974). In the mathematical language of graph theory, this duality is called a bipartite graph. Watts's (2004, 249) illustration of this idea appears in figure 8.11:

Formal affiliations based on statuses, organizations, or other formal memberships capture only one aspect of the modern social structures. Informal friendship and other kinds of relationships such as social circles also serve to cluster social networks.

Social Circles

We now come to the key idea that makes for the clustering that underlies social network small words. In chapter 3, we encountered the idea that networks had a "core." The notion of a degree of "coreness," and the difficulty in the karate club of drawing a clear partition, illustrated some practical difficulties in segmenting networks into regions or "communities." These apparent technical difficulties actually stem from important theoretical concerns. Social life is messy, and social networks are therefore far more complicated than the networks of electrical circuits that were the first applications of network theory and, as we said, different from recently studied biological or physical phenomena. First there is the problem of the penumbra—that is, the extent to which there are clear boundaries within society. With instituted groups or organizations the boundaries are fairly clear. We think we know who is a member of classroom x or organization y or even kinship group or moiety z. But if social life is conceived to be a skein or chain of relationships of potentially infinite regress—that is, a network—where do we draw the cut-points? How do we handle a classroom sociometric analysis for a student who shows up only occasionally? The standard bearer of change in modern corporations, the fabled U.S. General Electric Company former CEO Jack Welch, declared in an annual report to the stockholders that corporations were essentially "boundaryless" (General Electric 2000, 2). Customers, suppliers, and owners are all said to be "stakeholders" whose claims must be satisfied and who have recurring relations with the core of the organization that are ignored only at the peril of the organization. Then there is the "business group" and other extensions of corporate boundaries so familiar in Japan and Israel (Maman 1997; Smangs 2006). There are no neat "true" cut-points cast in stone. We make them relatively arbitrarily for a given purpose; designers of computer algorithms that struggle with how to partition networks are well aware of this.

Another practical difficulty with simple network models has profound theoretical implications. Any set of nodes in real life has multiple flows with other nodes, so there is never one single network connecting the nodes or vertices, but many. This is true at all levels: people, organizations, nations, and so on. We would like to construct *the* network connecting the nodes. Unfortunately, a theoretical calculus for indexing or adding one type of flow to another does not exist (unless they are all reduced to money, in which case social network analysis is severely limited). If this deficit is taken as an advantage, then an important task of network analysis is to develop propositions about the relationship between flows and/or between networks based on different flows. For example, in a study of the French financial elite, having attended the Grand Ecole ENA in the past was related to who certain individuals were friends with today; moieties based on friendship were related to who sat on the same corporate boards (Kadushin 1995). The French financial elite's connections, based on some long-standing friendship ties in part defined how financial decisions were made.

In an interesting extension of this analysis based on additional data on corporate deals, Frank and Yasumoto (1998) show that cohesive subgroups based on friendship were related to abstention from hostile business deals within the groups but not to support in business deals with others not in the group. This latter support (mainly in corporate takeover attempts) was interpreted as building up "social capital" based on exchange principles with financial leaders with whom the member in the subgroup did not have an "enforceable trust" relationship. That is, they were typical "brokerage" or "Godfather" relationships ("let me make you an offer you can't refuse") characteristic of situations with structural holes. The expectation being that when the debt was called, the individual who otherwise had no motivation to help would come through.

The phenomena of multiple flows, cross-cutting statuses, and the softness or fuzziness (fuzzy is the term mathematicians use) of clusters combine to produce problems for statistical analysis. Most statistics are based on the assumption that units are independent from one another or randomly distributed, the initial assumption of Barabási and Albert (1999). The social reality, however, is that many network clusters are composed of cross-cutting smaller units built up into larger ones which in turn overlap with one another, as we saw with the example of the karate club.[5] This view of society was first enunciated by Simmel (1955 [1922]), who saw society as a complex skein of partly overlapping, relatively loose networks that he called "social circles" (Kadushin 1966, 1976).

Social circles are characteristic of modern mass society and serve to integrate apparently disconnected primary groups within larger societies. Simmel observed that in metropolitan settings people have many different interests, activities, and characteristics and yet are able to find others who share them. This compensates for the alleged social isolation of the modern metropolis. In larger cities, individuals are able to construct a "do it yourself" kit of social life. Despite the unlikely combination of traits, an individual can be at the intersection of a variety of social circles such as opera lovers, skiers, and beer aficionados. Internet and online communities only further enhance the potential for integration. Distant interaction aside, the ability to form such diverse communities of like-minded people is one of the major draws of urban centers and may be a factor in the idea, "Once you have shown them gay Paris, how are you going to keep them down on the farm." Intersection of these circles, perhaps not so random, is one of the major forces behind the "rewiring" described by Watts's model.

To be clear, a circle is not a "group." It has neither clear boundaries nor a formal leadership. Rather, it is a denser region, not necessarily a totally connected segment, of a network. The nodes can be of any kind, but in Simmel's original idea they were people. The nodes are not necessarily directly linked. More often than not they are connected through two or (unusually) three steps. Thus, a social circle is a miniature small world and directly illustrates the small world scenario. At a gathering in which one apparently knows no one, one asks, "Do you know X?" as a way of locating both oneself and the people in the gathering. One asks this of several people. More often than not, the others know X. This is the sign that the person asking and the others are in the same social circle (that is how one happened to come to the gathering in the first place). If it turns out that after several tries no one at the gathering knows X, it is probably a sign to leave. One is in the "wrong" circle at the "wrong" party.

It is obvious that the concept of social circle is related to the small world. Because the world is clustered into overlapping social circles, it becomes both smaller and larger. If one belongs to the same circle, then distances between nodes are smaller, though density remains lower than for true primary groups. If one does not belong to a given circle, then the path distance between people in different circles may be much larger. We will show how this idea can be exploited in small world models.

The "flow" through the nodes of the social circle may be an interest in the same ideas, concerns, values, or in the case of an economic circle, in the exchange of valued commodities. There are entire industries that depend on a circle-like phenomenon. These are called external economy industries (see chapter 2) and are embedded within a variety of available resources upon which they depend to function. (Coser, Kadushin, and Powell 1982; Uzzi 1996). These include the arts and communications, but also the New York City high-fashion garment (Seventh Avenue) and finance (Wall Street) industries. Note the intentional geographic metaphor in the names. These are industries in which it is not economically viable to include within the organization all the factors of production (Williamson 1981, and see chapter 7). In the case of the high-fashion garment industry, for example, runs are short and must be timely. It is not reasonable to stock all anticipated fabrics and buttons or to own the sewing and cutting establishments. In publishing, it is possible to open a house with no more than a telephone and a computer. All other production factors including writers, editors, publicists, printers, and binders can be assembled to produce a book. Digital publishing and the internet are raising this external economy to new heights and traditional publishing feels under attack (Epstein 2010). But as Wall Street, even in the modern era of the internet, has discovered, there is no substitute for face-to-face interaction, at least to establish the basis for future non-face-to-face interaction and to develop or renew trust. Hence in the United States, all these industries have geographic names; Broadway, Hollywood, Madison Avenue,[6] Seventh Avenue, Wall Street, even though the actual places have changed and are less geographically centered. But the names suggest the availability of face-to-face contact.

The exchange of ideas and information underlies much of the circle phenomenon. So-called intellectuals are a paradigmatic example. In *The American Intellectual Elite* (Kadushin 2005a), I showed that 50% of the intellectual elite lived within about 50 miles of the Empire State Building, a radius I called "lunch distance," the distance which allowed a writer to come into the city, have lunch with his/her editor, and return home easily within the same day. Thus the distance is calculated more on means of transport than the actual distance in miles. Modern societies still retain some important aspects of community "social support," as Simmel and later Barry Wellman suggest (Wellman 1979, 1999a; Wellman, Carrington, and Hall 1988). The support is based on geographic, cultural, and virtual substrata.

In Simmel's original formulation, he noted that social circles can substitute for some of the attributes of primary groups, notably, the kind of social support that they offer. Importantly, social circles not only create the conditions for trust, but for enforceable trust. If trust is violated, there are sanctions that are expected and can be applied. For example, in the French financial elite (Kadushin 1995), in economic systems of new immigrants (Portes and Sensenbrenner 1993), and in Renaissance Italian elites (Padgett and Ansell 1993), nodes that are members of those social circles expect that trust is enforceable.

To summarize. Social circles are informal networks usually formed on the basis of common interests. Unlike small groups in which everyone is connected to everyone else, in social circles the links may not be direct but through a "friend of a friend." Lacking formal structure, circles have no formal leader. Some persons can, however, be more central than others because the now familiar phenomenon of an unequal distribution of links or degrees also holds within social circles; there is a "tail" of the distribution in which a few persons have many connections while most have fewer. Because the diameter of a circle is relatively small even in a large metropolis, they are miniature small worlds so that it is very likely that if we start with a person (ego) chosen at random within a circle, then any alter chosen at random who is not known to ego will know someone else who is indeed known by ego (our party example, above). Overlapping circles and communities serve not only to create the "short circuits" of the Watts-Strogatz model but also operate within smaller networks that are not the "whole world."

Social circles are related to or developed from various instituted forms and do not function completely independently. They are "pegged" to statuses, roles, and organizations. In addition, for the case of the cultural/intellectual circles of Berlin of the 1920s that Simmel discussed, the pegs were various "interests and common purposes." Peter Blau (Blau 1964; Blau and Schwartz 1984) developed a number of studies that used social demographic characteristics as proxies for direct measures of social circles and showed how the combination of demographic statuses could define their overlaps. McPherson (2004) suggests that what he calls "Blau space," in honor of Blau, can used to define the social distance of individuals from one another. He argues that this is a much better use than the way standard demographics of individuals in social surveys are commonly used to sort out their opinions and values, for example, "younger people tended to support Obama." Instead, he favors finding clusters of individuals who share the same social distance from one another in a "Blau space," formed by taking the standard demographics of surveys such as occupation and education and using those to calculate social distance between individuals. This measure then becomes a proxy for a large-scale mapping of social circles and their intersections. Opinions and values are shown to be a correlate of social circle membership. The idea is controversial and has yet to find wide application.

In addition to demographics, there are other more formal bases for network clustering, as Watts observed, that form bipartite graphs. People can be linked because they belong to formal organizational units such as boards of directors, because they are geographic neighbors, co-authors, or share the same status. For example, I am more likely to know other sociologists than I am corporate executives. These other "pegs" upon which connections are draped can be multi-dimensional, for example, a sociologist (status) who is at the same university. My co-author may be a co-author with someone else so the link between that other person is but one link away from me. The "bins" or "affiliations" can be arranged hierarchically, for instance, a co-author within the category sociologist within the same university. These kinds of networks can also form miniature small worlds.

Overlapping social circle clustering also potentially leads to a hierarchical structure, as Moody and White (2003) point out. Their method of clustering networks of any size was initially described in chapter 4. Here we give some further details. They draw their basic intuition from Simmel's idea that a group or a circle depends on particular individuals to retain its character. They quantify the idea by proposing a measure that is the "minimum number of individuals whose continuous presence is required to retain the group's connectedness" (ibid., 105). They call this concept "structural cohesion." More formally, they consider the connectivity of a graph or a sociogram. A component of a graph consists of all the nodes or actors that can be connected with each other by at least one path. A "cutset" is a collection of nodes that if removed would break the component into two or more pieces. A k-connected graph has no cutset of fewer than k nodes, as illustrated in figure 8.12 (Moody and White 2003, figure 8.1, 108).

Panel (a) has two unconnected components. Panel (b), with the same set of nodes as panel (a), has one cut-point, node 7 (in black) that is connected to nodes 11 and 13. Without this node's connections, panel (b) would look like panel (a) and with its two unconnected components. So panel (b) is defined as a graph with k=1. In panel (c), nodes 6 and 13 (in black) connect what would otherwise be the two components of

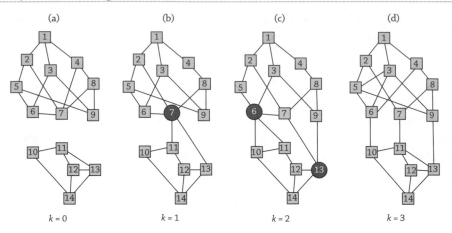

FIGURE 8.12 Examples of Connectivity Levels

Moody, James, and Douglas R. White. 2003. Structural cohesion and embeddedness: A hierarchical concept of social groups. *American Sociological Review* 68 (1): 108, figure 1. Copyright © 2003 American Sociological Association. Reprinted by permission of the ASA and the authors.

panel (a), so k=2. Panel (c) obviously has three connections between the otherwise unconnected components of panel (a), so k=3. Panel (c), which has two cut-points, is not dependent therefore on a single individual and, following Simmel, is a true social group and much more cohesive than panel (b).

The algorithm that illustrates this phenomenon produces some subgroups that are disconnected from one another but also some that overlap hierarchically. Moody and White's illustration (figure 8.13) is based on a cohesive group detection procedure for a network, G.[7] In the first level of the hierarchy the nodes do not overlap, but in the second level, node 7 is present in two groups.

Using the ideas of social cohesion and social circles, hierarchical connections such as those shown in figure 8.13, illustrating bipartite graphs and group overlap connections characteristic of overlapping social circles, one can show how apparently cohesive groups and circles can be connected and make a small world possible. It is important that the k-connections in social circles are usually are much larger than the two or three identified in the illustrations above. This makes for redundancy of the transmission of ideas and information that is not dependent on dyads. Redundancies (more k connections) make for cohesiveness, as Moody and White demonstrate in two examples, one regarding greater attachment to high school and the other concerning common political action among large American businesses. Cohesiveness is thus not necessarily the property of small groups but, though not visible by the "naked eye" as in the karate club, can result in a small world.

The Small World Search

If the Watts-Strogatz model is oversimplified for social networks, but the principle of rewiring is a sound one, what accounts for the rewiring that in social theory is *not*

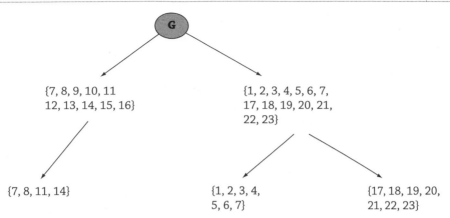

FIGURE 8.13 Hierarchical Yet Overlapping Cohesive Groups

Moody, James, and Douglas R. White. 2003. Structural cohesion and embeddedness: A hierarchical concept of social groups. *American Sociological Review* 68 (1):111, figure 3. Copyright © 2003 American Sociological Association. Reprinted by permission of the ASA and the authors.

random but rather a consequence of different kinds of social structure? Thus far, we have introduced a number of candidates for sources of the rewiring, any one of which could produce a small world. Common social circles are one. The circles themselves are not random but related to instituted social structures and interests. Common location in "Blau space" and common statuses such as occupation and education may serve as a link between what Watts called "caves." Common organizational memberships and location in an organizational hierarchy are all possible sources for rewiring. Movement, both geographic and organizational, brings a single individual into contact with quite different social systems (Martin 2009, 33). The mathematics of the small world reveals that a relatively small number of people with connections outside of their present circumstances is sufficient to produce the small world. But we still need to determine the likely links and the circumstances that make one connection more salient than the other. And finally, are the persons or organizations responsible for these links those with a high degree linked to others with a low degree, as in a preferential-attachment model, or those with high degree linked to others with a high degree, as in the assortative distribution or mixing model? Put another way, what kinds of people serve as the brokers and bridgers that through weak ties serve to hold the world together? In terms of Moody and White's diagram (figure 8.12), what are the social properties of node 7, the one who connects two arms of the hierarchy?

This brings us right back to the original Milgram small world experiment that sought to understand the bases through which people were linked to form a small world. People do tend to think in terms of hierarchies and social structural locations to locate a target person. For example, to find a target person, I might think of contacting someone I know in a similar profession in the same city to that of the target person. The networks that result from this model are highly clustered with short path lengths, and they are searchable (a flow is possible) in the sense that the probability of any message chain reaching the target is at least above some fixed value. In Milgram's study, the failure rate at each step was 0.25 (Watts, Dodds, and Newman 2002).[8] If this was set as the failure rate for the model, and the probability of success was 0.05, the longest path was approximately 10.4. Searchable networks are then modeled to be most effective when only two or three social dimensions are used over a fairly wide range of group homophily (ibid.). This corresponds to Killworth and Bernard (1978) who found in a reverse small world experiment (asking subjects how they would go about finding a particular person in a named city with a given occupation, sex, and ethnicity) that in choosing the category of the person who might help complete the chain, about half the choices were location and another half were occupation. Blau space was apparently invoked by most of the participants. The next variety of categories was less than 7%.

Milgram's original experiment has been difficult to duplicate. In a recent attempt using email, more than 60,000 email users attempted to reach 18 target persons in 13 countries, but only 1.6% of the 24,163 chains reached their target (Dodds, Muhamad, and Watts 2003). Judgments about the number of steps and the strategies used by participants, given the tiny proportion of completed networks, are dubious in my view. The difficulty of gathering empirical data on large-scale social networks is illustrated by this study.

One study, not of the whole world but an HP laboratory's email network of 430 individuals (still relatively large), with a median number of 10 acquaintances and a mean of 12.9, showed that the communications were largely pegged to the formal hierarchical structure; focusing on individuals with high degree was not an effective connection strategy, rather, one looked to the official hierarchy (Adamic and Adar 2005).

The general theoretical outlines of a small world theory have been laid down. It remains to discover how the small world really works. The next section offers an example of what can be contributed when we lower our sights to consider not the entire world, but a much smaller segment of it.

Applications of Small World Theory to Smaller Worlds

Beginning with Gaetano Mosca's (1939 [1923]) observation that an organized minority controls all regimes regardless of whether they are official "democracies" or not, a recurrent theme in political studies is the shape of political and policy influence. Notable figures in arguing whether Mosca is correct, and under what circumstances in what kinds of national states and local communities, include Mills (1959), Domhoff (1978), Higley, Hoffmann-Lange, Kadushin, and Moore (1991), Hunter (1953), Dahl (1961), and Laumann and Knoke (1987) among others. The Watts-Strogatz innovations in modeling the small world, Newman's methods for finding communities, the concepts of bridges and brokers, and types of relations (support and effectance or instrumental) all contribute to a more grounded discussion of the nature of political and policy influences.

Baldassarri and Dani (2007) studied civic organizations in two British cities and asked whether the networks of influence of these organizations were hierarchical and centralized (an organized minority) or horizontal and polycentric (more "democratic").

To discover this, they invoked the Watts-Strogatz "cave" or circle model of small worlds, shown in figure 8.14 (ibid., 741).

The diagram shows two ideal-typical representations of hierarchical and polycentric structures. The left diagram is hierarchical and the right one polycentric and similar to the small world graphs shown previously in which there is one link between otherwise isolated networks. These are not mammoth small worlds but represent possible ideal-typical arrangements of 124 civic organizations in Glasgow and 134 in Bristol. The question is: Are the actual networks in each city more like the left model or more like the right? To have a network there must be connections between the civic organizations. The authors distinguish between social or affective bonds that reinforce identities and solidarity within similar organizations, and instrumental ties, or transactions that bridge different kinds of organizations in the manner of weak ties. These are the equivalents of support and effectance discussed in chapter 5, "The Psychological Foundations of Social Networks." Unlike data gathered from databases or internet crawls, determining ties between organizations required careful intensive field work. Watts and Strogatz's clustering coefficient, C, that measures the density of local relations and L, the average shortest path length, discussed earlier were tested on the networks that resulted from the field work. Also tested were measures of hierarchy and connectedness. For each real city, the observed index of hierarchy was far lower than expected by chance, and connectedness was higher, as was clustering. These, taken together, were indicative of small world graphs. Since hierarchy was low, high connectedness suggested that it was not the result of a few central organizations, but rather connectedness within the circles. On the other hand, average path length was higher than would be expected by chance, suggesting that there was some segmentation that had to be bridged.

The method of testing has interesting theoretical implications. The indexes from the actual networks can be computed and compared with an "alternate world" (my concept, not the authors') of 1,000 random networks with the same distribution of de-

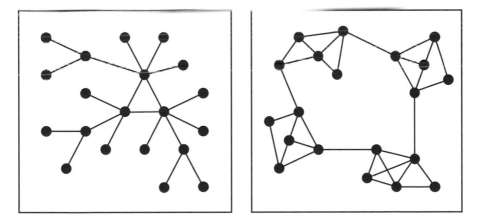

FIGURE 8.14 Ideal-Typical Representations of Hierarchical and Polycentric Networks

grees and the same size. This is necessary because there is no practical way of sampling 1,000 cities. Even if sampling were possible, there would likely be key differences with Bristol or Glasgow.

The intuitions suggested by the quantitative indices are born out by clustering into "communities" of organizations and the pattern of social bonds and transactions between and within the clusters of organizations. Detailed analyses show that organizations within the same cluster are more likely to be linked via informal social bonds, whereas organizations from different clusters are more likely to be linked through formal, instrumental transactions. This observation confirms the intuition that social bonds operate within clusters, and transactions serve as bridges.

Finally, the "rewiring" ideas of small world theory come into play in another consideration of "alternate worlds." By selecting edges (connections) of the observed network at random and "rewiring" (connecting them) to a randomly chosen organization, the observed clustering was reduced and the level of hierarchy increased. This is because random patterns of interaction reduced the observed tendency toward balanced interdependence of ties (I interact with you, and you interact with me). Therefore, random rewiring especially affected social bonds. But random rewiring, because it ignored the ties created by social structure, also increased path length.

This brings us to the nuanced social theory implications of polycentric versus hierarchical networks. From one consideration, the ideal-type polycentric network, as is in the Moody and White measures of cohesiveness, is not dependent on single actors or single ties. It has many cut-points. A hierarchical network can be destroyed by "taking out" key actors and/or key ties or cut-points. Good for control, but fragile. Students of terrorist networks as well as community action networks should take note. On the other hand, an extreme reliance on support or social bond ties within clusters results in a fragmented network of disconnected circles that destroy society. Dense interaction, because there are few paths that lead outside a circle, curiously, also leads to "Bowling Alone," perhaps the very opposite of Putnam's original theory (2000). As Simmel in his theory of cross-cutting social circles originally pointed out, bridges between different statuses and circles serve to integrate society (1955 [1922]). The bridges in the Baldassarri and Diani study (2007) are formed mainly through instrumental transaction ties. We come back to the necessity of both support and effective networks for community political action. The delicate balance between them is best explored via the new concepts and theories of the small world. The limited example of Bristol and Glasgow do not settle the controversies about structures of political influence. But they do show a path to future theoretically based research.

Where We Are Now

The following appear to be the presently known foundations of large social network theories about the small world. That everyone is linked to everyone else in a surprisingly few steps—though in more steps than chance alone would suggest—seems a well-supported proposition. This is the result of seven fundamental principles. First, contributing to the linking of almost everyone to everyone else is the fact that the average person in the modern world knows almost 300 people, perhaps double that, thus making possible the linking of interpersonal environments. Second, we saw that the distribution in the population of this number is highly skewed; a small number of people (or other kinds of nodes) have a very large number of connections. Third, the actual number of paths in small world experiments is larger than would be expected solely on the basis of the number of connections for each node. Fourth, there are clusters (circles, organizations, countries, etc.) of individual units and barriers between them such that the number of paths between units in different clusters is beyond the number than might be expected by chance. Fifth, a major factor accounting for barriers and structures are social circles formed on the basis of homophily of interests and attributes. The circles are embedded within organizations, social classes, and others structures of societies. Sixth, there are overlaps between the structures, and these intersections serve to produce the small world. However, the extent of overlap and barriers is not currently measureable except in relatively small communities. So, seventh, various models have been proposed that predict a small world but do not depend on the size of the interpersonal environment. Nonetheless, the parameter—how many people one knows—is useful in additional contexts because it can help social scientists estimate the size of otherwise unknown or hidden populations, for example, people living with HIV or heroin users.

Whatever the size of the interpersonal environment and on whatever basis it is formed—informal as in social circles or formal as in hierarchical organizational and work group membership—we know on the basis of mathematical models that in principle, through "rewiring" connections between otherwise isolated circles, groups, and organizations, it takes but a few links to connect just about the entire social world. However, small world models have not as yet systematically explored the *attributes* of the nodes or vertices that produce these connections or the obverse—the social barriers that might prevent connections. We do know that linkers are likely to be those with more connections than the average person or organization—those at the end of the skewed tail of the distribution of contacts—and are likely to be more "cosmopolitan" by definition because their connections include many different worlds. Links may be made by nodes with a cumulative advantage, nodes with few links that are connected by those with many. "Assortative distribution," on the other hand, describes connections in a small world made through elites that have many links to one another. Assortative distributions seem more common in social networks than cumulative advantage distributions, though there is disagreement about this. In any case, the models do successfully predict a small world. The details of how this actually comes about in social systems as opposed to physical systems remain to be filled in and constitute a critical area for further research.

There are some very important practical applications of the small world theory to the study of different kinds of flows: cascades, diffusion, epidemics, and the role of "influentials" that will be explored in the next chapter. Still, the nature of the links, determining the key linkers or brokers and their socially structured distribution, remains largely unaccounted for. As is typical for certain stages in the development of theory, much of what is holding us up is our ability to gather data with which to confront theoretical speculations. Almost all the "data" in small world theory is simulated or computed. As yet, we have very few really large social networks against which to test our theories that will stimulate new ideas and insights. The difficult work of finding ways to gather large interaction networks, other than data mining of email and telecommunications or semi-social interactions (as in co-author or co-citation networks), is still in its infancy. For example, networks of who makes telephone calls to whom are now in the realm of possibility, but as our final chapter on ethics suggests, more than technical problems are raised by this possibility. On the other hand, as suggested by the example of two cities' civic organizational structure and the Moody and White study of cohesiveness, the ideas of the small world can be effectively applied to smaller settings.

Some of the critical ideas of small world theory are explored in a different context in the next chapter on diffusion. That chapter examines how connections diffuse ideas, innovations, and disease. While not necessarily explicitly invoking small world concepts, diffusion depends on the extent to which nodes are connected and under what circumstances. The topics of connectedness, clustering, density, centrality, and brokerage that we have previously encountered will come up again in this topic which, perhaps unlike the small world theory, has immediate practical applications to a wide range of issues from marketing, opinion formation, and the control of disease.

9 Networks, Influence, and Diffusion

Networks and Diffusion—An Introduction

The distribution and transmission of culture and social systems across geographic areas, times, and generations are arguably the main engines of civilization. Culture's "spread in area is generally called diffusion" whereas "internal handing on through time is called tradition" (Kroeber 1948, 411). We have evolved from hunting and gathering with primitive stone tools to our present high-tech society; from social systems based on small kin groups to national governments and international global systems. In the process, we have transmitted what we have learned—both the good and the bad—to the next generation through formal and informal systems. We have also spread disease through biological and social means. Networks are involved in all these transmissions. At a basic, subjective social level something may be transmitted or diffused through (1) contact that involves some form of influence, persuasion, or coercion—for example, someone teaches me something or influences me to do something, to think a certain way, or provide me with a new tool; (2) contact that involves some kind of emulation—e.g., my friend has an idea or a tool that I think it would be useful to have; or (3) adoption or emulation without direct social contact—for example, I hear or read about something that I like. These situations all involve a decision or an action on the part of the recipient of the transmission.

The diffusion of agriculture into Europe about 10,000 years ago could have occurred through the migration of a population that had already adopted the innovation, termed demic diffusion or through presumed imitation or adoption of what must have been considered a superior system , termed cultural diffusion (Armelagos and Harper 2005; Pinhasi, Fort, and Ammerman 2005). The precise details are not available to us today, but social networks lie at the heart of this key diffusion.

Anthropologists remind us that the social context of diffusion must be considered. For example, without an infrastructure of roads, automobiles would not have wide distribution. Further, transmission or diffusion may not require an actor's subjective assent or dissent. People move into a neighborhood bringing with them something older residents did not have before. Or, a person catches a cold because someone next to him or her on the airplane sneezed. Epidemiology, the study of biological diffusion, is the intellectual home for tracing this latter kind of contact. Finally, independent inventions do not involve diffusion. A classic example comes from anthropology and the "principle of limited possibilities" (Goldenweiser 1922).[1] An efficient way to move a boat or raft through the water is to use a paddle or an oar with a blade attached to a shaft that is narrower than the blade and therefore lighter and more easily managed together with some sort of handle attached to the shaft. Throughout the world in regions with apparently no historic connection, paddles and oars have proven to be somewhat alike because of the common constraints of the physics and anatomy of rowing or paddling. But with such exceptions, the history of civilization, whether in terms of incidents of plagues or the development of agricultural and industrial technologies, is the story of diffusion through networks (Armelagos and Harper 2005; Pinhasi, Fort, and Ammerman 2005).

This chapter seeks to apply the basic ideas of social networks to diffusion and epidemiology. The connection ideas of the small world models that we just studied are obviously involved. After a brief introduction to basic diffusion models that are essentially non-social and the structural influences upon them, we will establish the subjective social character of diffusion by reviewing the field of social influence, mass media, and marketing. The concepts of structural holes and density developed in chapter 5, "The Psychological Foundations of Social Networks," are important to an understanding of social influence and opinion leadership. Small groups and leadership studies help us to understand how opinion leadership works. Social circles have a key role in understanding the social systems of adolescents and how they affect what they learn or do not learn in high school. Then we will examine epidemiology. We will discover that, surprisingly, the social network approach is relatively new in epidemiology. Previously, epidemiologists had been able to model diffusion simply by assessing what proportion of people in a population had a disease at a given time, what proportion remained at risk for the disease, and what was the likelihood of recovery if they contracted it. Similar models have been employed in the study of adoption by organizations of innovations. The dynamics of networked social connections between people became increasingly relevant with the growth of HIV-AIDS.

Two key but elusive concepts in diffusion, "tipping point" and "threshold," will be explored. A tipping point occurs when an epidemic or an innovation "takes off" and needs no further stimulation from outside forces or influences. The small world connects individuals on its own, as it were. A threshold occurs when a balance between acting and not acting is overcome in response to a combination of internal propensities and the influence of external events, such as the perception that "everyone is doing it." The drawback to these seductive and important concepts is that both tipping points and thresholds are usually discovered in retrospect and are difficult to predict. Nonetheless, modeling and network theory are helpful in understanding when and how a diffusion process breaks out of a local social circle and, by means of rewiring (see chapter 8), can spread throughout an entire social system. In just the last several years, these ideas have led to models suggesting how epidemics might be curbed.

THE BASIC MODEL

Diffusion is a process through which elements are transferred, borrowed, or adopted into a social system. Disease, ideas, opinions, values, traits, physical objects, or practices are examples of these elements. A stylized model of diffusion is shown by figure 9.1 below (fromValente 2010, table 10-1).

The figure assumes that a few people will adopt a new idea or practice during the first period. Then they interact randomly with the rest of the population and persuade a constant small proportion in the next period. This scenario is repeated over a number of periods. The proportion who have adopted with each period increases, until everyone has adopted the idea or practice. The proportion of new adopters rises as more people are available to transmit the innovation, but then falls as there become fewer who have not already adopted the innovation. This produces the classic "S" shaped curve of diffusion. We have put this in terms of an innovation, but the spread of a disease can be modeled in the same way.

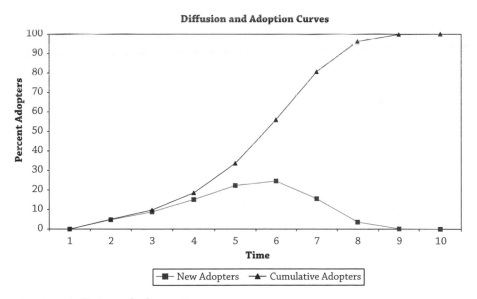

FIGURE 9.1 Diffusion and Adoption Curves

Based on Valente, Thomas W. 2010. *Social networks and health: Models, methods, and applications* New York: Oxford University Press. By permission of Oxford University Press, Inc.

The stylized model can be altered by conditions that have an impact on the nature of the network. The shape depends in part on the characteristics of the transmitters as well as those of the receivers and the possible links between them. Since the processes take place over time, historical and other macro factors also affect the curve.

The S-shaped diffusion curve assumes that a network connects potential adopters; that is, potential adopters "imitate" previous adopters. Otherwise, if the potential adopters hear about an innovation from a central source that reaches some fixed proportion (but not all) in each time period, a modified exponential curve describes the process and does not have the initial convex segment. As figure 9.2 shows, the exponential (non-network) model A reaches half the population much sooner than the diffusion model B, which eventually takes off at a much faster pace than the central source model.

There are several processes that can produce an S-shaped curve (Geroski 2000). The one most popular in the literature is the earlier described simple epidemic or contagion diffusion that depends on the aggregate adoption rate. It is particularly sensitive to macro effects rather than the individual characteristics of potential adopters or the connections between them. More complex is what statisticians call a probit regression model that adds to the contagion model an explanation of the differences in time of adoption by considering individual characteristics of the receivers, including their values, goals, needs, and resistances. Models of information cascades or "bandwagon" effects also produce an S curve. In this process, adopters at early stages evaluate the utility of an innovation. Later adopters imitate what they see as the successful adoption by the initial users, as with those who strive to "keep up with the Joneses." Further, an S-shaped diffusion curve can be produced by the population ecology model that is driven by density and competition between firms (Hannan and Freeman 1989). Since this is not a network-based explanation, it will not be considered here.

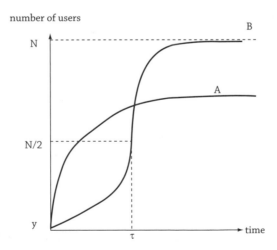

FIGURE 9.2 Plots of the modified exponential (A) and logistic (B) diffusion functions.

EXOGENOUS FACTORS IN ADOPTION OF INNOVATIONS

The telephone and the automobile, two icons of American culture and technology, illustrate the effect of exogenous factors on the diffusion process. Imitation or contagion was aided by marketing and government policies (Fischer 1992). Automobiles were first marketed as a leisure activity for the rich, then as prices fell, they were marketed as a business and family necessity. Telephones were originally marketed as a business device, not as a way to connect socially. The Bell system had little interest in marketing the telephone as a means to overcome rural isolation. The U.S. government protected the AT&T monopoly until 1984. Rather than aggressively seeking new customers in rural areas, AT&T advertisements focused on protecting the Bell system monopoly. Unlike Canadian and European governments who owned their telephone systems, the U.S. government did not subsidize telephone service to rural areas. By building networks of roads, however, the U.S. and state governments promoted and in effect subsidized automobiles, and thus aided auto, but not telephone, adoption by farmers.

In non-biological diffusion, individual actors (including corporate actors such as organizations) make the decision to adopt a new practice—whether these individuals are the prehistoric peoples adopting grain cultivation or herding in preference to hunting and gathering or subscribers of telephone services. Fischer notes, "People decided whether or not to subscribe [to telephone services] based on their tastes and needs" but, oddly, "the telephone companies themselves encountered difficulties in understanding how to sell" residential telephone service (Fischer 1992, 261). The telephone company at the time lacked the conceptual and methodological understanding of how to study individual actions, a matter to which we now turn.[2]

Influence and Decision-Making

Diffusion does not occur unless some people learn of adopt a new artifact, behavior, or idea. Underlying any theory of diffusion therefore is some schema, either implicit or specific, of how people learn or decide to do something. In the chapter on motivation to network we skirted around this idea. Here we directly address it.

In the new age of mass advertising, it is not surprising that decision-making processes about adoption were first applied to consumer buying. As early as 1935, Kornhauser and Lazarsfeld (1955 [1935]) reviewed a number of studies of buying behavior and proposed that they could be broken down to the characteristics of the individual such as the state of his/her knowledge at the time, his/her motivations, and the situation—the attributes of the product, the way it was sold, as well as various influences on the individual. The researchers made influence, personal and otherwise, an explicit part of the situation. Lazarsfeld was interested in accounting for the reasons why people acted the way they did. One way of doing this was to lay out the elements that went into the decision and ask respondents to weigh the alternatives. He described the basic technique in his oft-quoted article, "The Art of Asking Why" (Lazarsfeld 1972

[1934]). He applied this method to such mundane acts as buying soap or, perhaps more consequentially, voting. Lazarsfeld attempted to sort out the relative impact of the perceived attributes of a soap or a candidate, the impact or influence of media messages about these attributes, as well as the impact of other persons in the actor's environment who attempted to influence the decision. If the researcher simply asked, "Why?" without further specification, she or he might get an answer that addressed only one of these dimensions, whereas in fact they all were involved. After ascertaining the relevant factors that entered into the decision-making, the actor was asked to evaluate which was the most important. This technique developed into the idea that influence flowed from media to "influentials" and thence to the consumer or voter and was called the "Two-Step Flow" of communications (which was later expanded to consider multiple-step flows). Elihu Katz (1957) reviewed the history, logic, and findings of early social network diffusion studies of the Lazarsfeld school and some of the limitations of the method. Katz (1960) later noted that similar work was taking place in rural sociology, which studied the processes by which farmers adopted new practices.

The early problems of the rural sociology and the personal influence schools remain. One is the difficulty of tracing the influence process over time: the practical problems of finding the influencers, the theoretical problems of modeling the source and nature of the influence, and distinguishing between the effects of media and the social environment and specific individuals who might inform or persuade (or both). The other key challenge is establishing causality. Cross-sectional analysis can establish a difference in adoption by those exposed to a given medium or individual influence and those who are not. Note, however, that those who are favorable to a position or an idea are more likely to expose themselves to media that promotes it. Those favoring a particular candidate in an election, for example, are more likely to listen to that person's speeches. This produces an association between the media and the action, but the association is as much caused by the actor's predispositions as it is by the effect of the content of the media. When it comes to personal influence, the homophily principle holds: individuals are more like to associate with others who share their views or social characteristics (see chapter 2). Again, a correlation between friends and opinion may reflect differential association (the tendency of like-minded people to associate with one another—the homophily principle explained in chapter 2) but not the direct influence of the friends. Nor is it clear that panel studies or studies of the same individuals over time can necessarily overcome the difficulty of determining causality. Randomized experiments "solve" the problem in laboratories, but experiment results are not easy to generalize because the social elements of the real-world situation are an inherent part of the diffusion process. Assessing the role of influence and homophily remains a key intellectual problem in studies of diffusion.[3]

Lazarsfeld often resorted to qualitative assessment of those who had adopted or taken an action, asking a respondent to evaluate the impact of the different sources of influence and potential reasons and motivations elicited in an interview (Kadushin 1968b). This can be difficult and time consuming, especially for complicated decisions. For example, in attempting to understand why people chose to undergo psychotherapy, a decision that may have taken place over a number of years, self-help books and the mass media were a factor, but the role of other people, especially significant others, was very important to defining one's self as having a psychological problem and critical in finding a place to seek treatment. However, the influence of others was less important in the final decision to show up for treatment (Kadushin 2006 [1969]). In addition, being embedded in a circle or network of friends knowledgeable about psychotherapy and psychoanalysis was extremely important in the decision (Kadushin 1966).

Targets of diffusion are frequently described as passive recipients. But even in the early *Personal Influence* study we see targets playing an active role. Young women, for example, were hypothesized to be eager seekers of the latest fashions. Their active interest influenced the process. Those who actively searched for ideas, opinions, and products, were more likely to obtain advice from others in their personal network. Seekers for psychological help asked their friends for referrals.

Interestingly, there is recent experimental evidence that the communicator or sender merely by talking about something does more to convince himself or herself than the target of the influence (Kashima et al. 2010). Missionaries and preachers may be more effective in convincing themselves than in converting the heathen.

THE CURRENT STATE OF PERSONAL INFLUENCE

What is now known about personal influence? It depends how personal influence is specified as well as how it is measured.

Conceptually, there are three possibilities in the process of personal influence. (1) the recipient solicits the influencer(s) for advice; (2) the influencer actively attempts to persuade the recipient to take the action or make the decision or simply informs the recipient; (3) the influencer serves as a model—uses the product or has an opinion about it but is not directly connected to the recipient. The first two possibilities actually form a four-fold table (see table 9.1) and the consequences are clearly different.

The studies on diffusion and personal influence are often not clear about which of these four situations has taken place; the extent of the recipient's active searching really makes a difference. The third possibility, product endorsement by authorities or celebrities, is a frequent tactic of marketers (Amos, Holmes, and Strutton 2008; Dean 1999).[4] This does not require a direct connection between the recipients and the influencers, though marketers often call this "opinion leadership."

TABLE 9.1

Typology of Influence

	Solicit Advice from Others	
Was Persuaded by Others	No	Yes
No	Passive	Informed
Yes	Persuaded	Convinced

More interesting from a network point of view is the controversy created by Ronald Burt's (1987) reanalysis of the Doctors and New Drugs study (briefly discussed in chapter 5 on the "Psychological Foundations of Social Networks"). Burt contends that direct contact between an earlier adopter of the new drug and the target of the adoption is less effective than the structural similarity between the physician who adopted a drug earlier and the later adopter; physicians' drug prescriptions followed those of persons who occupied a similar position in the network in terms of their connections with other physicians. This is a "keeping up with the Joneses" phenomenon and similar to the "bandwagon" explanation of the S curve noted above. In a more recent interpretation of the Doctors and New Drugs study, Burt finds that contagion or diffusion through cohesion or actual personal contact and diffusion through structural similarity have complementary functions:

> Opinion leaders are more precisely opinion brokers who carry information across the social boundaries between groups. They are not people at the top of things so much as people at the edge of things, not leaders within groups so much as brokers between groups. The familiar two-step flow of communication is a compound of two very different network mechanisms: contagion by cohesion through opinion leaders gets information into a group, and contagion by equivalence generates adoptions within the group. (Burt 1999, 51)

A reanalysis of Burt's data by Valente (2010) offers a new model that allows both cohesion and structural similarity to be measured with the same network methods. This examination suggests that direct ties or cohesion and similar position or structural similarity are of about equal importance. Contrary to previous analyses, neither was especially effective in producing prescriptions for the drug.

The hypothesis of the importance of personal influence has been recently challenged empirically and conceptually through network simulation (Watts and Dodds 2007) and marketing studies (van den Bulte and Joshi 2007). Van den Bulte and Lilien (2001) explain, "The Medical Innovation data set [from Doctors and New Drugs] is reanalyzed and supplemented with newly collected advertising data. When marketing efforts are controlled for, contagion effects disappear" (van den Bulte and Lilien 2001, 1429). In other words, the original ignored some exogenous factors in explaining network diffusion. Others have seriously questioned the two- or n- step process in which influentials pass along ideas or knowledge they have received from the media on to other individuals who are the recipients, or who in a chain process pass this on to other potential adopters (Lang and Lang 2006). Emphasizing context and exogenous factors, the Langs and others maintain that the personal influence hypothesis and accompanying research has seriously hampered the understanding of the pervasive and long-reaching impact of the mass media that continues to have a major effect on setting the agenda in culture and politics.

Both these arguments have been countered by Valente, who in summarizing many studies in different fields on personal influence concluded:

> The importance of opinion leaders is hard to overstate. It is also important to note that opinion leaders are not necessarily the earliest adopters of innovations.

Opinion leaders need to reflect the norms of their community and they cannot deviate too much from what is accepted in the community otherwise they will lose their privileged position in the network. Thus, they can lead, but not too far ahead of the group. Typically the earliest adopters are innovative and often on the margins of the community, they innovate because they are different. The opinion leader then translates this innovation for the rest of the community. This is their skill, they are admired by many and are good at scanning the environment because they are connected to lots of people. (Valente 2010, 180)

The difference in the findings has much to do with how a study goes about finding opinion leaders and how opinion leadership is measured. In addition, the opinion leaders' position in a network can now be examined. Earlier efforts were hampered due to the lack of network analysis technology. Also, those studies in which there is an intervention and opinion leaders are trained and active rather than passive are different from those without these additional factors. The "Doctors and New Drugs" study and most political and marketing studies of opinion leaders did not train or target opinion leaders. Rather, opinion leaders were those found naturally in the target population. The experimental evidence about deliberate interventions to find, create, and inform opinion leaders is overwhelmingly favorable to the effective influence of opinion leaders (Valente 2010). One reason for this is that these are situations in which (1) being proactive or seeking solutions is a value; (2) the innovation is not trivial so being shown "how to do it" is required; and (3) persuasion rather than merely making information available is important. Much of recent literature about interventions is found in the health field. The early diffusion studies of the impact of county agents on farmers on decisions to use new technologies (cited by Valente 1995, 2) also fit this model. The evidence is more mixed on happenstance or naturally occurring opinion leaders not specifically targeted by an intervention.

Influence is a transaction between people, so influencers who actively attempt to persuade others have their counterparts in those in the target population who actively seek information or solutions. Evidence subsequent to the Columbia University voting studies (Berelson 1954; Lazarsfeld, Berelson, and Gaudet 1948) suggests that opinion leaders in politics are effective among active advice seekers, but those who do not discuss politics tend to get their information and ideas directly from the mass media (Weimann 1994). Direct mass media persuasion apparently works well enough for the "couch potato," though sorting out the effects of exposure to media that already agrees with one's position as opposed to media that converts a non-believer remains a challenge for studies of influence.

SELF-DESIGNATED OPINION LEADERS OR INFLUENTIALS

While this is not a "how-to" treatise, measurement issues are inescapable in assessing whether or not opinion leaders have an impact (Valente and Pumpuang 2007). Since diffusion is a matter of tracing the flow of a new idea, product, or practice, network-based methods are clearly the best way to assess the place of personal influence in the chain of events. But network data collection is arduous and for the most part impossible in very large systems except where one relies on transmissions that leave a record such as email. Sample surveys can ascertain who claims to be exposed to various media and can trace the effect on the respondent of others in his or her immediate circle, but cannot "connect the dots" between the respondents. Simulations or experiments are useful but have real-world limitations.

We discussed earlier the use of celebrities as de facto opinion leaders or at least as role models. Finally, there are survey scales that directly ask respondents to assess how influential they are. For example, respondents are asked whether people turn to them for advice, whether they like to lead, and so on. One example is the PS (Personality Strength) scale (Weimann 1994), another is the engagement scale constructed on the basis of the Roper ASW scale (Nisbet 2006). While these self-assessment techniques may seem naïve, they are not without merit, as we shall see.

Each method has its own biases that can make imputation of influence problematic. In the famous *Personal Influence* study which sampled women in Decatur, Illinois, it was difficult to locate persons named as influential to follow up on their characteristics, and there were other difficulties, as Katz and Lazarsfeld reported with "our very cautious, but adventuresome excursion into 'survey sociometry'" (Katz and Lazarsfeld 1955, 329). Asking respondents to evaluate the impact of various influences on them was also hampered by not including all the relevant factors in the questionnaire. On the whole, the authors were actually more cautious about their findings than others who commented on the work. This pioneer study has, however, inspired considerable further research and has been cited over 700 times in the Science Citation Index.

The PS scale seems to be an influence rather than an opinion leader scale since the sheer quantity of media consumption that would characterize opinion leaders in a two-step flow is absent; rather, those high on the PS scale tend to read higher quality publications and say they are more likely to be asked for advice. Those high on the scale are said to be "the 'multipliers,' the trend-setters, the source for guidance and advice, the human transmitters of mass-mediate climate of opinion, issues, and agendas" (Weimann 1994, 286). As seen in the *Personal Influence* study, influence and opinion leadership are by and large not generalized personal attributes but specific to a particular field. Fashion leaders are not necessarily leaders in public affairs. Recent research further suggests that the scale does not work well in traditional societies (Weimann et al. 2007).

A self-report scale of engagement behavior in politics was tested in the ESS survey in 15 European nations as a type of self-report opinion leadership measure: "In contrast to media behaviors, interpersonal political discussion, the key communicative mechanism of opinion leadership that embodies both information-seeking and information-giving behaviors, was universally predictive across all countries in the study" (Nisbet 2006).

In sum, recent research confirms the practicality of self-identified opinion leadership, but its utility seems limited to more advanced Western countries. The more blanket notion that information from general mass media consumption is passed on interpersonally is not supported. Also, in the current studies, influentials tend to be exposed to more upscale media rather than constitute the omnivorous mass media consumers of an earlier era. These studies are mainly cross sectional and the few panel studies are not sociometric, so the full chain of influence is never verified. Finally, there is the potential for influencers to be much more widely diffused and "democratized" as blogs, Facebook, and YouTube become widespread (Kadushin 2005a, new Introduction). "Companies with names like Klout, PeerIndex and Twitter Grader are in the process of scoring millions, eventually billions, of people on their level of influence—or in the lingo, rating 'influencers'" (Rosenblum 2011). While this is presented as something new, the technology that underlies this could have been developed by anyone who read our chapter 3 where we discussed power.

CHARACTERISTICS OF OPINION LEADERS AND INFLUENTIALS

Who are the influentials and the opinion leaders? That is, are there specific social positions that they tend to occupy? The answer depends in part on how opinion leaders and influentials are identified. Although the original *Personal Influence* study found that Social Economic Status (SES) did not really matter and that there were opinion leaders in every stratum, more recent studies suggest that especially for the PS scale, higher SES is associated with somewhat higher PS scores. Consistent with leadership theory (see chapter 6, "Small Groups and Social Networks"), "Leaders are often of slightly higher status than their followers but not much higher... This happens because most people like to look up to others that are like themselves, only a little better" (Valente 2010, 98). When group sociometric studies were accompanied by PS scoring, higher PS scores were associated with greater sociometric centrality (Weimann 1994). This might seem obvious, because to be an opinion leader one has to be well connected to potential followers. Consider the dynamics of the diffusion of new or novel ideas or information, however. Central individuals embedded in a system of strong ties not only have a high potential for transmitting ideas, but can also send messages to those who share those ideas or practices. Another kind of centrality is the betweenness that links groups that might otherwise not be connected. The less "constrained" broker or person who bridges structural holes (Burt 2005) can be a very effective opinion leader. New ideas are also more likely to come from the periphery or a network and are likely to be unconventional, especially in the early stages of the diffusion of a new idea or practice. But because opinion leadership is a balance between having new ideas and an ability to reach others, those high in opinion leadership tend not to be the earliest adopters. As we saw in the chapter on small groups, leaders tend to exemplify the norms of the groups to which they belong. They therefore cannot be too far ahead of the curve. There is a tendency to glorify early adopters, especially by those in product development who would like to know who the early adopters are and use them to spread the word. But early adopters are by definition mavericks.

Research and development laboratories are a good example of the early adopter as a hero. By and large, those with the most patents are those who have good antennae for the latest findings. They transmit the results of their scan of the environment and the literature to others in their laboratory: "There is then evidence of a two-step flow of information, in which about six individuals act as technological gatekeepers for the rest of the laboratory...In both laboratories, the gatekeepers held significantly more patents, had published significantly more papers than their colleagues, and tended to be first-line supervisors" (Allen and Cohen 1969, 18).

These persons can be found through sociometric questionnaires and subsequent analyses. They are indeed bridgers in both common sense and technical network terms (Allen 1978). But the method used to locate these leaders can affect the results. In an effort to apply these findings, Allen went to supervisors in other laboratories and asked them to identify opinion leaders or brokers.[5] When they were identified, they became the special recipients of memoranda and information. Contrary to research findings, the intervention had no effect. Allen was perplexed. Upon further inquiry, it was discovered that the supervisors purposely named the wrong persons, lest their natural leaders be inundated with too much information and thereby lose their effectiveness (Allen 1977).

There is another kind of influential opinion leader, people in elite circles who influence one another and whose ideas "trickle down" to the public. These circles affect national policy along with corporate fashion, and set the current agenda of ideas. Elites in different domains such as politics, business, media, and intellectuals tend to pay attention to other elites in their circles and form opinions and policy views in reaction to others in their circles (Higley et al. 1991; Kadushin 1968a, 2005a; Laumann and Knoke 1987; Steinfels 1979; Useem 1984). This phenomenon is not usually intellectually located in the realm of studies of diffusion, though network methods are the basis of most of these studies. New ideas, on the other hand, often enter from elites who are oppositional or peripheral, as in the case of the American intellectuals' opposition to the war in Vietnam (Kadushin 2005a). Despite the very practical importance of understanding the role and impact of opinion leaders in the diffusion of innovation, ideas, values, opinion, and consumer products, however, and after over 50 years of research, it is apparent that much remains to be nailed down.

GROUP INFLUENCE

Thus far, we have focused on an influential as an individual. But the earliest work on influence concerned the impact of groups on individuals' opinions and decisions; a review of this research formed the first part of Katz and Lazarsfeld's *Personal Influence*. Particularly among adolescents, peer group influence is considered a major factor in forming aspirations and values, often in contrast to those advocated by parents and schools (Coleman 1961; Friedkin and Cook 1990). Fashions, ideas, as well as drugs, alcohol, and delinquent behaviors are spread through peer groups. Facebook is now ubiquitous among teenagers and produces virtual peer groups; the implications are just beginning to be studied though it is beginning to be clear that there is a "digital divide"; persons of lower social class are less likely to have access to computers and the internet (boyd 2008; Hargittai 2008; Subrahmanyam and Greenfield 2008).

A more traditional research field has been the study of delinquent youth and the effect of peer groups on delinquency: "Many studies find that the relationship of peer delinquency to self-report delinquency exceeds that of any other independent variable, regardless of whether the focus is on status offenses, minor property crimes, violent crimes, or substance use" (Haynie 2001, 1014). The theoretical battleground has been over the causes of this statistical association. Is the correlation found because delinquents tend differentially to associate with other delinquents and be selectively recruited to such groups, or is it because they lack the social controls exerted by attachments to parents, schools, and more conventional teens?

The social network data required to sort this out has been lacking until recently. Adolescents, like people of other age groups, generally "do not belong to a single, densely knit, isolated friendship clique, but instead are affiliated with many loosely bounded friendship groups with varying degrees of cohesion and permeability" (Haynie 2001, 1014). Simply counting the number of reported delinquent friends is too crude a measurement. A complete map of adolescents' networks is an obviously difficult task, though one accomplished for a relatively small number of high schools in James Coleman's *The Adolescent Society* as early as the 1950s (Coleman 1961). A more recent extensive survey, the Adolescent Health longitudinal study (Institutes of Health 1997) revisited adolescent networks. About 90,000 students from grades 7 through 12 at about 145 schools were surveyed in the first wave in 1994–1995. Data on self-reported delinquent behavior of both the respondent and those nominated were available for a sampled subset of 120 randomly selected schools. Included in the survey were approximately 13,000 students' ego networks (up to the five best friends of each sex) who completed both a school questionnaire and a home interview (Haynie 2001). It was found that "the delinquency-peer association exists and remains robust regardless of controls for numerous other factors" (ibid., 1048). Network factors affect the extent of this correlation. The extent to which the friends of ego are friends with one another is especially important. A cohesive network of delinquents leads to greater delinquency on the part of the focal person. This observation supports our intuitive sense that social influence is most effective when it comes from all directions. Social influence often requires concentrated exposure.

An even better way of discovering the extent to which friends in high school influence one another was found in the Adolescent Health study's complete friendship sociometry of about 15,000 students over three waves of data collection. This allowed for clumping or segmenting groups of friends in each high school studied. (The topic of network segmentation was introduced in chapter 4.) These clumps, clusters, or positions are a key to the influence process. Though the idea of an adolescent gang is a popular one, it overstates the extent to which social structure in high schools is formalized. In his pioneering network study of high schools, Coleman suggested several social categories which had a familiar ring—"nerds," "jocks," and "the leading crowd." These categories clustered students' relationships to one another and therefore their orientation to high school life. Beyond social categories—named either by the participants or by observers—are circles formed on the basis of common interests, activities, or places to hang out. These circles create bases for interaction which, in turn, further create or solidify the circles. This is Simmel's original idea of social circles described in the previous chapter (Kadushin 1966; Simmel 1955 [1922]) and what Feld (1981) called a social focus. The circles are characterized by direct or indirect interaction though a friend of a friend. These circles are not a formal structure, group, gang, or even a clique, but they nonetheless exert a strong influence on "members." Simmel wrote discursively about circles, but they have been difficult to measure. They require simultaneous measurement of settings, occasions, or interests as well as the network of people involved in the settings.

Recent advances in computation as well as the statistical conceptualization of multiple levels of analysis (Raudenbush and Bryk 2002) have allowed for the systematic simultaneous analysis of these circles and their individual members. In high school settings, a local position was defined as "a group of adolescents who, by virtue of their coursetaking, share a social and academic space in school" (Frank et al. 2008, 1648). Using data from the Adolescent Health survey, they correctly predicted that this "position" or circle would affect students' choice of taking courses in mathematics: adolescent peers who are not directly friends but are "members" of such a position were "influential because they provide important information or opportunities (for example, knowledge about the nature of a math course or advice on performing well in it)."

Groups, circles, and social positions thus may be more effective in social influence and diffusion than single individuals, a matter that recent research in social networks as applied to epidemiology will argue.

Epidemiology and Network Diffusion

We now turn from studies of social influence to biological diffusion more directly known as "epidemiology." The Center for Disease Control (CDC) defines epidemiology as "the study of the distribution and determinates of diseases and injuries in human populations" (2010). The distribution is the result of two factors: incidence—the number of new cases in a given period; and prevalence—the number of total cases that are present in a given population at a given time. In an epidemic, there is a sharp rise in the incidence of the disease. Epidemiologists have traditionally modeled epidemics as S curves (see figure 9.1). The terminology of epidemiological models is slightly different from the adoption of innovation models described at the beginning of this chapter because epidemiology typically models "SIR" (Susceptibility, Infection, Recovery). The "recovery" part in innovation consists of adopting the innovation and removing the adopter from the population at risk for "infection" or adoption.

SOCIAL NETWORKS AND EPIDEMIOLOGY

Since incidence (new cases) is frequently caused by contagion—colloquially, one person "catches it" from another—social network theories and methods should be a natural tool for epidemiology that leads to preventive policies. For example, differential prevalence of a disease in a population may be related to differential diffusion through a social network. In HIV-AIDS this characteristic is notable. The disease is partly spread by contagion through shared needles. Reducing needle sharing by distributing free needles is an "obvious" intervention that has a strong effect on incidence of the HIV, but has not proven easy to achieve in the current social and political climate (De et al. 2007). The application of social network theories and methods in epidemiology ought to be obvious, but as Rothenberg noted, "There is a curious disconnect between the worlds of social epidemiology and social network analysis... references to social networks from the literature of social epidemiology are rare" (Rothenberg 2007, S149). Valente observed, "the use of social network methods and theory in public health has been limited until now. It was not until the mid-1990s that sociometric techniques were published in the flagship public health journal *American Journal of Public Health*" (Valente 2007, 154). It may be that part of the reason is that epidemiology produced interesting models of S-shaped diffusion curves that did not depend on understanding the dynamics of network social diffusion, but rather on the aggregate adoption rate and various macro factors, as we noted above in discussing social influence (Geroski 2000). But the field is rapidly changing and is itself an example of the diffusion of ideas and the development of a tipping point. Symptomatic is the appearance of a review of social networks in a recent *Annual Review of Public Health* (Luke and Harris 2007).

Public attention to HIV served to activate and renew interest in social network approaches to epidemiology. In 1985, just as the American public was becoming aware of AIDS, Klovdahl, a pioneering network methodologist who had developed innovative ways of mapping very large social networks, worked with data collected on 40 cases of AIDS in ten cities "to illustrate the potential usefulness of a network approach in evaluating the infectious agent hypothesis when studying a disease or disease outbreak of unknown etiology and in developing strategies to limit the spread of an infectious agent transmitted through personal relationships" (Klovdahl 1985, Abstract). But a continuing handicap to studying HIV transmission networks has been the perceived devastating consequences to an individual from a disclosure that he or she has AIDS or is HIV positive (see chapter 11, "Ethical Dilemmas of Social Network Research"), and hence the reluctance of AIDS activists and public authorities to develop partner notification systems for this epidemic. (Physicians are currently required to notify the CDC of new cases of HIV.) Notification of public health authorities and partner notification is required by law in many jurisdictions for tuberculosis or STDs such as gonorrhea.[6] Klovdahl (1994) worked with colleagues in public health and epidemiology in Colorado and developed interesting and ethical ways of collecting and analyzing data on large HIV-AIDS networks. The Colorado study led to the extension of these approaches to epidemiological studies of other STDs and to tuberculosis. The Centers for Disease Control (CDC) now states:

> Shared sites of drug or alcohol usage (e.g., taverns and crack houses), [as they are in HIV spread,] have been implicated as sites of *M. tuberculosis* transmission. Potential factors are close person-to-person proximity, repetitive exposure, and poor ventilation. Routine interviews might not generate a complete contact list for these settings, and the patient's social network should be explored for other information sources. (Centers for Disease 2005, 29)

Traditional epidemiological contact tracing methods typically failed to find much more than 10% of the patients who were linked by a common biological "fingerprint" (they had the same DNA markers of TB; Klovdahl et al. 2001). In contrast, network hypergraph principles (see chapter 6, "Small Groups, Leadership and Social Networks") were used in tracing an outbreak of TB in Houston: "A tuberculosis outbreak network, thus, can consist of persons, places and the relevant links connecting them" (Klovdahl et al. 2001, 684). The network approach traced over time both persons and places and assigned them centrality scores: "Had it been possible to eliminate place-associated transmission early in this outbreak, over 90% of the cases caused by the Print 4 organism [the DNA marker] may have been prevented" (Klovdahl et al. 2001, 689).

Social networks principles were used in tracing a syphilis epidemic in a community of teenagers who would get high together and have sex. Partner notification has been the cornerstone of prevention and control in the United States. But this study showed the limitations of traditional partner notification approaches.

> The network approach demonstrated that the results of interviewing infection and uninfected people were virtually identical for the purposes of discovering infected contacts. In this outbreak situation, the probability of being sexually connected to an infected person was the same regardless of whether one was infected. In a closer examination of the clinical presentation and temporal data of people with syphilis, the concept of "source and spread" cases has little meaning. The likelihood of having contracted syphilis from a particular person might appear to be based more on the probabilities of transmission from multiple infected partners than on single transfer of treponeme [the bacterium *Treponema pallidum* that causes syphilis].
>
> The traditional ... epidemic curve—would fail to capture the growth and complexity of the sexual substrate from which these cases of syphilis came. ... disease intervention had little impact on the underlying network behavior that generated these cases. (Rothenberg et al. 1998, 159)

The concept of "concurrency," which we will now explain, underlies both the importance of place and the apparent failure of traditional methods of tracing contacts.

SOCIAL NETWORKS AND HIV-AIDS

An additional area of inquiry concerns the situation where contact tracing is much more difficult, such as with HIV-AIDS. To be sure, what is known is tentative, because the social network approach is difficult in this field. Still, there have been some significant methodological advances in the epidemiology of social networks as applied to HIV-AIDS and sexual relations (Morris 2004) and this has led to better estimates of its prevalence and its differential location among youth and African Americans (Morris et al. 2006). Here are some findings.

First, a few facts on the biology of HIV transmission relevant to social networks. Contrary to some popular beliefs, a single contact does not necessarily lead to infection:

People with HIV are much more infectious during the period of primary infection after they are first infected with the virus than they are during the ensuing long latency period during which their antibody response limits the number of viral particles in their blood, semen and/or vaginal secretions. This makes it possible for those seropositives who have already entered the latency period to function as "firewalls" in risk networks such that the entry of a new case of HIV into the network (with its attendant high-viral load) cannot lead to rapid and widespread further transmission because viruses that are transmitted enter into "firewall" members with their antibodies already developed. (Friedman et al. 2007, 644)

Even during the initial primary infection period, the probabilities of further transmission are not 100%, because many other factors come into play. This means that network trees in which contacts are serial are less effective transmitters than concurrent contacts in a "community" in which an infected person can transmit to several people who in turn can submit to several more. Note that the word "community" is often not used in the HIV literature because it carries a positive connotation. But there is indeed a positive side to communities in populations at risk for HIV. Word about precautions and reduction of high-risk activity spreads through social influence and opinion leaders in these communities. Further, members of a community of drug users can distribute clean needles in ways that authorities cannot.

How does HIV get out of the "communities" so that some "rewiring" (see chapter 8) takes place and the disease spreads? Basically, through weak ties.

The unstable relationships in IDU [Intravenous Drug Users] networks have implications for the spread of HIV and for prevention. To the degree that these unstable relationships represent weak ties to other IDU networks, they may increase the probability of exposure to HIV. High-turnover networks may increase the rapidity with which HIV spreads Thus, short-term relationships may carry HIV across long-term networks and, thereby, across social categories. (Neaigus et al. 1995, 34)

Friedman also points out that variations in infectivity mean that variations in frequency of taking risks are extremely important—indeed, that a key parameter in population spread of HIV is what proportion of a population switches from high- to low risk behaviors. As with TB, sites are important. Prostitutes, crack houses, bars, and bath houses provide sites for the establishment of weak ties—hanging out with people with whom one would not otherwise associate. As a network phenomenon, people are linked to places or institutions that help in the transmission of disease; places encourage concurrent rather than tree contact. Finally, though users who share needles generally share them with their strong ties, those ties are not permanent but change. This variability leads to transmitting HIV out of what appears to be a close circle of users (Valente and Valahov 2001).

The importance of concurrency cannot be overemphasized. We saw how important it was in the transmission of TB. It is even more important in HIV-AIDS. Morris and Kretzschmar summarize their findings:

Concurrent partnerships exponentially increase the number of infected individuals and the growth rate of the epidemic during its initial phase. For example, when one-half of the partnerships in a population are concurrent, the size of the epidemic after 5 years is 10 times as large as under sequential monogamy. The primary cause of this amplification is the growth in the number of people connected in the network at any point in time: the size of the largest "component." Concurrency increases the size of this component, and the result is that the infectious agent is no longer trapped in a monogamous partnership after transmission occurs, but can spread immediately beyond this partnership to infect others. (Morris and Kretzschmar 1997, Abstract)

Concurrency, combined with assortative mixing (same kinds tend to stay together, on which see chapter 8), can cause, over time, the observed strong epidemiological differentials between non-Hispanic Blacks and non-Hispanic Whites in their prevalence of STDs, as statistical simulation (see figure 9.3) over a ten-year period demonstrates (Morris et al. 2009, 1025, figure 9.1).

TRANSPORTING DISEASE—LARGE-SCALE MODELS

The social network epidemiological findings reviewed earlier are mainly derived from field studies. Simulation and large-scale social network modeling using small world methods have been quite successful in developing ideas and findings about many contagious diseases, as suggested by the example given above for STDs.[7]

Air-transportation-network properties are often responsible for the global pattern of emerging diseases. This network is the origin of the heterogeneous and seemingly erratic spreading on the global scale of diseases such as severe acute respiratory syndrome [SARS] (Colizza et al. 2006). The timing of the arrival of diseases worldwide can be effectively modeled using transportation connection data and small world theory and models (Gautreau, Barrat, and Barthélemy 2008).

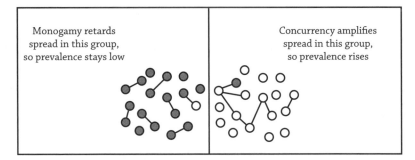

Assortative mixing reduces spread between groups,
so a prevalence differential can be sustained over time

FIGURE 9.3 Assortative Mixing and Concurrency

Morris, Martina, Ann E. Kurth, Deven T. Hamilton, James Moody, and Steve Wakefield. 2009. Concurrent partnerships and HIV prevalence disparities by race: Linking science and public health practice. *Am J Public Health* 99 (6):1025, Figure 1. Copyright © 2009 The Sheridan Press. Reprinted with permission.

Restricting travel between municipalities could have a beneficial effect on the speed of transmission of a highly contagious disease, geographically and in absolute numbers. This is true for a wide range of plausible values of the inter-municipal infectiousness. Even in scenarios of compliance as low as 70%, travel restrictions are effective (Camitz and Liljeros 2006). The traditional public health method of quarantine is validated. On the other hand, quarantine is difficult to enforce. Similarly, models show that decreasing the size of day care centers from 16.7 to 13.4 children predicts a reduction in the spread of strep pneumonia by as much as 85% in Norway (Karlsson et al. 2008). Small class size has implications beyond facilitating learning.

There are some interesting findings about vaccination strategies for flu. An obvious strategy, but as it turns out a wrong one, is vaccinating individuals who are sociometric stars. The less obvious strategy follows from small world theory: vaccinating people who are tightly knit with one another is less effective than vaccinating people at random (Hartvigsen et al. 2007). If a tight knit group is immunized, then because of assortative mixing, the effects are less likely to spread out of the group. Random vaccination reaches a wider group because those immunized are weakly connected to a chain of others who are not connected with each other. The immunized person can break a chain of infection.

Tipping Points and Thresholds

A tipping point occurs when a trend, an idea, or an infection appears to take off on its own. The growth curve begins slowly and then, as shown in figure 9.1, a certain point is reached in which the proportion that is infected or adopts the idea seems to shoot up—the tipping point—eventually leveling off as almost everyone adopts the idea or becomes infected.

Malcolm Gladwell's *The Tipping Point* (2000) brilliantly popularized this idea borrowed from epidemiology and applied it to many phenomena from crime to social policy to advertising. The book is said to have sold over two million copies and is still on the *New York Times* paperback bestseller list. The idea itself, once confined to specialized communities of experts, took off. It makes a great deal of intuitive sense. There are some problems with his analysis, however. Although the observation of a tipping point is an exercise in reading a mathematical graph, Gladwell offers no formal definition of tipping point. So how are we to understand what he is saying? Without Gladwell's persuasive rhetoric, we must look into some of the mathematics that underpin the idea. In keeping with the goals of this book, we will rely mainly on pictures and graphs to make the point.

The classic S or sigmoid growth curve is illustrated by figure 9.4:

It is a logistic (based on logarithms rather than straight lines) distribution. The mathematical "inflection point" is at $x=0$, on the vertical line. You might "eyeball" the curve to decide that -2 is the point where the curve appears to take off, and $+2$ where it appears to level off, but there is no substantive or mathematical justification for this. To be more meaningful from a diffusion or epidemiological point of view, we

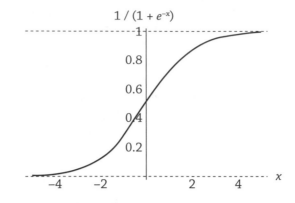

FIGURE 9.4 Classic S or Sigmoid Growth Curve

need some further information about the diffusion. We begin with the basic idea that contagion or imitation results in the observed S curve. Second, we need to add the now familiar idea of influence: that which gets people to adopt an idea or introduces a new disease into the population. After it is introduced, the idea or the disease takes off on its own as a result of imitation or contagion. In this model, both contagion and influence operate simultaneously but not on the same individuals: "In early time periods, most new adopters adopt due to external influence: It is obvious, and easy to prove, that imitation produces the greater fraction of incremental new adopters in each subsequent period as well. This simple and intuitively appealing result indicates a meaningful tipping point..." (Phillips 2007, 721). The tipping occurs when the adoption or the disease is self-sustaining without any external input. This can be modeled as shown in the following set of curves that Phillips uses as an example that have a tipping point at t 1, where t is the time period and x the proportion adopting or infected (figure 9.5).

The middle curve (in grey) shows the effect of cutting off external influences or advertising at the inflection point. The growth is slower than the top curve (in light grey) where external influence was continued. The bottom curve (in black) tests the inflection or tipping point. It is slower than the middle curve because external influences were cut off two periods before the inflection point. A variant on this model adds a price multiplier such that later adopters are more sensitive to price or the cost. That is, they will adopt only if the price is lowered. In short, we can discover a tipping point, after the fact, by observing what happens when we stop a direct intervention. Using mathematics, however, we can project what would happen under different intervention scenarios.

Problematic, however, is that the model assumes that one is either susceptible to outside influence or imitation but not to both. This notion of either/or seems unrealistic, though as Phillips pointed out, the model "worked" and, among other things, has been responsible for the "dynamic pricing" in which the same seat has a different price depending on how many people have already booked on to the flight. Phillips adds to the first two assumptions, contagion and influence, a third factor: resistance to

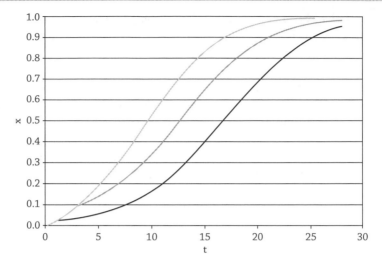

FIGURE 9.5 Tipping Points

Reprinted from *Technological Forecasting and Social Change* 74 (6): 721, figure 2, Phillips, Fred. 2007. On S-curves and tipping points. Copyright © 2007, with permission from Elsevier.

adoption, change, or disease.[8] The infection point occurs when imitation overcomes resistance. Most formal models of diffusion and influence tend not to incorporate resistance to innovation and disease, although it is an "obvious" factor.

This inevitably brings us to the nagging question of how does one set the parameters for the models? Typically, only after the fact, on the bases of some epidemiological studies or other data. Yes, there are tipping points, but we do not know what they are until after they have happened. We can see what happens, for example, if we stop an intervention. But the tipping point model does not tell us *when* to stop the intervention. We would have to have done the field work or the research in advance *before* we could set parameters to predict what eventually happened.

THRESHOLD

Threshold is often used interchangeably with tipping point. As the jacket cover for Gladwell's *Tipping Point* puts it, "The tipping point is that magic moment when an idea, trend, or social behavior crosses a threshold, tips, and spreads like wildfire." There is actually more to it than that. As we have seen, a tipping point can be a collective phenomenon in which contagion rules and eventually conquers without any further outside influence or input. That is, the spread reaches a certain threshold and then takes off. One does not have to presuppose any characteristics of individuals to model this growth. Individuals as well as groups can experience tipping points in which enough influence or perception of what is taking place in the environment leads people to make a decision or to take an action. Usually this is called a threshold. It is the final "reason" that leads to the action, and the concept ties individual decision-making and action to collective phenomena. Individuals can have personal thresholds: the point at which an individual buys a product, joins a riot, or votes.[9] Notably, a population is heterogeneous with respect to individual thresholds—that is, there is some distribution of these thresholds. In now classic papers, Granovetter developed models of threshold behavior that are "apt in situations where people's decisions or actions depend on other people's previous ones" (Granovetter 1978; Granovetter and Soong 1983), which is typical of most diffusion. He offers riots as an example:

i) At any point in the progress of a riot, whether one decides to join depends in part on how many others are currently involved, as it is riskier to join when few others have—chances of being apprehended are greater. ii) Some individuals are more daring than others (a personality factor); some are more committed to radical causes (ideological influences); some have more to lose by being arrested (rational economic motives: e.g., the employed vs. the unemployed).

Combinations of such influences give the result that while one individual might be prepared to join very early—in the risky stage—others might not be willing to join until the behavior was quite safe, nearly universal. Call these, as in common parlance, low versus high threshold individuals.

iii) The state vector—telling us by 1's and 0's, for example, who is and is not rioting at time t—changes over time, and results, at any time, in part from the configuration in the previous time period. (Granovetter and Soong 1983, 167)

From the model's point of view it does not matter whether the source of the threshold is self-interest, conformism, or any other motivation. Interestingly, because this is network connection behavior, very small differences in the distribution of thresholds can lead to very large changes in outcomes. Granovetter and Soong offer the following example: Suppose in a population of 100 individuals, there is a uniform distribution of thresholds from 0 to 99. Should the person with a 0 threshold start a riot, the one with a threshold of 1 may join and a person with a threshold of 2 will join until everyone participates. But if there is no one with a threshold of 1, then the "riot" stops immediately. In terms of individual dispositions, the crowds are nearly identical, but the network produced outcomes that are entirely different. In practice, threshold models are more complex than it would appear, precisely because variations in the distribution of thresholds, the sociometric as well as spatial connections between individuals with different thresholds all contribute to dramatically different levels of adoption.

The snob effect is another kind of threshold related to level of adoption, according to Granovetter and Soong. One does not want to adopt something that has become too popular. As has been attributed to Yogi Berra, "It's too crowded, nobody goes there anymore." For this situation, formal modeling offers two possibilities, neither of which is intuitive. An innovation catches on quickly, has staying power, but then succumbs to the snob effect. We are looking at the difference between two cumulative distributions: one for those whose lower threshold (the adopters) has been exceeded and another for those whose upper threshold (the snobs) has been exceeded. The resultant cumulative distribution is unstable and oscillates unpredictably. But an innovation that catches on slowly but also has an immediate snob effect reaches a stable solution.

For simplicity's sake, Granovetter assumed that each actor was fully aware of all the others' actions in deciding whether or not to act. But in reality, from the point of view of any actor, to paraphrase the late Speaker of the House Tip O'Neill, all networks are local. The actor is directly responsive to those around him or her not to the total system. There are few empirical studies that measure individual decision-making thresholds. One study relies on time of adoption relative to extent of exposure; the proportion of adopters in ego's personal network serves to indicate a threshold (Valente 1996). For example, one person may adopt an innovation if 25% of their social network has adopted, but another may adopt only if 50% have adopted. The first person is said to have a lower threshold than the second person even though we do not have a direct measure of the person's "threshold psychology." Two persons with the same individual psychological threshold may adopt at different times depending on how many others in their network have adopted. Further contextualizing threshold, there is a total network threshold (the proportion who have adopted given the proportion in the total network who have adopted) and a local network threshold (the proportion who have adopted given the proportion in one's direct interpersonal environment who have adopted). This gives additional meaning, but necessary complication, to the concept of innovation:

> [There are] individuals [who] *are innovative with respect to their personal network or [those who are] innovative with respect to the social system.* Those with high network thresholds who adopt early relative to the social system are only innovative relative to the social system, not relative to their personal communication network. Low network threshold adopters are individuals who adopt early relative to their personal network yet may (though not necessarily) adopt late relative to the social system. (Valente 1996, 73 [italics in the original])

Valente (1996) reanalyzed three classic studies: doctors and new drugs (Coleman, Katz, and Menzel 1966), Korean village contraceptive adoption (Rogers and Kincaid 1981), and Brazilian farmer hybrid corn adoption [unpublished report]. By and large in the three cases investigated, individuals who adopted early relative to their local network were also likely to adopt earlier than most of the entire network.[10]

There are few observational studies on thresholds and diffusion. Simulation, however, is another possible source of data. Of particular interest is the method of computer Agent-Based Modeling (ABM). In this method, the researcher creates an artificial population of "agents" (they could be people, organizations, or microbes) that "interact" on the basis of certain rules. The interaction takes place over a number of time periods. The results can be tracked. This is not the place for instruction,[11] but the results clearly depend on the rules that are created. As we know, social system interaction can produce unforeseen results and unanticipated consequences and this is why we learn from ABM. Through this system, we can create simulations that have agents with differing thresholds, with different degrees of connection with one another, different degrees of clustering, and different small world properties.

Valente (2010, 224–231) and Chiang (2007) offer some examples and arrive at similar results. In common with some of the epidemiological modeling we have cited, random networks have more rapid diffusion than one might naively expect. They provide short overall paths in the network. Just a little clustering creates bottlenecks. The network neighbors of any node chosen at random have more connections than the random node, leading to greater propagation (your friends have more friends than you have [Feld 1991]). As theory suggests, clustered networks speed diffusion within the cluster but impede it overall because diffusion becomes concentrated within the cluster. Highly central nodes, if they are marginal to clusters, are very effective in propagation because of the structural hole effect. Valente included in his simulation a real network. Diffusion in the network was slow because of the network's natural clustering. Rumors spread more rapidly in random networks but since the networks were not clustered, the rumors tended not to come back to the individual being rumored about and hence (unfortunately) were not correctable.

Chiang modeled a situation in which individuals or in modeling language "agents" "rewire" their networks, that is, choose a new neighbor in the network with either greater or less similarity in their thresholds. The S curve generally applies in this scenario. Adoption "is maximized when agents' neighbors include both some agents with rather different thresholds and a core group of similar others" (Chiang 2007, 64). If the agents are extremely dissimilar, adoption levels are relatively low. On the other hand, in these models it is possible for an agent with a high threshold to adopt earlier than those with a low threshold because that agent is surrounded by actors with diverse thresholds, whereas some agents with low thresholds are trapped in a pocket of others with low thresholds. Diversity and balance help in diffusion. Chiang finds the model consistent with some empirical cases that he suggests. For example, in the growth of Christianity in the Roman Empire, moderate levels of contact with non-believers may have been beneficial to Christianity's diffusion. During recruitment dinners in the Unification Church, new prospects are always surrounded by old members.

Basic network theory seems to explain these simulation-based findings. Homophily plays a role when agents or actors are surrounded by similar others who have similar thresholds for action. When actors are surrounded entirely by others with similar thresholds, the cascade may stall since it will become self-contained. To break out of a closed homophilous circle, one needs actors who are different. We do not learn anything new by hanging out with people who are just like us. Again we are faced with the dualities of support and density versus bridging and structural holes (See chapter 5, "The Psychological Foundations of Social Networks") and Simmel's important principle regarding the ways in which cross-cutting social circles create a cosmopolitan view (Simmel 1955 [1922]).

These families of ideas deal with exogenous thresholds, that is, those that are characteristic of individual agents. There has also been considerable work with thresholds that depend only on how many individuals have already adopted an innovation rather than on their personal predispositions. These models are useful in that they emphasize system externalities. For example, people adopted fax machines when there were others who could receive them. This kind of threshold creates a cascade or snowball effect. There is another consequence to the network effect: the product which is first adopted tends to drive out the others. Suppose there are two competing products with different standards. If the products are very much dependent on connections with others such as fax or teleconferencing, then early adoption of one standard drives out the other (Kornish 2006). Facebook's early successes in moving far beyond the young person's niche of MySpace created huge a volume of users, eventually dooming MySpace, whose unique visitors in May 2011 were 22% of those of Facebook [my calculation], which in May 2011 reached 73% of the United States internet population (Lispman 2011).

Where We Are Now

This chapter has covered a great deal of ground so it is useful to summarize and draw some conclusions about social network theories of diffusion. To begin, the basic model for diffusion, oddly enough, conceals more than it reveals. Diffusion more or less follows an "S" or Sigma curve with the y axis representing the cumulative proportion who have adopted and the x axis representing the time of adoption. In the early stages, the proportion who adopt something or who are infected rises slowly, then later rapidly takes off as more and more in the population adopt or succumb to a disease, and finally tails off. Why? The classic explanation leaves the origin of the idea or innovation as an unexplored phenomenon to be explored by some other theories. But once the seed is planted, a few actors (people, organizations, or national states, for example) take it up. Subsequent rapid growth is driven by contagion—the higher the percentage in the population at risk, the more likely those who have not already adopted or "infected" interact with the growing number who have. But growth tails off because as more and more adopt, there are fewer available individuals at risk, that is, those who might adopt.

This chapter attempted to unpack this account. Given that we are not able to answer for the origin of an idea or disease, we still must account for the dynamics that lie behind a given contagion and its rate of growth. Many mechanisms could cause contagion, most of which are at the heart of network theory. A tipping point, where an innovation takes off on its own, is characteristic of most diffusions in a population. Individual thresholds determine when a particular person or a set of individuals overcome their resistance to change or to disease. Social and cultural contexts can impede or speed adoption or provide an end to it. Some diffusion takes place until the entire population has adopted it, but in other instances diffusion seems to reach a ceiling where no further adoption takes place.

Network interaction theories of course cannot explain all aspects of diffusion. There are exogenous factors. Government intervention for example helped expand the use of the telephone in Europe and the automobile in the United States. Marketing and advertising efforts do have a network component, however, and have been of interest to network theories since the 1930s. We have discussed theories of decision-making that include input from media, attributes of a potential innovation, and the influence of others in the network that surrounds the actor. This unpacks one aspect of contagion, personal influence, which is important in the adoption of new practices, ideas, votes, and products, especially when potential targets are active seekers of advice. Whether this influence is caused by direct contact or by emulating others who are structurally similar, as in "keeping up with the Joneses" or both, has been a matter of controversy. Current research suggests that both direct contact and emulation are about equally important, though exogenous factors such as marketing and media are also important. The size of the circle of influence or structural similarity that surrounds the potential adopter is critically important to the theory of influence. Most often, influence comes from the immediate surround of the actor or at most two or three steps removed. Informal social circles based on mutual interests and activities that surround actors are keys to the influence process.

Embedded in the concept of personal influence is the notion of opinion leader—the person who influences others to adopt. While as a result of computer modeling there has been recent skepticism about the effectiveness of opinion leaders, much of the recent evidence suggests that opinion leaders are particularly effective in the health field if they are specially targeted, selected, and trained. On the other hand, naturally occurring opinion leaders, as is true of other types of leaders (see chapter 6), cannot be too far out of step with their followers. Opinion leaders do tend to be of somewhat higher social status and better informed. We do not have full sociometric data for most opinion leadership studies, but those we do have, along with some computer modeling, suggest an interesting balance in successful diffusion between being peripheral (mavericks can be early adopters) and being central (central agents can reach many others). In successful diffusion, there is also a balance between the embeddedness of the leader in a dense group that promotes the innovation or having a position as a bridge between groups, so that an innovation diffuses out of its original circle. The matter of balance and tradeoff is crucial to theories of diffusion.

The concept of opinion leader is central to the idea of a multi-step adoption process in which opinion leaders obtain their views from media or from experts and then transmit these views to their immediate circle, which further passes them along to their respective circles in a networked cascade of influence. So called "viral marketing" makes use of this idea. But the n-step opinion leadership chain is now not so clearly supported by the available evidence. Part of the reason may be that the full chain of network data is not available for any of these studies.

Epidemiological models were traditionally content with the unpacked idea of "contagion" as a function of the number of persons remaining at risk and the number already infected. Social network ideas that detailed the kind of interaction necessary for transmitting a disease were superfluous. Studies of HIV-AIDS, however, made it obvious that social contact through sex and needle sharing were responsible for contagion, and the network mechanisms involved were important to understand. Social network analysis added to the epidemiologists' tool of contact tracing (not an easy matter with HIV), the familiar social network idea of the duality between persons and groups. Circles, communities, and sites were critical to the spread of disease. We saw how circles of teenagers engaged in multiple concurrent sex partnering spread syphilis, communities of drug users sharing needles lead to HIV infection, bathhouses and prostitutes spread HIV, and places to hang out spread TB. We also noted that circles and communities can also be a source of education and intervention as well as negative contagion.

Social network ideas derived from recent small world modeling have been recently introduced into epidemiology modeling with very promising non-intuitive results. Modeling suggests that the spread of SARS (Severe Acute Respiratory Syndrome) can be vastly curtailed by air travel restrictions even with far from perfect compliance. Decreasing the size of day care centers can cut the spread of childhood infectious diseases.

Tipping points and thresholds are the last frontier, but they are like the future—notoriously difficult to predict even with sophisticated modeling. They are typically evident only after the fact. It is hard to pinpoint just where on the diffusion curve a tipping point should be placed. Modeling the consequences of individual adoption thresholds has been more fruitful and raises important issues in social network theory.

Explorations in varying individual's thresholds and their distribution through Agent-Based Modeling have led us to the very edge of network theory. Diffusion is simultaneously sensitive to the interpersonal environment network that immediately surrounds an individual and affected by global network characteristics. Balance between them is the key in ways yet to be fully explored. Similarly, centrality in a dense network and centrality as a bridge have different effects with the latter more likely to lead to fast diffusion, though random seeds are also effective. Rewiring small worlds is a major way disease and innovation can spread. The center of gravity in most diffusion theory is the individual actor (either a person or an organization) as source, innovator, or opinion leader. But it may well be that conceptualizing diffusion as taking place through a circle or focus-based clusters is a more fruitful way to proceed. The entry of social network theory and methods into epidemiology is but 15 or so years old. The juncture of social network ideas and methods into this applied field will certainly enrich diffusion and epidemiology theories. Working out the details in an applied field will surely feed back upon and enrich the theoretical base.

If we think about the positive aspects of diffusion, the spread of useful material things, ideas, and innovations, we realize that individuals and organizations have potential access to a far wider range of matters than those that lie within them or are part of their standard repertoire. The reach and availability of commodities, ideas, and influence beyond those immediately at hand is the central concern of "social capital" to which we now turn.

10 Networks as Social Capital

Introduction

Social capital is a fitting topic for summarizing the field of social networks. Central to the concept are the consequences of social networks, mainly positive but sometimes negative.[1] To oversimplify, social capital implies that "social networks have value" (Putnam 2008). It brings us back to the fundamental premises of social networks, the tradeoff between the comfort and support individuals derive from dense networks of social relationships and the benefits achieved by going beyond local circles and forging bridges to wider universes. Characteristic for a social network–based idea, social capital operates on several levels. Networks in social systems may be nested, for example, organization networks within industry networks. There are also individual actor networks. At each level, social capital has two main consequences: social capital investment and individual social capital. Social capital investment, as is the case for financial capital, can lead to even greater social capital. For example, high voluntary organization participation increases community voter turnout. Individual social capital increases individual well-being—typically, physical and/or mental health, or adjustment and a sense of well-being. Individual social capital can also lead to financial well-being and social and/or occupational upward mobility. Further, social capital has cross-level consequences. For example, high community-level social capital can lead to individual well-being. These are impressive claims and social capital is a complex concept. In this chapter, we will unpack the concept, raise measurement issues, and review data on the consequences of social capital at different levels. We will discover that although the idea seems relatively straightforward, once explored, the concept raises a host of issues.

According to Putnam (2000, 19) the concept of social capital was introduced as early as 1916. Yet the term "social capital" has come into widespread use relatively recently. Whereas the Web of Science retrieved seven "social capital" citations for the year 1990, a search for social capital articles in 2010 revealed over 12,000 (see figure 10.1).

The inclusiveness of the phrase "social networks have value" has aided this outpouring, and many recent articles on social capital begin by noting the varied definitions of the term. While praising Putnam's *Bowling Alone* (2000) as putting an important issue on the agenda (as of June 2011, the Web of Science shows well over 700 citations to the book), Claude Fischer noted that social capital "is not much different from saying that social capital is everything psychological and sociological about a person." As a past editor of the American Sociological Association's journal *Contexts* he put "social capital" on his do-not-use style-sheet (Fischer 2005). But there are precedents for poorly defined key sociological concepts, for example, anomie. In some ways, anomie as a negative concept is the mirror image of positive social capital and is also a two-level concept. Anomie at the societal level is sometimes defined as a lack of moral standards in a society, or at the individual level, as a personal state of isolation and anxiety resulting from a lack of social control and regulation. Anomie was introduced into social analysis by Émile Durkheim (1951 [1897]) over 100 years ago. His argument, put in modern network terms, was that anomie occurs when network ties are loosened, either at the individual or the societal level or both. Nonetheless, exactly what anomie means, its implications, how is it measured, and its causes remain controversial. Subject to almost endless definitions and reconceptualizations, the concept has

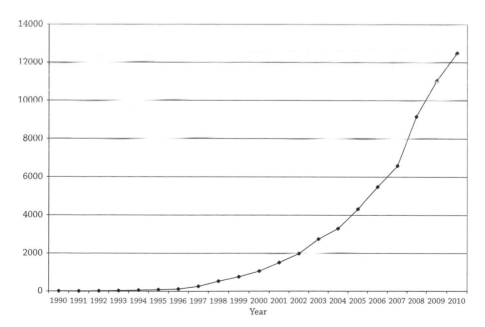

FIGURE 10.1 Number of Social Capital Citations in the Web of Science

generated an outpouring of research and garnered the attention of leading minds in social science. Anomie is cited in introductory sociology texts, yet the concept remains difficult and subject to a variety of interpretations and conflicting evidence.[2]

Before we enter into the definitional complications of social capital, I offer a story about social capital that illustrates many aspects of the concept.

THE GENERAL IDEA OF SOCIAL CAPITAL

In the midst of baking a cake, I run out of sugar. I can, however, go to my neighbor next door to get some. It was worth being nice to that neighbor even though I did not particularly fancy her. Do I have to give back to her an equivalent amount of sugar? Maybe she can borrow my lawn mower the next time she needs to mow her lawn and that will count as a return of the favor. Maybe the value of the sugar is trivial enough not to require repayment. Now I need a recipe for a new cake. My neighbor has just the right recipe for me. But there is really nothing to return except for good will because in giving me a copy of the recipe my neighbor retains one for herself. The same day a guy three houses down the street who I do not know has heard from my neighbor that I know something about computers and asks me to help him. I am busy but feel obligated to at least try to help because we all live in the same neighborhood. Someday I may have to ask that neighbor, maybe a different one, for help in fixing that darn lawnmower. What goes around comes around. In fact, I am really in a bad mood because the cake wasn't very good, the new recipe was of no great help, and besides, my lawnmower is broken. A long-term friend just happened to call me up on the telephone, and I let loose some of my frustration on him. He told me a bunch of silly jokes and made me feel much better.

The concept of "social capital" is said to cover all these situations. I don't have to have the sugar because my neighbor has some. I may even be able to return the favor not with sugar but with something of equal value. I did "invest" in that relationship by being nice to my neighbor in the past. The guy down the street counts on my help even though he hardly knows me because we live in the "neighborhood," and we therefore have something in common. And I "cast my bread upon the waters" in helping him, because I believe someone in the neighborhood may eventually help me. This is a neighborhood rich in resources—for example, sugar, recipes, mechanical knowledge of small engines, and computer savvy. Not only do I personally have "social capital" but so does the neighborhood through its collective resources. Finally, social capital does not have to be accessible solely through geographic propinquity. I received some "social support" long distance. Other than actual resources, Glanville and Bienenstock (2009) suggest that social capital may also imply the presence of trust—at the individual level my neighbor does not believe I intended to rob her, and collectively, this is a neighborhood in which people trust one another and share values from the importance of home baking to respect for others.

Social networks have value because they allow access to resources and valued social attributes such as trust, reciprocity, and community values. There are two fundamental types of access to resources: the first is illustrated by my borrowing a cup of sugar when I did not have one. These are resources that could be available to an individual as a product of her or his social network. The second type, with a long tradition in social science, are the resources created by "community." The resources of my neighborhood in the story were made available by the sense of community that the neighborhood seemed to have. Sadly, community resources are often most appreciated when they are taken away, when communities are destroyed through natural or human-made disasters (Erikson 1976).

Community is as diffuse a term as social capital and is itself the subject of a plethora of definitions.[3] I shall describe the phenomenon of social capital as community after I investigate how individual social capital resources (e.g., wealth, power, or reputation) are embedded in the social networks from which an actor may borrow.

Most sociologists define social capital as resources made available through social relations. "[R]esources and relations facilitate information flow, influence flow, rendering of social credentials and affirmation of self-identity... which in turn can be used to generate returns in the marketplace" (Lin and Erickson 2008b, 4). They conclude that "A theory of social capital... focuses on the production and returns of social capital and explicates how individual and collective actors invest in social relations through which they gain access to diverse and rich resources for expected returns" (ibid.).

Putnam observes (personal communication) that, in addition to the social resources that accrue to those who invest in them, community-level networks benefit from "the shadow of neighbors." Reputations, actions, and benefits (a neighbor raking his lawn so that the leaves do not now blow over onto mine) become visible and available to others who have not necessarily themselves invested in social relations. Collective problem solving is thereby facilitated.

SOCIAL CAPITAL AS AN INVESTMENT

Since social capital is an analogue to financial capital, we will briefly review the principles of capital as used by economists. Marx's theory of "surplus value" represents the price of the product extracted by exploitation of workers, minus the cost necessary to keep them alive. It has two components: the current revenue that can be used to repeat the current production process and sustain the consumption style of the capitalists, and one that is saved for future investment, thereby incrementing the valued resources. The first of these is called "capital." Adam Smith also had the general idea but did not actually use the term "capital." However, he had reservations about the relationship of labor to capital creation. He considered "productive" labor as that which augments the stock of "capitals" versus "unproductive" labor which does not.

To be sure, modern economists do not cite Marx on capital, though of course the other "giant" upon whose shoulders he stands, Adam Smith, is still referenced. This is not the place to enter into theories of capital—for that would take us from Adam Smith, John Stuart Mill, the "Austrian School," John Maynard Keynes, and Joan Robinson, to the post-Keynesians. That would be the subject of another book. At the minimum, everyone agrees that entrepreneurs try to estimate what they can earn if they hold back current resources and invest them in factors that aid production of still more resources rather than consume them immediately.

There are endless debates about calculating this "surplus value," determining its sources and who should be the recipient of it, evaluating how surplus value relates to labor and consumption, and identifying the entrepreneurs. There are also differing views about how investments are discounted, who sets the discount rates, and the consequences of different savings rates for the total economy. If all this were clear, we might not have had the financial meltdown of 2008, and we would have better ideas about how to quickly create a turnaround. The crisis reminds us that the investment process is embedded in a social system, for like social capital, financial capital depends on social structure.

For the moment, we will ignore the subject of the financial or social capital of nations, communities, and organizations and concentrate on individual persons as "entrepreneurs." The idea of denying immediate gratification in favor of an eventual return is clear in the concept of "human capital," a term developed by economist Gary Becker (1964) who was awarded a Nobel Prize, in part for this idea. According to his theory, workers can invest in skills and education that would enable them to negotiate for higher wages and thus gain for themselves some of the surplus value created in the production process. The social capital analogue to human capital is that investment in networked resources gives an actor advantages in the market. Acquiring general education or technical or manual skills can be arduous and costly. While these human capital accumulations are being acquired, an actor puts off immediate returns in favor of future gains. The extent to which individuals actually invest in social relations in anticipation of future gains is more problematic. In my example, I was nice to my neighbor not because I might eventually get something from her, but because of general social norms. Social climbers, those engaged in office politics and civil politics, may consciously invest in social relations in the anticipation of eventual personal gain. This investment is sometimes regarded as gauche, as the pejoratively tinged "social climber" suggests.

Recently, as a consequence of the popularization of social network ideas, the noun "networking" has been added to the lexicon. The *Oxford English Dictionary Online* (June 2011) offers a fourth usage: "The action or process of making use of a network of people for the exchange of information, etc., or for professional or other advantage." It finds the first examples in the late 1970s. In the introduction to this book, we noted the rapid development since 2002 of social networking websites to make connections between people. But the social capital implications of these sites, as of this writing, have not been extensively researched.[4] The extent to which most individuals consciously invest in social relations in anticipation of some material or symbolic gain may be limited. The analogue to financial capital of deferred gratification may also be somewhat overstated in human capital theory. Many people consider education a pleasurable experience in itself, regardless of its long-term market value, as liberal arts advocates often maintain. As for social capital, most people probably derive immediate gratification from making friends.

Actual demonstrations of the effectiveness of investment strategies in social capital are rare. As Fernandez and Castilla observe, "if the term 'social capital' is to mean anything more than 'networks have value,' then we will need to demonstrate key features of the analogy to 'real' capital. If 'social' capital is like 'real' capital, we should be able to isolate the value of the investment, the rates of return, and the means by which returns are realized" (Fernandez and Castilla 2001, 85). They investigated a firm that gave bonuses to existing workers for referring potential employees: "The firm's $250 investment (in the form of a referral bonus [for persons hired]) yields a return of $416 in reduced recruiting costs" (ibid., 101). The referrals did get an applicant who was more appropriate for the job, thus saving screening costs. On the other hand, over the long term, once a person was hired, having come from a referral did not reduce turnover. From the employee's perspective, persons with better jobs were more likely to refer others and thereby reap the benefit of the bonus. The authors argue that it is likely that the instrumental value of getting the bonuses was discovered after employees discovered themselves in these better positions, hence "it is misleading to think of occupancy of these positions as *investments*" (ibid.; authors' italics). There are also qualitative studies of investment in social capital. In *Friends of Friends*, Boissevain (1974) devotes an entire section to "brokers" (his term) who reap a profit from their investments in their networks. The subtitle to the book includes the word "manipulators." In popular literature, we are familiar with the Mafia capo who invests in favors for people in the expectation that at some point he will make them "an offer you can't refuse." There are still not enough studies of investment strategies in social networks and their possible payoffs, though ongoing work on social network sites may yield better information

The analogy of social to financial capital may be limited,[5] but this limitation has not prevented the widespread application and use of the term social capital. Deficiencies of the analogy notwithstanding, the implications of networked resources and improved capability of collective action are enormous. Tapping into the evidence behind the theory of the value of social networks to individual or collective actors has proven to be an interesting challenge and one we have met before. Assessing an individual's or a community's networked resources requires mapping the full network, ascertaining the resources available in various domains to each member of the network, and finding the ways that these resources are or are not made available to various individuals and to the community as a whole. Because of the potential number of connections in a total community, mapping an entire community is at this point not feasible, nor in some ways desirable because of the lack of focus and clarity that such a project entails. However, some ingenious ideas and tools that focus on key aspects of social capital and how to measure it have been developed. Because the devil is in the details, in this chapter more than in the previous ones, we will pay attention to the relations between the basic concepts involved in social capital and the indicators that are used to measure that concept.

The salience and importance of investment in social capital is another key issue that lurks behind all the analyses that follow. Some individuals and communities have more social capital than others. How did this come about? Did the individuals or the communities consciously invest in the creation of social capital or were they structurally situated so that they had more social capital but not as a result of their own investment strategies? Rich people often claim the rewards of wealth as their due because of wise investments. In reality, they inherited their wealth or benefited from a structural location that allowed them to accumulate more wealth. The unequal distribution of wealth is generally an unfair distribution. As has been often said in this book, social networks are essentially unfair. We can work to improve our connections, but those who gain entry to elite colleges, for example, and thus a ticket to a better life, have had the benefit of cascading connections that they themselves have not made. Communities vary enormously in their resources: being well connected in an African village is certainly helpful, but being well connected in New York City certainly conveys greater material advantages. Assessing and accounting for "the wealth of nations" is a task that has baffled economists ever since Adam Smith (1778) raised the topic.[6]

The analyses that follow are divided into two parts: those that concern the social capital of individuals and those that examine the social capital of social systems, communities, or organizations. The division is necessary for exposition, but the two are necessarily related. Individuals within social systems having significant social capital tend to have more social capital themselves. Analyses that move from one level to another will be presented in the section on social system social capital. Within each section we will take up problems related to conceptualization and measurement, and the importance, or lack of it, of investment in social capital.

Individual-Level Social Capital

SOCIAL SUPPORT

One important aspect of social capital is social support. As the Beatles song framed it, social support entails "a little help from my friends" (1967). Social support was one of the first practical matters studied by network researchers and others who did not think of themselves as students of social networks. Initially, social support was not called social capital, and those who study social support do not necessarily invoke the concept. More popular than social capital, in 2011 the term "social support" retrieved from the Web of Science over 28,000 citations.

Indicators of social support favored by social network researchers mainly rely on "name generators." A name generator is a question used in a survey that asks respondents to name people they are related to in particular ways, people whom they feel close to, people they can call upon for particular help. Most famously the question, "Who are the people with whom you discussed an important matter with?" has been used in the General Social Survey (Bailey and Marsden 1999; Burt 1984). With the names in hand—usually just initials or a first name—the survey asks about the characteristics of those named, such as gender, age, education, how the respondent came to know them, and which of those named know one another. The last question can be used to construct a network of those persons who surround the respondent, technically called the ego network.

Social support is as fuzzy a concept as its relative, social capital. Support can include the perception that one's friends, relatives, partners, or community feel positive toward one or, using a name generator, can include a count of the number of individuals a person believes could or would provide support for general or specific matters (lend you a cup of sugar, help with computers). Finally, social support includes the structure of the network within which the person ("ego") is embedded.

Much of the research literature on support concerns illness and other stressors affecting a person who might need help. Studies of stress raise the issue of whether a person has a support network in place before confronting a stressful situation. A support network might be something like an inoculation, making stress less likely to occur among those who are socially supported. This is known as the "buffer" hypothesis. Alternately, support might follow the experience of stress, thus helping a person to cope with it. Both kinds of support can occur. The literature on social support is so extensive reviews of the reviews have been published.

Most of the recent work on social support tends to be in the health and mental health fields, although there are reviews about workplace issues such as adjustment on the job and financial help. A recent review in the health field (Smith and Christakis 2008) draws a distinction between social network studies, which tend to be structural and extend beyond a person's direct contacts, and studies of direct social support. As the review reports, "[s]ocial support studies assess the quality or quantity of a person's social ties, social network studies treat the ties themselves as objects of study potentially relevant to outcomes of interest, and thus draw them explicitly" (ibid., 407). The authors favor a two-level analysis in which the structure of social relations has outcomes for individuals. The authors note that recent work shows that individual level social support, as traditionally defined, not only has a "feel good" aspect, but even affects basic biological mechanisms related to morbidity and mortality: "For example, higher levels of social support improve global immune functioning, as evinced by a fourfold relative risk reduction in susceptibility to experimental rhinovirus inoculation" (ibid., 406). They report that "in the case of spouses, there is compelling evidence that the health of one member of a dyad can affect the health of the other" (ibid., 409). Recent reviews of reviews conclude that the evidence on the effects of individual-level social support and networks (now read social support as social capital) is more robust than other individual psychosocial factors. The reviews decry the often fuzzy definitions of the independent and the dependent variables as well as the quality of some of the research. The more robust reviews point to strong evidence that both the quality of social support as well as the size of the networks of support may be associated with lower risk of coronary heart disease (see below) and cancer. For elderly populations, support from a spouse and wider community social networks may be associated with better health (Egan et al. 2008).

Does social support reduce the likelihood of "catching" a disorder, as in the case of global immune function, ameliorate the effects of a disorder once it is experienced, or both? In most studies, the timing and relationship of support to stress and illness is difficult to determine. It is easier in studies of Post Traumatic Stress Disorder (PTSD), especially combat-related PTSD where the timing of the stressor is relatively easy to determine. Social network factors prior to combat, including the much cited but erroneous "finding" that group cohesion in combat reduces the probability of combat-related PTSD, have little effect on the incidence of PTSD on combat veterans (Lerer and Kadushin 1986), but many studies show that social support, variously measured, ameliorates the longer-term effects of post-combat PTSD (Charuvastra and Cloitre 2008). This meta-review also reports that social support was one of the stronger correlates of PTSD, with more social support correlated with fewer effects of PTSD, though the precise timing of support was apparently not studied (ibid.). The review data also suggested that subjective accounts of being supported are more likely to have positive effects than structural network measures. The authors suggest that a sense of social bonding and safety following the trauma may account for the observed effects.

The technique of name generators has a number of drawbacks. First, there is a limit to the number of names one can ask for—often no more than five, especially if some additional data on the reported supporters are solicited. Further, since support can entail personal costs to the supporters, the names elicited tend to be close ties rather than weak ties. As noted earlier, one of the major impetuses for research on social capital derived from the finding that white-collar jobs were more often found through weak ties rather than strong ties (Granovetter 1973). Weak ties may therefore be important in social support. Finally, in terms of concept-indicator theory (Klausner 1964), social support is just one example of social capital. There are of course many others.

INDIVIDUAL NETWORKED RESOURCES: POSITION AND RESOURCES GENERATORS

Another way of measuring aspects of social capital is to utilize a rule or theoretically derived indicator and combine it with inductive empirical testing. A classic example from physics is the measurement of temperature. The theory, developed over two hundred years with many observations by many different scientists, is that matter, if not confined, expands as the temperature rises because of the increased molecular activity that accompanies a rise in temperature or energy. Alternately, if a gas is confined so that expansion is not possible, the pressure rises as the temperature rises. But how empirically should we observe the expansion? We are familiar with the column of mercury confined in a glass tube, though many other materials that expand have been proposed. Scientists sought to find the constants in the equation, and decided to set measurement points, such as the freezing point, which is zero degrees, and the boiling point of water, which is 100 degrees (Gillies 2008).

The "position generator" is both a theoretically and empirically derived indicator of access to networked resources. As developed by Lin and Dumin (1986), the theory begins with the proposition that given the nature of social stratification, valued resources are more likely to be found in the higher reaches of the occupational structure. Second, the success of an instrumental action is more likely if higher valued resources can be accessed by an actor. Therefore, third, the higher the position one is able to reach, the greater the likelihood of accessing valuable resources, such as recommendations for a job. Hence, those who can access higher positions either through inheritance or achievement should be able to secure better jobs. (The classic: "It isn't what you know it's whom you know.") Further, the strength of weak ties proposition suggests that those whose relatives or close ties do not have high status can nonetheless achieve higher status through mere casual acquaintanceship with high status individuals. A corollary to the theory developed later was that a wide range of positions could also lead to positive instrumental gains because lower statuses might have access to skills and knowledge that higher statuses might not possess (such as repairing lawn mowers in the story with which we began), and thus an acquaintanceship with a wide range of statuses may result in cultural cosmopolitanism which could prove valuable in some higher status occupations (Erickson 1996). It was further hypothesized that even potential access could result in valuable instrumental consequences. It was not necessary to demonstrate that these resources were actually used. In the original 1986 formulation, access to valued networked resources was not called "social capital." Only later was it reconceptualized as social capital.

This theory rests on the foundation of the functional theory of stratification (Davis and Moore 1945). Higher status persons have more resources because "the collectivity, or the community, promotes its self-interest by conferring relatively higher statuses on individual actors who possess more valued resources" (Lin 2001, 31). Hence if an actor knows high status persons, the actor can utilize the more valuable resources of those individuals. While the functional theory of stratification has been widely criticized (Hauhart 2003), the utility of its application to the position generator rests first on measurement issues and then on its predictive value. We will now address these issues.

The same kinds of calibration challenges faced by efforts to measure temperature are also characteristic of the "position generator." The challenge is to find a wide range of occupations (but not so many as to tire out respondents—20 turns out to be the efficient number) about which to inquire and which are immediately recognizable by respondents in various societies. The formulation of the question depends on the goals of the study. For example, the question, "Among your relatives, friends, or acquaintances are there any in the following kinds of work?" elicits a wide range of ties from weak to close. Whereas the request, "Please think of people you know by name and by sight well enough to talk to" concentrates on strong ties (Lin and Erickson 2008b, 10). In addition to the position generator, a "resource generator" has been developed (in a Dutch version) that asks, "Do you know anyone who... Is handy repairing household equipment... Can work with personal computers... Who can babysit for your children" and 30 other items (van der Gaag, Snijders, and Flap 2008). In this study, respondents are asked about relatives, friends, or acquaintances. In addition, a number of scales were developed in this study that used a standard position generator. For the position generator, the maximum prestige, the range in prestige, the number of positions accessed, the gender mix of an occupation, and the total accessed prestige were developed. In most populations, all these were highly correlated. Several reliable scales were derived from resource generator items such as a personal support or a personal skills scale. The authors conclude that "whether there is any effect of the presence of social networks on an outcome of interest can be answered with any instrument" (ibid., 44), but that for specific inquiries into potential accessed resources, different scales might be useful. The position generator is more effective for instrumental effects (e.g., getting a job), but less so for expressive actions (e.g., understanding other people's values).

Lin and Erickson (2008b) further point out that position and resource generators can (and should be) adapted to different social contexts. The same occupations in different societies have different meanings. Some important occupations such as "lama" in Mongolia, mine manager in coastal British Columbia, or Communist party official in China do not exist in other societies or are not prestigious. Gender stratification, however, exists in all known societies, and each prestige level may have different valences by gender. Access to these resources will therefore differ by gender. In multicultural settings, knowing people in occupations both in one's own and other ethnic groups may be important.

CORRELATES OF INDIVIDUAL SOCIAL CAPITAL

Social capital, defined as access to networked resources, has many observable correlates. Getting a good job, the original hypothesized outcome of the position generator set of indices, has been widely confirmed as a correlate of network diversity and/or the prestige of the positions an individual can access (with appropriate controls for an individual's prior social prestige). The way this works may differ by society. Strong ties, for example, are more useful in China than the weak ties found by Granovetter in the United States. In the Netherlands, "The better a person's access to occupations rich in economic capital, the higher the economic capital (but not cultural capital) of the person's occupation" (Lin and Erickson 2008b, 6). More diverse networks lead to a wider range of interests and information, which is in turn related to political activities, as well as different opinions. Diverse networks are associated with membership in voluntary organizations, though the direction of causality is not clear.

A persistent finding in social network research is often ignored in the excitement about the utility of social networks and "networking." Social networks are exclusionary and unfair. Since people tend to associate with others like themselves (the homophily principle; see chapter 2), the networks that they form tend to be with people who have the same characteristics. If people have lower prestige, socio-economic status, or are the target of discrimination, then their networks will tend to be composed of people with lower prestige, socio-economic status, and who are otherwise disadvantaged. It stands to reason, then, that the networked resources available to the disadvantaged in any society will be less potent than the networked resources that can be accessed by the advantaged. This can be put in a positive way that lends further credence to the utility of the concept of social capital: "We find that, even after controlling for demographic characteristics, including supervision, occupational class, and income, access to social capital still significantly contributes to current status. 'Who you know' adds to status attainment over and above one's prior status" (Cross and Lin 2008, 377). But it is also true that who you know is constrained by disadvantage. The same authors found in their U.S. data that racial/ethnic homophily led to a deficit in social capital among the disadvantaged that limited their opportunities and chances for upward mobility and integration into the wider U.S. society. The same considerations should hold for women. They are historically disadvantaged and, based mainly on strong tie evidence, have less social capital (Marsden 1987; Marsden and Hurlburt 1988). They are also, like racial/ethnic minorities, disadvantaged in the kinds of networks they can form in the workplace (Ibarra, Kilduff, and Wenpin 2005). Yet, in a careful analysis of their own data and a review of other North American position-generated social capital data, Cross and Lin (2008, 378–379), do not find substantial evidence that men and women have unequal access to social capital. Perhaps, as they suggest, activation rather than mere potential is the issue, since resource generators measure only potential but not actual access. They also note that at present there are few studies that follow the full access to resource mobilization as a factor in status attainment.

OTHER INDICATORS OF NETWORKED RESOURCES

Position and resource generators attempt to ascertain the extent and range of networked resources available to individuals. The idea can be extended and varied by using other indicators of networked resources. Here is an example to suggest the kinds of extensions to the basic idea of networked resources that can be developed. The 2000 Social Capital Benchmark Survey (http://www.cfsv.org/communitysurvey/index.html) analyzed by Son and Lin (2008) included 11 items that asked, "Thinking now about everyone that you would count as a PERSONAL FRIEND, not just your closest friend—do you have a personal friend who ... Owns their own business?; Is a manual worker?; Has a different religion than you?; Is a community leader?"; and similar targets covering a wide range of social statuses. Son and Lin suggested that "[a]lthough the items are apparently not systematic indices of individual social capital, they capture a variety of characteristics in friendship ties (i.e., bridging and bonding aspects of social capital), including some occupations, economic status, and race of a respondent's friends. In other words, the items represent both diversity and richness of embedded resources residing in the friendship networks in terms of socioeconomic status." Since the research went beyond close friends, some weak ties were included. Summing the 11 items gives a measure of individual diverse access to social resources.

Another kind of networked resources is an individual's connection with voluntary organizations. Earlier, we noted that diverse networks are related to membership in voluntary organizations. The number of voluntary organizations to which a person belongs may therefore indicate the extensiveness of resources available to them. Further, the larger the number of types of organizations to which a person belongs (for example religious, political, sports, etc.), the greater the indication of network diversity. Similarly, the demographic, gender, and ethnic character of the organization can be another indicator of diversity. Organizations also access different degrees of resources. Factor analysis suggested these several indexes can be combined into a single one indicating the total networked resources that an individual can access through membership in a voluntary organization.

Diversity of organizations, and the number of organizations to which an individual belonged, predicted the individual's involvement in expressive civic affairs (such as preserving values or standard of living). Diversity, but not the number of organizations, was a predictor of individual involvement in instrumental activities (gaining specific advantages). In general, indicators of individual social capital other than organizational memberships were a consistent predictor of instrumental civic activity.

Indicators of access to resources tested the theory that information provided by former migrants to prospective migrants decreased the latter's costs of moving (Garip 2008). Looking at both the village and household level and using longitudinal surveys, focus groups, and field work observation, Garip examined the distribution of the occupations and destinations of those who migrated from rural villages to urban settings in Thailand. As with the more quantitative studies of the utility of networked resources, she found that the patterns of migration depend on a variety of factors. As she wrote, "The diversity of resources by occupation increases the likelihood of migration, while diversity by destination inhibits it. Resources from weakly tied sources, such as village members, have a higher effect on migration than resources from strongly tied sources in the household."

The Son and Lin and the Garip examples show how the general concept of networked resources can be applied to investigations of the consequences of these resources to gaining valued outcomes. Standardized instruments are useful, but so are applications that use the idea in novel ways to develop new indicators built on the standard instruments.

There are a variety of other studies that found networked resources work in different ways depending on the context. Some examples are:

- Teams working in exploratory product development completed their projects more quickly if they had a social network structure composed of many non-redundant external ties; teams exploiting existing knowledge took longer to complete with this same type of network structure mainly because external ties not needed for the task had nonetheless to be maintained (Hansen, Podolny, and Pfeffer 2001).
- In investment clubs, the number of instrumental ties that members had with one another prior to joining the club were positively and directly related to a club's financial performance (with appropriate controls). Exactly why is not clear: in these clubs task orientation was improved, organizational heterogeneity was increased as might be expected, and this led to a greater task orientation. However, heterogeneity was negatively related to performance (Harrington 2001). This is a cross-level analysis in which the social capital of the individuals increases the group-level social capital.
- In the emerging software industry in Israel, both network centrality and geographic propinquity were related to engaging in similar strategies (Gabbay, Talmud, and Raz 2001).
- In a large health organization in Finland, employees with sparse networks (structural holes) were more likely to name a person who could solve a problem for them who was not directly connected to them. Employees thus acquired some

instrumental benefits from sparse networks, but work units benefited from internally cohesive networks by having greater trust. Indirect networks attenuated the flow of information critical in triage decisions. Neither maximally sparse nor maximally dense social networks lead to optimal outcomes. Developing an optimal level of cohesion appears to be complicated (Johanson 2001).

• And from (Lin, Cook, and Burt 2001, 228): "Forms of social capital that are valuable in one environment may be useless or even harmful in another." Individuals with more education generally have access to more resources. But this relationship does not hold in all situations. For example, in a hurricane, the less educated relied more on kin and received more informal support (Hurlbert, Beggs, and Haines 2001).

Social Capital as an Attribute of Social Systems

Social capital has also been viewed as an attribute of social systems themselves. The network structure of the social system may endow the system with important benefits, though it may also have negative consequences. This "focuses on social capital at the group level, with discussions ... on (1) how certain groups develop and more or less maintain social capital as a collective asset, and (2) how such a collective asset enhances group members' life chances" (Lin 2001, 22).

At the group level, there are propositions about how one aspect of social capital enhances other assets of the group. In other words, social capital can create more social capital. Group-level social capital is an idea specified in various ways by such great theorists as Tönnies, Marx, Weber, Durkheim, Pareto, Simmel, Kroeber, Parsons, Lévi-Strauss, and Merton. It should be obvious that a very wide range of concepts and theoretical orientations and propositions as well as empirical findings are involved. The broad sweep of connotations and denotations of social capital as an attribute of social systems has led to a vast range of propositions as well as to problems in measurement. Here we will review some of the major contributions to the theory.

THEORISTS OF SOCIAL SYSTEM SOCIAL CAPITAL

Pierre Bourdieu was the first social scientist who presented definitions of social capital that were structural. He interpreted them as networked resources both for collectives and individuals. As he stated, social capital is "the aggregate of the actual or potential resources which are linked to possession of a durable network of more or less institutionalized relationships of mutual acquaintance or recognition" (Bourdieu 1985, 248).[7] Bourdieu further explained that social capital is "made up of social obligations ('connections') which are convertible in certain conditions to economic capital and may be institutionalized in the form of a title of nobility" (ibid., 243). In a seminar discussion of the concept of capital (including economic and cultural or informational capital), he added to his earlier definition that social capital resources might accrue to either groups or individuals (Bourdieu and Wacquant 1992, 119).

James Coleman offered this functional definition: "Social capital is defined by its function. It is not a single entity, but a variety of different entities having two characteristics in common: They all consist of some aspect of social structure, and they facilitate certain actions of the individuals who are within the structure" (Coleman 1990, 302). In Coleman's view, social structure consists of relationships. Social structure becomes social capital when it is appropriated to further an actor's goals. Sandfleur and Laumann (1998) identify three kinds of benefits in Coleman's social capital theory: information; influence and control; and social solidarity. Though analytically distinct, they can operate together.

Group-level social capital provides individuals with information that is timely and trustworthy. Coleman offered examples of trust generated by closed network systems. In New York's Diamond District, cheating would be immediately visible because of the tight networks of the Hassidic Jews who dominate 47th Street. This environment allows handshake deals over gems worth thousands of dollars. Surveillance by friends and neighbors over children in tight-knit neighborhoods allows children to play safely even when their parents are not available. The ethnic enclave gives immigrants social capital advantages in helping one another and offers employment. The enclave also has negative consequences: outsiders are barred, there are serious consequences for individual freedoms, and there is a tendency to try to keep individuals from joining the mainstream or be "too white" (Portes and Sensenbrenner 1993; Waldinger 1996). Tight networks can also lead to a loss of privacy. Another odd disadvantage, at least to the public, is that tight-knit neighborhoods can protect criminal elements from outside prosecution in a "negotiated co-existence" (Browning 2009).

We saw in chapter 7, "Organizations and Networks," how a system that has structural holes allows key players to make rapid use of information from diverse sources. Because social networks are exclusive and "unfair," systems with many structural holes give advantages to those who can manipulate access to information.

Influence and control, in Sandfleur and Laumann's view, can be regarded as legitimate (see chapter 7) when people accept directives because the authors of the directives are worthy of being obeyed. Trust is a foundation of such authority and is an attribute of social capital that allows for various social actions to take place—some desirable but others not so desirable. Thus the influence and control aspect of social capital promotes decision-making and action.

Social solidarity is the most general aspect of social capital at the group level. The theory is that mutual trust and commitment arise from group norms, from repeated interaction, or both. Since the development of trust and values is a process that takes place over time and feeds back into the development of social networks, it is a process that generally cannot be directly observed. Simulation, however, can offer clues as to how this takes place (Glanville and Bienenstock 2009). In Glanville and Bienenstock's simulation, indirect or generalized reciprocity tends to increase over time. Generalized reciprocity means that helpful acts to others are performed as a collective obligation, not in the expectation of an immediate reward (see chapter 5). Generalized reciprocity is an important consequence of social solidarity and the development of trust. Frontier society barn raising is a typical example. Social capital is therefore seen as the basic glue of society and community.

BOWLING ALONE

Social capital as a social system attribute is an idea popularly associated with Robert Putnam's *Bowling Alone*. Putnam, who builds on Coleman, begins by saying,

> [T]he core idea of social capital theory is that social networks have value... social contacts affect the productivity of individuals and groups. [Further,] social capital refers to connections among individuals—social networks and the norms of reciprocity and trustworthiness that arise from them. In that sense social capital is closely related to what some have called "civic virtue." The difference is that "social capital" calls attention to the fact that civic virtue is most powerful when embedded in a dense network of reciprocal social relations. (Putnam 2000, 19)

Putnam's accessible prose is responsible in part for the widespread impact of his book. At the same time, his style makes the formal relations between his concepts and indicators difficult to trace. Here is an effort to unpack some of the ideas.

His basic argument is that participation in political, civic, religious, workplace activities, volunteering and informal networks leads to a culture of social trust and to networks with generalized reciprocity that bridge different groups. This is social capital. The outcomes of social capital are democracy, tolerance, and civic community participation. Social capital also results in low crime, safer neighborhoods, less tax evasion, better schools, and economic growth. But communal participation in the United States has been declining (hence the metaphor—people do not bowl in teams and leagues, they bowl alone) and so the amount of social capital is on the decline, and this leads to less positive outcomes.

Social capital and social networks in this argument are latent concepts, that is, they are not directly observable. Networks are both indicators of social capital and also are a process that leads to social capital. Networks in the sense used by Putnam are a latent variable, because as was noted earlier, while in principle one might draw all of the social networks in a community, in practice this is impossible; no one could make sense of the result even if one were able to do it. As in Coleman's theory, what concerns us not just any network but those characterized by reciprocity and trust. Reciprocity is best when it is generalized as in net generalized exchange (see chapter 5). One does something for another person but does not expect something directly in return. Rather, one trusts that the social system or the group will eventually reciprocate. Since these kinds of networks are almost impossible to measure in a large social system, there are a series of indicators for them, most of them referring to some kind of social participation. As noted, in Putnam's theory, social participation produces social networks. Participation also leads to trust and to a general culture of trust which in turn promotes participation in a virtuous circle. Trust is thus an attribute of social capital. Participation and a culture of trust are indicated by such actions as working for a political party, entertaining at home, or the attitude—believing that most people can be trusted. The consequences of a high level of community social capital lead to various positive outcomes, such as lower community crime rates. That is, if *individual* people in a community are, in the aggregate, politically active, entertain at home, and think most people can be trusted, community crime levels tend to be lower. In statistical terms, this is a two-level model: *individuals* who do various things or believe in them, and, at second level, *community* crime. In *Bowling Alone*, all the outcome variables are community variables, but most of the predictors are individual-level variables or aggregated individual-level variables.

Putnam's conceptualization has some problems. Some of the indicators, such as those involved in democracy, are both causes of democracy and also outcomes of the social capital process, which has led to an accusation that the arguments are circular (Portes 1998). But the relationship can also be interpreted as saying social capital can produce more social capital in a virtuous spiral, and the reverse, less social capital can lead to less social capital. This important point is not made sufficiently clear in *Bowling Alone*, though Putnam has said this elsewhere (Putnam, Leonardi, and Nanetti 1993). Some of the outcomes of social capital, such as greater health, are not tautological, however. Health per se is not an indicator of social capital. Thus some of the concepts and indicators are circular while others can be empirically tested. Putnam cannot be both tautological as has been claimed and also empirically wrong. In *Bowling Alone*, the extensive tests of the outcomes of social capital are suggestive. Since they are at the aggregate state level but also imply individual attributes and outcomes, they suffer, however, from an "ecological fallacy." An ecological fallacy attributes correlations among attributes of individuals to the correlations between those attributes at the aggregate level. For example, individuals who live in states with more social capital (as indexed by Putman) are supposed be happier. The implication is that individuals with more *individual* social capital are also happier. This may or may not be true. Statisticians have long held this kind of correlation to be a fallacy (Robinson 1950). There is a cure for this problem: multi-level analysis that Putnam has employed in later work, but which is not evident in *Bowling Alone*.

RECENT FINDINGS ON SOCIAL SYSTEM SOCIAL CAPITAL AND ITS CONSEQUENCES

Research since the influential *Bowling Alone* has tried to unpack the community-level social capital syndrome with varying degrees of success. The Social Capital Community Benchmark Survey, used by Son and Lin, is a useful example because it includes a number of separate individual- and aggregate-level indicators that are subjected to various types of scale analyses with the selection of key independent and dependent variables. But as they and others have pointed out, conclusions about aggregate community-level consequences of social capital, based on the consequences of various indicators of social capital for individuals, requires complex multilevel analyses such as HLM (Raudenbush and Bryk 2002). Such analyses simultaneously examine both aggregate and individual data—something *Bowling Alone* and most of the studies based on it did not do.

Some research has built directly on James Coleman's ideas. One of Coleman's hypotheses about social capital was that "closure" among parents and children promoted the well-being of the children (Coleman 1990, 590–600). Using indicators similar to those of Coleman in data from the Mother-Child Data of the National Longitudinal Survey of Youth (NLSY79), Dufur, Parcel, and McKune (2008) examined the effect of family social capital investment in their children as compared with the effect of school social capital on the behavioral problems of first- through eighth-grade children. Family investment in social capital included how many of their children's friends they knew by name, how often they knew who their children were with when they were not at home, child church attendance, and parental usual hours of work per week. The principal of each school judged additional measures such as the extent to which the child's parents were involved in advising the school, participated in program design, engaged in policy decisions, and volunteered in after-school programs. Note that these are different kinds of indicators than networked individual resources. Rather, they are indirect indicators of investment in two kinds of aggregate social capital with a return to individuals. With these measurements indicating the two latent variables—family social capital and school social capital, and with appropriate controls—family social capital was negatively related to behavioral problems, but school social capital was not. The study findings seem to back Coleman's original claim about the importance of family social capital, though other studies favor school social capital over family social capital. The issue is not yet resolved.

"Generalized trust" is often measured with the survey question, "Generally speaking, would you say that most people can be trusted or that you can't be too careful in life?" (General Social Survey since 1972) or similar variations dating back to 1950.[8] Trusting people appears to be an ambiguous item since, to paraphrase Abraham Lincoln, "You can trust all of the people some of the time, some of the people all of the time but you cannot trust all of the people all of time." It appears that the generalized trust question, with Lincoln's reservations, is not as unreliable and invalid a survey instrument as it might appear to be. It is fairly reliable on the aggregate country level. The validity of the measure as a correlate of civic virtue as hypothesized by Putnam is another matter: "Most empirical studies have not been kind to the civic society [voluntary organization activity either as cause or consequence] explanation of generalized trust" (Nannestad 2008).

Part of the problem with trust is that it is taken as synonymous with access to resources. But some environments are rich in resources and others are not; some are high in reciprocity and trust while others are not. Glanville and Bienenstock (2009) show that both dimensions can vary and suggest some outcomes of these situations, as illustrated in table 10.1, based on their figure 10.1 (ibid., 1518).

TABLE 10.1

Typology of Reciprocity and Trust

	Reciprocity/Trust	
	Low	**High**
High Resources	High transaction costs	Efficient Markets, Social Support
Low Resources	Job information but poor jobs	Revolving credit, Social Support

Reprinted from Glanville, Jennifer L., and Elisa Jayne Bienenstock. 2009. A typology for understanding the connections among different forms of social capital. Copyright © 2009 SAGE Publications. Reprinted by permission of SAGE Publications.

If the social system is characterized by low levels of trust but high resources, there will be much trade and many transactions but high transaction costs, meaning there are plenty of goods but both buyer and seller must be wary. If both reciprocity/trust are low and there are also few resources, then whatever jobs are passed on (in Granovetter's weak tie situation) are likely to be not very good jobs. Social support accompanies high levels of trust but is of little help in an environment with low resources. Markets are useful and efficient when trust is high and there are lots of resources (Coleman's example of the Diamond District). But when resources are low and trust is high, poor people's revolving credit associations are common.

The World Bank has been much taken with the idea of building aggregate social capital (Feldman and Assaf 1999). For example, there are social funds: "multi-sectoral programs that provide financing (usually grants) for small-scale public investments targeted at meeting the needs of the poor and vulnerable communities, and contributing to social capital and development at the local level." However, recent work suggests that social funds, rather than building new social capital, utilize existing social capital and build on existing relationships rather than creating new ones (Vajja and White 2008). On the other hand, a randomized intervention in rural South African villages found "higher levels of structural and cognitive social capital in the intervention group than the comparison group, although confidence intervals were wide" (Pronyk et al. 2008). The jury is out.

There have been a large number of studies in the past few years that attempt to connect community-level social capital to individual health. The findings are mixed. "The association between community social capital and health differs . . . [by] health outcome, study population and location. This underlines the need to take such diversity into account when aiming to conceptualize the relation between community social capital and health" (van Hooijdonk et al. 2008). Part of the variance in findings is caused by different definitions and measures of community social capital, measures of individual-level health and the absence of true multi-level modeling.

The following recent study of the relationship between heart attacks and membership in voluntary organizations is an exemplar of "how to do it." The study illustrates the improbable, far-fetched "magic" of network theory: how the number of people employed in voluntary organizations affects the probability of heart attacks. The empirical question is the association between community-level social capital and the recurrence of coronary heart disease. Community-level social capital is distinguished from individual-level social capital, which is conceptualized as individual-level access to resources embedded in his/her own social networks. The authors (Scheffler et al. 2008) note that individual-level social capital overlaps with the idea of social support, as we discussed earlier. The model hypothesizes that community-level social support (1) increases the level of available information on treatment and preventive measures; (2) lowers the effort required to organize politically and therefore to bring more health facilities into the community; and (3) makes social support more accessible. These three outcomes of community-level social capital, which is not directly measured but implied, in turn lead to better health (see figure 10.2).

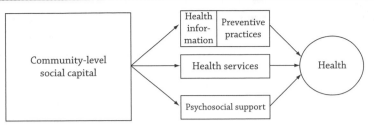

FIGURE 10.2 Pathways between social capital and health

Reprinted from *Social Science & Medicine* 66 (7):1604, figure 1. Scheffler, Richard M., Timothy T. Brown, Leonard Syme, Ichiro Kawachi, Irina Tolstykh, and Carlos Iribarren. Community-level social capital and recurrence of acute coronary syndrome. Copyright © 2008, with permission from Elsevier.

One aspect of community social capital in Putnam's theory is the vibrancy of voluntary organizations. Rather than aggregate individual-level voluntary organization participation, the study by Scheffler and colleagues uses the Petris Social Capital Index (PSCI). It is derived from the Census County Business Patterns (CBC) report on the number of persons employed in voluntary agencies. The voluntary organizations selected for the index are those listed in the index of Putnam's Social Capital Community Benchmark Survey. The index computes the number of persons employed in these organizations per county population (Brown et al. 2006). This is therefore a theoretically derived indicator that points to, but does not directly measure, community networked resources. It is clearly on a different level from individual measurement. The individual-level dependent variable is derived from Kaiser Permanente records, as reported by medical personnel, and none is based on individual self-reports.[9] A number of individual attributes were controlled as well as other medical conditions. Census block-level attributes such as income, income disparity, and racial concentration were also examined. Thus, three-level statistical analyses were employed. The essential point of this complex study is that community-level social capital is associated with a 9% reduction in the relative risk of acute coronary syndrome recurring. There is an interaction effect because this holds true only for individuals living in areas with less than median household income, even after controlling for a number of key factors in coronary risk (Scheffler et al. 2008, 1611). The authors point out that although the association is not large, it nonetheless has potentially important public health implications, since acute coronary syndrome is the leading cause of mortality in the United States, affecting almost 14 million people. The fact that the effect occurs mainly in low-income areas is an important part of the debate in the United States about health care.

Where We Are Now

Social capital is a diffuse concept. At the heart of the idea is the hypothesis that "social networks have value." Unlike financial capital, the analogue, in which money is the value that one invests in order to have more money, social networks do not have a universal coin. They have many forms and the values they produce are extremely varied. The two underlying assumptions of the theory of social capital—(1) that actors actively invest in their social networks in anticipation of future advantage; and (2) that social networks contain resources that actors can draw upon for their own benefit—are rarely directly tested. Rather, it is hypothesized that those actors whose networks, whether achieved or ascribed, have greater value, as a result, enjoy greater valued outcomes than actors whose networks are of lesser value. *Potential* access to resources is the key. Very rarely is there an account of the investment process itself or the actual activation of the needed resources. The story with which we began this chapter remains just a story. Nonetheless, the claim that social networks have utility is obviously very attractive and has garnered much attention, research, and support. There is substantial evidence that, when adequately defined, some network structures and attributes can dependably be associated with some valued outcomes.

As usual, the devil is in the details. There are two levels of networks: community or group and individual. The latter is easier to handle so we began with it. The most successful and widely tested specifications of social capital are those of Nan Lin and his colleagues who found that people who have a large number and/or a wide range of friends in different occupations, or who have friends in high-ranked occupations, have improved occupational outcomes. The implication, not directly tested, is that they are able to draw on the resources provided by their network of friends to gain better occupations. Given that the intervening mechanism—actually accessing these networked resources—is not typically measured, these are impressive findings. There is also some cross-level analysis, suggesting that individuals whose communities are richer in occupational resources tend to have better occupational outcomes. The studies of migration and immigrant enclaves show the two faces of tight social networks as a resource. In some cases, the individual or community network helps migrants find jobs in a new country or region. Once an immigrant community becomes established, members typically find jobs through their close tied ethnic networks. On the other hand, the ethnic network's very focus on the ethnic community can limit connections to the outside world. The same double-edged sword occurs in organizational networks in which a tight network gives access to internal resources but also limits access to wider spread resources.

In the health field, social capital may be conceptualized as social support given or potentially made available by one's social network. There is such a large literature on social support, much of it predating the widespread use of the concept of social capital, that we have had to resort to meta-analyses of reviews to keep track of the findings. The reviews point to problems in the conceptualization of individual support networks—just what kinds of networks offer the best support. There are also varied health-related dependent variables. They can range from self-definition of being in good health or relatively free of worries to very particular physician-specified diagnoses. There is also the issue of timing: does social support prevent a disorder or alleviate it? On the whole, the findings show positive outcomes for social support, however defined. Problems in conceptualization and measurement of the independent and dependent variables, support and health, seem not to deter researchers and scientific journals. Articles showing the utility of social support in different circumstances and under varying conditions continue to be regularly published.

Community-level social capital research has been dominated by Putnam's *Bowling Alone*. His contention is that communities in the United States have increasingly experienced a reduction in social capital as indicated by decreased voluntary organization activity, political participation, trust in others, and other indicators of civic virtue and that this trend has had many unfortunate social consequences. While some observers claim circularity of argument, the analogue to financial capital in Putnam's argument may be apt: the rich get richer and the poor get poorer. Social capital can create more social capital, or the reverse, declining social capital leads to even less social capital. Despite what many feel is Putnam's inadequate formal conceptualization and measurement of community social capital, the concept has attracted much attention. The attractiveness of the basic idea has led to some new interesting multi-level research. For example, communities with greater diversity tend to be those in which there is less interpersonal and inter-ethnic trust. Counties with less social capital have a greater number of recurring coronary heart attacks in low-income neighborhoods.

There is one glaring lack in social capital network research. Community-level social capital has been much bemoaned as increasingly suffering from a deficit, though if true, it is not clear what to do about it. More directly staring us in the face is the unequal distribution of individual social capital, whether by race, ethnicity, gender, or income. The touted use of social networking sites and the internet as sources of social capital has generated a "digital divide" that has merely increased the advantages of those who have versus those who have not. Social capital inequality has serious consequences, which remain largely unexplored. Perhaps social capital research could use some of the Marxist zeal that has characterized some of the research in social stratification.

As noted in the introduction to this chapter, social capital has much in common with the concept of anomie developed long before the concept of social network was invented. Without the concept of anomie, one would not even think of relating the percentages of Protestants or being not married to higher levels of suicide as did Durkheim (1951 [1897]). (Whether the association has proven correct in the long run is another matter). Controversial and difficult to pin down, anomie nonetheless generated a great deal of theory and research. Social capital seems to be doing the same thing. There is more work to do. Recent specifications of the concept are promising in that they point to further ways of unpacking the concept and examining the relationships between the various indicators of social capital.

To begin with, while almost all network analyses could have a social capital interpretation, not all social capital propositions necessarily involve networks either explicitly or implicitly: "Only 4.5% of abstracts for articles [reviewed in their study] on social networks mention social capital, and just about 2% of those on social capital explicitly mention social networks" (Moody and Paxton 2009, 1491). There are cultural and psychological aspects of social capital as well as network aspects. Baker and Faulkner (2009) propose the concept "double embeddedness" to express the idea that economic, political, and social actions in communities, organizations, and markets are simultaneously embedded in social structural networks and culture. They argue that sometimes culture and social structure feed back upon one another, but sometimes they operate at cross purposes. There is much further to explore in pinning down this double em- beddedness. The macro-micro aspects of social networks and social capital deserve much more analysis. Glanville and Bienenstock call attention to the fact that, for ex- ample, macro dense social networks lead to norm enforcement while micro dense net- works are associated with individual social support. It is all well and good to talk about neighborhood social capital in general, but a careful survey of Chicago neighborhoods suggested that the concept had at least four dimensions, themselves composed of a number of specific survey items (Sampson and Graif 2009). Mere contact with others is not an exact enough indicator of general social capital because it depends upon whom the contact is with, because contact not only indicates social solidarity but social influence as well (Cote and Erickson 2009). The effect of network structures on social capital needs further investigation. For example, many of the advantages of social capital occur when resources flow between subgroups and accrue to the larger social system (Frank 2009). While this may appear to be a familiar epidemiological contagion mechanism, Frank suggests that the flow can occur as a result of a "quasi- tie" which results from cognitive or psychological identification with the larger system rather than a direct network phenomenon.

The upside to the diffuseness of the concept of social capital is therefore its very richness. This richness, however, means that much further conceptual exploration and empirical research are required further to develop and ground the implications of social capital. There is much to which we can look forward

11 Ethical Dilemmas of Social Network Research

Networks as a Research Paradigm

As readers of this book have learned, network analysis is neither a study of individuals nor a study of groups, organizations, and institutions. It is both. The embeddedness of individuals within larger contexts creates special challenges for research ethics with roots in medical studies of individuals. In network studies, research about an individual has implications for all the persons he or she is connected with. Facebook, which uses network principles and algorithms, can lead a person to contact someone designated a "friend" even though that friend has never heard of the initiator and the friend does not want to share information. Recently, Iranian immigration-control officials checked Facebook for the name of a traveler entering Iran, and recorded the names of all of her friends who were in Iran (Morozov 2009). Network information can expose individuals who did not answer a network questionnaire in a survey and also has implications for any organizations that person is connected with. Likewise, data on particular organizations has implications for the individuals networked to it.

This chapter discusses the standard guide for research ethics, The Belmont Report (National Commission 1979) which is the basis for the Federal Human Subjects Code (Regulations 2010). Though laudable, as we shall see, the principles of the Belmont Report are difficult to adapt to social network research and for that matter to social science research.

The Belmont Report and the ensuing regulations on the protection of human subjects and the creation of Institutional Review Boards (IRBs) had their origins in abuses of human subjects in biomedical experiments during the Second World War as detailed in the Nuremberg war crimes trials and the ensuing "Nuremberg Code" which, among other matters, insists that medical investigators alone cannot set the rules for the ethical conduct of research, even when guided by beneficence and the Hippocratic ethics. There was also the infamous American Tuskegee Syphilis Study. For over 40 years, the United States Public Health Service observed the development of syphilis in untreated poor African-American men without making available to them, in order to maintain the study's protocols, penicillin (which by 1947 had become the standard and effective treatment for syphilis). The study continued until 1972 and led to deaths and the contraction of the disease by the wives and children of these men. Also controversial was the research of small world theorist and experimenter Stanley Milgram, who in an investigation of obedience to authority, asked volunteers to "shock" apparent subjects (Milgram 1974). Nobody was actually shocked for there were no real subjects, just actors. Milgram showed that a significant number of the actual subjects (the volunteers who supposedly did the shocking), complied with the experimenter's request to apply increasingly painful shocks. The real subjects were debriefed, but the dramatic experiment was considered by many to be unethical. An important study in social conformity was also based on deception. In 1951, Solomon Asch successfully misled the subjects into believing they were judging the length of a line. Confederates of the experimenter gave the wrong answer, and one-third of the actual subjects went along with the wrong answer (Asch 1951). Influential social psychologists of the 1960s and '70s, such as Stanley Schachter and Philip Zimbardo, also engaged in deception of subjects in experiments that, although they would not now be allowed today, produced findings that are still widely cited. The extent to which deception should be allowed in experiments continues to be debated, and the cost-benefit ratio has been invoked as a partial solution. Does the benefit to society outweigh temporary discomfort to subjects? What must a subject be told about the procedures of a study as "informed consent?" A difficult calculus.

The basic principles invoked by the Belmont Report (National Commission 1979) attempt to set this out. They are:

1. Respect for Persons.—Respect for persons incorporates at least two ethical convictions: first, that individuals should be treated as autonomous agents, and second, that persons with diminished autonomy are entitled to protection...
2. Beneficence.—Persons are treated in an ethical manner not only by respecting their decisions and protecting them from harm, but also by making efforts to secure their well-being...Two general rules have been formulated as complementary expressions of beneficent actions in this sense: (1) do not harm and (2) maximize possible benefits and minimize possible harms.
3. Justice.—Who ought to receive the benefits of research and bear its burdens?

Several specific requirements that seem especially relevant to network research follow from these general principles:

1. Informed Consent.—Respect for persons requires that subjects, to the degree that they are capable, be given the opportunity to choose what shall or shall not happen to them. This opportunity is provided when adequate standards for informed consent are satisfied...

2. Assessment of Risks and Benefits...risk/benefit assessments are concerned with the probabilities and magnitudes of possible harm and anticipated benefits...Risks and benefits of research may affect the individual subjects, the families of the individual subjects, and society at large. (ibid.)

These principles have been incorporated into the Federal Human Subjects Code, and specifically into the requirement that Institutional Review Boards be set up so that independent parties can assess investigators' research protocols to ensure that these and other such principles are followed. In practice, Institutional Review Boards (IRBs), which are not national but specific to each research organization or university, often rigidly apply rules designed for biomedical research and experiments that are ill suited for survey and network research. Problems securing IRB approval are frequent complaints on social network listservs. The National Academies' panel on Institutional Review Boards, surveys, and social science research reports found that many of the then-current rules did not translate well into social science research and inhibited and delayed research unnecessarily (Council 2003). Some of their concerns have resulted in the decision that signed written consent can be inappropriate for some kinds of social research, including surveys. By its very nature, survey research poses questions to respondents who are told that they may refuse to answer any specific question—so that consent is in fact required and given not only generally but for every question on a survey, including questions on naming their friends. By and large, network questions on surveys do not seem problematic to respondents.[1] Questions on income generate more "no" answers than questions about networks of friends. The National Academy panel also noted that concerns about privacy need to be reviewed in an age in which so much about individuals is available through the internet.[2] We will have more to say about this new world later. Issues on informed consent and privacy are complex when it comes to network studies. Embeddedness of individuals in organizations is an issue which largely escapes IRBs and which we will address when we discuss research on organizations. Who benefits from the research is naively addressed in the Belmont principles. Finally, some network analysis and research into criminal and terrorist networks intentionally aim to harm individuals. Since ethics are never merely an abstraction, these issues will be illustrated with case examples.

Anonymity, Confidentiality, Privacy, and Consent

In social science research, anonymity and confidentiality are routinely granted to respondents, informants, and subjects in experiments and observations.[3] In large-scale survey research with at least several hundred respondents, these guarantees are easy to keep.[4] The researcher has no interest in the particular names of respondents, except in the case of panel studies when prior respondents need to be contacted again. Identifying the respondent serves no purpose whatsoever.[5] In smaller scale qualitative studies, often organization or small-community studies, the identity of the respondents, despite promises of anonymity, may be obvious to both potential readers and the social scientists. The latter often cannot successfully analyze the data without knowing who the respondents are. Publication usually involves changing the names of respondents as well as information such as age, occupation, and sometimes gender. The concern that these characteristics might reveal the identity of the subjects outweighs the importance of their backgrounds for the narrative. When it comes to the comparative organization or community studies there are further difficulties because it may be impossible or even undesirable for analytic purposes to disguise the names of the organizations or communities. Organization consultants, whether academically based or not, face the additional dilemma that the observations or surveys that they produce may have unanticipated consequences for the individuals surveyed or observed (Borgatti and Molina 2003). Some firms use network data to identify employees who are obstructive as well as those who promote and disseminate good ideas.

Social network data have one troublesome and distinctive attribute: the collection of names of either individuals or social units is not incidental to the research but the very point. Further, the network analyst in collecting information about who relates to whom is not confined to the names of respondents or informants within the study, for they may give the names of others who have no idea that they are being named (Borgatti and Molina 2003). In studies of elites, for example, it is common practice for a connection to be considered as valid between two individuals who are not respondents if they are both named by a respondent within the study (Alba and Kadushin 1976; Alba and Moore 1978; Higley and Moore 1981; Moore 1979; Moore 1961). A relationship or tie between individuals on politics and policy is obviously pertinent to a study of influence on public policy; but more private matters such as who are friends with whom can also be very important to the making of policy (Kadushin 1995). In organization settings, while who one works with might seem a legitimate topic, who one is friends with probably lies outside the purview of an employer (Borgatti and Molina 2003). Recent developments in social networking sites such as Facebook, Myspace, and Twitter, however, suggest that most respondents, especially those under 40, routinely post the names of their friends, making the request for names by researchers a matter of little consequence.

Researchers do not necessarily have to ask respondents for information. There are publically available databases that can be ransacked to produce ties between individuals and groups. Network analysis does its "magic," however, by making visible what was not visible before and reveals connections between individuals and groups who may not have wanted this information to be made public. It is one thing to map the network of electric power grids, yet another to map terrorists, criminals, corporations and their executives (not that they are all on the same moral plain) on the basis of data that were in principle there to be mined. The purpose of any statistical analysis, including network analysis, is to make visible that which is not apparent to the "naked eye."

Ronald Breiger (personal communication) offered the example of a regression analysis of posted faculty salaries that are available for many public universities. If the analysis includes the names of outliers—those whose earnings are two standard deviations below or above the expected values for persons with the same qualifications—has the privacy of those individuals been violated? The data are legally available, and no laws are broken by doing the statistical analysis, but the individuals whose names are used probably do not expect to have their salary status compared in this fashion with their colleagues.

There is an obverse point of view, however, rooted in the history of the social network field. The inventor of sociometry, Jacob Moreno, insisted that sociometric data were not valid unless the subjects knew that their answers would have consequences. That was the principle behind his and Jennings's famous study of the cottage system of delinquent women teenagers. One of the first applications of network analysis was in the early 1930s, when sociometry (Moreno's original name for network analysis) showed how to artificially construct primary groups of adolescent young women incarcerated in separate cottages at the same institution. The aim was to place women who liked one another in the same cottage rather than having cottages populated by warring cliques (Moreno 1953). When grouped in cottages with greater group cohesion, the women were less likely to be cantankerous. Moreno successfully constructed primary groups, or natural cliques, or what were described above as "strong ties" that substituted for the lack of functioning families in this situation. Since Moreno, the general tendency in the network field, however, has been not to reveal individual identities. For example, the famous Bank Wiring Room study omitted details that would have revealed the identity of the subjects (Roethlisberger and Dickson 1939).

Informed consent is more complex in network studies than it might seem. Earlier we observed that Facebook names might be used by government agencies in ways the account holder might not anticipate. According to the *Christian Science Monitor*, only 20% of Facebook members rely on privacy settings to regulate content (Farell 2009). Facebook has been struggling with privacy issues. It is generally true that third parties may get one's name and email address from social networking sites. Such persons may or may not be those with whom one wants to have anything to do. Further, in network studies if enough of the context is known, it has been shown that the identity of the individuals in the study is not very difficult to determine. "Deidentified" phone calling data can be "reidentified" if you have a little information to start with. To include the complexities of network possibilities in a consent statement might be simply confusing; millions of social network site users ignore such possibilities. I am unaware of any research protocol that explains these issues to respondents.

Who Benefits

From an ethical point of view, a fundamental issue is who benefits from the network analysis. This is the basis of the ethical judgments of government-required Institutional Review Boards on cost versus benefits—usually the costs to the subjects (the respondents in most network research) and the benefits to society at large and to science, though as we shall see, the interests of all the key stakeholders are not necessarily taken into account. For academics, abstract ethical issues are often overshadowed by the bureaucratic need to submit all research proposals to a Protection of Human Subjects Institutional Review Board (IRB). Human Subject Review Committees are frequently dominated by researchers from a medical background. Often their primary concern is that subjects not be harmed by research. In many cases, the committee concludes in the case of network studies that hazards to the individual outweigh any benefit to science. Further, many IRBs believe that any means of identifying individual participants is illegitimate and unethical. When viewed in this way, with privacy as an absolute right, network data collection is harmful regardless of any possible benefits. When "science" is not involved and IRBs are not consulted—as in the examples of interrogation of suspected terrorists or in some other national defense–related studies; attempts to discover the "real" leaders of an organization; or pursuit of dates, business contacts, or sales advantages from the linking of names—the issues become even more murky. Network researchers are concerned that a blanket application of individual rights to privacy will ultimately torpedo the entire social network field. There have been many instances on the Social Network listserv of researchers asking for help after an IRB rejected their research proposal. Sometimes, when the researcher explains how confidentiality will be protected, IRBs relent. Network researchers attempt to explain that anonymity cannot be given, but confidentiality can be protected. When an IRB provides guarantees of confidentiality and an institutional structure that enforces these guarantees, the willingness of respondents to participate may actually increase, thereby improving the research. The guarantees requested by IRBs usually spell out the nature of network research and ask for the respondent's written consent. In contrast, the usual practice in survey research is to require some kind of assent to being questioned, a statement about the general nature of the research, and the right to opt out of any question, but written consent, except for minors (parents have to give consent), is impractical and not required.

In addition to subjects, respondents, or science in the abstract, there are many other stakeholders who may benefit or be harmed: the state or the government in the search for terrorists and criminals, management in organization studies, gay and drug-using communities in HIV epidemiological studies, and civil libertarians in all the studies. Ethics are also politics. The investigators and researchers themselves have a key stake in reputation, prestige, and ego, not to mention salaries and promotions (Merton 1973). Finally, an obvious point may be overlooked, for there is another dimension to the concern with subjects that IRBs do not necessarily consider: the reactions of literate "natives" to the revelation of details about their lives and interrelations in a social science report, article, or book. This is not so much the lack of privacy or confidentiality, but rather the overall interpretation of the setting or the findings. This is a problem for all social science research, not only network studies, but it may be especially a problem when cliques or informal structures are discussed. In the end, ethics is not an abstract issue, but one that is best understood by examining specific cases and examples, to which we now turn. Since the details of decisions about ethics are often not available in the published reports of specific studies, I will also report some of my own experiences.

Cases and Examples

SURVEY RESEARCH

Surveys and network studies pose special problems of their own. Network analysis, as shown in chapter 9, has wide use in tracing illnesses especially in AIDS research, subject to the safeguards that can serve as a model for all network research (Klovdahl 2005). The fact that HIV-positive status is often hidden for understandable reasons raises a number of problems (Shelley et al. 2006). Contact tracing had been the modus vivendi of work with TB and venereal diseases. In the beginning, HIV-positive status was tantamount to a sentence of a short and painful life and considerable stigma. As a result, in the early years of the discovery of the disease, it was virtually impossible to introduce studies that depended on contact tracing. Gay Men's Health Crisis (GMHC), for example, was and still appears to be strongly opposed to such work, though it cites and reviews much epidemiological research on HIV. The organization notes on its website that "New York State's HIV Confidentiality law prohibits health care providers and social service providers from disclosing your HIV status without your written consent." But many states now require contact tracing or what is also called partner notification. I have not been able currently (as of September 2011) to find anything on the GMHC site about epidemiological contact-tracing research, though the organization has been opposed to mandatory contact tracing in the past. Posted on the GMHC site are the National HIV/AIDS Strategy for the United States and the National HIV/AIDS Strategy: Federal Implementation Plan. Neither mentions contact tracing as a strategy.

Rarely does a survey include in its methodological appendix an account of the ethical problems involved in the survey, so here I offer some examples from my own experience. Sometimes an ordinary survey involving network data can lead to unexpected problems. One of my first forays into network research in a survey was in a study of Juilliard School of Music in the early 1960s (Kadushin 1969). The intent was not to study ego networks but to use the data to construct a network of the entire school. We actually would have been satisfied with the characteristics of the network that surrounded each person, rather than the network of the entire school. We asked, in a mailed questionnaire, "who are your 'three best friends?'" (the format used in those days). This question apparently was responsible for a rumor that I was trying to discover who was homosexual. Response rates in some departments suffered, and the question was unanalyzable because of extensive missing data. This was before the days of IRBs. In retrospect, the IRB apparatus, had it approved of the method, might have alleviated some suspicions, but perhaps not. It is one thing to gather data from schoolchildren, but another from young adults.

Elite and power surveys are another set of traps. In the late 1960s I worked with a team from Columbia University's Bureau of Applied Social Research and the Yugoslav Opinion Research Center on studies of elites in Yugoslavia. Later we were involved, together with colleagues in Czechoslovakia, in studying the Czech elite. In the same time period, I studied the American intellectual elite (Kadushin 2005a). Each study contained data on who the respondent talked with about what. These data were used to develop very large computer-constructed sociograms (Alba 1973; Alba and Guttman 1972). Obviously, we needed the names to construct the socio-grams. During the 1968 student "revolution" on the Columbia campus, I took the data home for safekeeping, since I was fearful that the Yugoslavia data, together with the names, would be publicly circulated. A book was eventually published, with analyses of the characteristics of different kinds of Yugoslav elite circles, but the sociograms were not (Kadushin and Abrams 1973a, 1973b). When the Russians reentered Czechoslovakia in August after the famous democratic spring of 1968, the data were temporarily placed in a safe deposit box. The box and the codebooks were eventually retrieved and sat in my home office until Pat Lyons at the Institute of Sociology at the Czech Academy of Sciences recently asked about them. I found a shop which collects antique computers and was able to read old punch card data and transform them into an electronic file. The file along with the codebook was shipped to the Academy. I am pleased that a report using these data has recently been pub-lished (Lyons 2009).

Later we collected similar data on the general American elite as well as the Australian and German elite (Higley et al. 1991). Oddly enough, elected officials are in a special "exempt" category—subject to review by IRBs but routinely exempt from the usual restrictions on confidentiality. Of course, many elites are not elected. My most recent foray into elite studies was collecting data on the French financial elite in 1990 (Kadushin 1995). In none of these cases did we have to contend with an IRB. But we did have potentially sensitive, if not dangerous, data. Of course, people can dissemble about their contacts. While interviewing members of the American elite, one of the key figures in the Watergate scandal (not yet broken) was interviewed. That individual described as his major political/social concern issues pertaining to the environment (partly true), and he provided us a list of contacts in that field. Needless to say, his con-tacts involved in trying to cover up the scandal were not mentioned! Sometimes, things are just too "hot" to attempt a network study. I do not know if we would have inter-viewed some of these individuals had we known about Watergate because their con-tacts might have been too sensitive. I did withdraw my proposal to study the American intellectual elite after I first proposed it in the mid-sixties because there was a Senate investigation into the loyalty of prominent American intellectuals who were beginning to be opposed to the war, and I wanted to use the war as a network "tracer." The Senate investigation was dropped, and I submitted the proposal a year later. It was eventually funded by NSF and became *The American Intellectual Elite* (Kadushin 2005a).

In that book, I published a list that summed up the top 70 names mentioned on seven network questions that asked who influenced the respondent and who were gen-erally most influential on various topics. The names were listed in four ranks, the top 10, the next 10, ranks 21–25, and 26 though 27. The latter two sets had numerous ties. Within each set of ranks, names were listed alphabetically so as to minimize invidious comparisons. Among the top 10 was Daniel Bell, who was then noted by careless re-viewers as the leading American intellectual, though among the top ten he was leading only by virtue of the alphabet. Since interviews and links between people were anony-mous, the intent of the list was to indicate the kind of people being studied. I do not think the list violated any privacy concerns, but it retrospect it was at least an intellectual error. Readers and reviewers paid more attention to the list than to the content of the book. I would not (and did not) repeat this mistake. A sociometric list of leaders can present the attributes that correlate with leadership rather than the names themselves. This is a good rule, both from an intellectual and ethical standpoint. That said, having the names on a sociogram helps the analyst interpret the data. Which people are in which positions can give the analyst, who knows the original scene, many clues as to the formal properties of the network or the attributes of the clusters that can then be formally tested. The names are then removed for publication. In the computer-generated sociogram on intellectual circles as published in the *American Intellectual Elite* (Kadushin 2005a, 85, fig. 1), the people (or their intellectual or biological children) clustered on the right turned out years later to be the core of the neo-conservatives. Their placement on the right of sociogram was of course pure accident. Since I am the only one who knows who the names, and their attributes alone do not entirely predict their politics 25 years subsequent to the sociogram, I cannot publicly make such a claim. But their personal associations as depicted in the network turned out to be excellent predictors.

My study of the French financial elite posed several ethical problems. The research was done at the request of a journalist who had access to elite French circles. We made a deal: she would conduct the interviews according to my specifications with respect to the network questions and the sample design; I would analyze the data for her in return for the right to publish the data in an academic journal. She would publish the data as a book. There was no IRB review. Her access meant that we could ask whom the respondent socialized with—critical for this population. We agreed that interviewees would be promised anonymity at least for the network part of the interview. But when it came time to publish the book, the journalist wanted to put names to the nodes in the sociogram. We had quite a row. The list of names was important to her, since the book was intended as a description of the French financial institutions and the way they worked. Who made what kinds of deals with whom, most of which was part of the record in any case, constituted an important dimension of the book, and the publisher would not accept it otherwise. We compromised: the names as located on the sociogram were printed in the book, but none of the edges were, and thus who was connected with whom could not be determined, though the general clustering of persons could be adduced. It was assumed that the readers of the book, bankers, and investment capitalists in the Anglo-Saxon world, would never read the *American Sociological Review* (Kadushin 1995).

The general rule for network diagrams is that the labels are often a numerical ID starting with 1 and ending with N, as recommended by Steven Borgatti (in exchanges on the Social Networks List) and as automatically implemented in his UCINET (Borgatti, Everett, and Freeman 2004). Even numerical IDs can be problematic in that, for most research, a key must link the number to the actual name so that data can be tracked. There is an elaborate protocol required by the federal government for handling sensitive data that involves several linked keys accessible only in an encrypted, locked, and protected computer in a manner especially reviewed and approved. In the published article,

I did not use numerical IDs but instead added information for each node about his/her political party orientation (four possibilities) and whether she or he graduated from the most relevant grand école. Any number of people could fit the combination. When Frank (Frank and Yasumoto 1998) asked for the data set so that he could reanalyze it, he added many details about corporate relations and deal making that he obtained through laborious research of his own. With this additional information, it was apparent that he could easily link the names to the sociogram. We agreed that he would not do so, even though this made for some awkwardness in the analysis.

ORGANIZATION RESEARCH

Organization network analysis as depicted in chapter 7 focuses on improving organization design, efficiency, and communication. Worthy goals. But as we saw in the classic study of the Bank Wiring Room, there are perceptions as well as the reality of winners and losers in this endeavor. This is especially true if one of the goals is to discover leaders, persons who are likely to disseminate good ideas, innovators, or attributes specific to particular individuals. Here matters can get dicey if people are named and their careers and rewards are at stake. One strategy is to be explicit about these possibilities in a consent form. Experienced network organization researchers have put it this way:

> Perceptions held by management and/or coworkers about an individual may be altered by the study, and could have a dampening effect on the individual's career (including being fired). Thus, the consent form has to be a little bit more explicit [than is usually the case in survey research]. In addition, because network analysis is not terribly familiar to most respondents, it may be quite difficult for them to foresee the pain that the analysis of such simple data as "who do you talk to" can bring. Thus it would seem necessary in the organizational network case to expand the consent form to include examples of network analysis so that potential respondents can make a fully informed decision. Our personal experience with writing truly informed consent forms is instructive: we hate to do it. This is because it feels like we are giving away the store, and because it makes us wonder why anybody would fill out the network questionnaire. We would be much more comfortable hiding this information from the respondent. This is the surest sign that conducting a social network study without truly informed consent is deceptive and wrong. (Borgatti and Molina 2005, 211)

Borgatti and Molina recommend a "Management Disclosure Contract" (MDC), signed by management and the investigators and given to the respondents as part of the consent form. The MDC specifies what the management will see, what the respondents will see, how the data may be used, and what decisions may be based on it.

Organization data collection has become more sophisticated than distributing questionnaires, whose real-time validity may be questioned. The MIT Media Laboratory directed by Alex (Sandy) Pentland collects cell phone data and places electronic badges on workers to track their interactions (Olguín et al. 2009). As they observe, however,

Privacy concerns also must be discussed whenever this type of sensing technology is employed. It is important to anonymize sensitive data so that it cannot be traced back to a specific individual, and this anonymization must occur before the data is stored. Similarly, we must offer tools that allow users to easily select which portions of their data to publish. Not only will this keep users more engaged in the study, but it will prevent serious breaches of privacy and lead to subjects that are more comfortable with their participation. (Waber et al. 2008)

I avoid identifying specific people except to discuss in general ways the characteristics of leaders, innovators, and disseminators, and what can be done to improve the effectiveness of such persons. I oppose doing research that will have direct consequences for employment and rewards unless it is specifically part of a general "360 Feedback" consultation. Through this tool, employees have the opportunity to receive job performance feedback from supervisors and supervisees. Employees are then given a chance to react to the feedback, change, and improve. If after a certain time it is apparent to both the employee and his/her supervisors that things are not working out, the employee may be encouraged to move on. "Three-Sixty Feedback" is a part of human resources management; network research is not and should not be used, in my view, as a human resource tool. Not only is it unethical, but in the end counterproductive, as employees learn to "game" their network responses, rendering the studies useless.

Nonetheless, feedback to employees of a firm is complicated. Often, employee surveys are presented to employee respondents as a way of improving the firm and making progress. If nothing happens as a result of the survey and the network analysis, employees will be less motivated to participate the next time they are surveyed. A regular survey program is a good tool for improving management. Feedback, especially at the work-group level, can change conditions and help respondents feel that their participation in the survey was useful and had consequences. But feedback, even when general, can pinpoint some respondents, especially those in leadership positions. A balance needs to be struck between feedback and finger pointing. One firm with whom I consulted had a rule of 25. In addition to having feedback professionally managed, no feedback could take place with work groups of 24 persons or less.

TERRORISTS AND CRIMINALS

Now we come to an area not envisaged in the Belmont Report or in federal regulations. Network analysis and research can be conducted with the premise that the aim of the research is to harm particular individuals or organizations who are "bad guys." This research and analysis is designed to benefit society and protect against criminals and terrorists. As recent disclosures suggest, however, some of the work in the name of protecting American civil society may have actually harmed it.[6] Some work in this field involves secret interception and wiretaps, but important work in social network analysis of terrorists can be done with public databases or archived material that can be transformed into a database. An example of what can be done in this field using network tools, is the work of Valdis Krebs (2002). Krebs, a respected organization consultant, analyzed networks of 9/11 terrorists based on publicly available data. He suggests:

What do you do with these [identified] suspects? Arrest or deport them immediately? No, we need to use them to discover more of the al-Qaeda network. Once suspects have been discovered, we can use their daily activities to uncloak their network. Just like they used our technology against us, we can use their planning process against them. Watch them, and listen to their conversations to see...
> who they call/email
> who visits with them locally and in other cities
> where their money comes from. (Ibid.)

Not all network analyses of terrorists rely on public data. Rather, intelligence agencies start, as he suggests, from observable entry points and then use standard investigative techniques to connect the dots. What is new is the network method of making connections. This method was apparently used in August 2006 to locate a terrorist group that aimed to blow up planes crossing the Atlantic. Krebs assures that massive "big brother" data mining of phone and financial records was not involved (Krebs 2008). Does Krebs's work raise ethical problems? I think not. Do his suggested applications invite problems? Perhaps. It is in the interests of public safety to employ network analytic techniques. Problems may arise, however, in how "standard investigative techniques" are used. They may result in error, identifying the wrong people, a matter to which we will return. Or they may involve torture of informants—an unethical and illegal practice which also usually leads to incorrect information.

Networks and Terrorism: The CASOS Projects

The Center for Computational Analysis of Social and Organizational Systems (CASOS) at Carnegie Mellon University, headed by leading network sociologist Kathleen Carley, utilizes publicly available sophisticated network analysis tools to conduct research for, among others, the United States Department of Defense, the United States Navy, the Office of Naval Research, DARPA (Defense Advanced Research Projects Agency), the Army Research Lab, the Air Force Office of Scientific Research, the Office of the Chief of Naval Operations, as well as NSF (National Science Foundation) dissertation and training grants.[7] The chief software tool of CASOS, used in many of their publically available papers (for example, Carley, Reminga, and Kamneva 2003), is *ORA (Organization Risk Analyzer): "*ORA is a risk assessment tool for locating individuals or groups that are potential risks given social, knowledge and task network information."[8] CASOS further suggests that an individual's "removal" from a given network "debilitates" it. *ORA is available for free download and includes many innovative and powerful network analysis methods. DyNet is a tool connected to *ORA and is "intended to be a desktop system that can be placed in the hands of intelligence personnel, researchers, or military strategists."[9] There is also "NetEst [which] will provide recommendations for which actions these law enforcement organizations should take to destabilize the network and cripple its ability at minimum cost."[10] No software is currently available.

Another prominent network researcher, James Fowler, whose work was cited in the introductory chapter, has recently circulated a request for people to apply to work with him on an Intelligence Community (IC) Postdoctoral Research Fellowship Program which was established in 2000 to fund basic research in areas of interest to the intelligence community. It is not clear whether parts of the work are classified, though proposals are specifically required to be unclassified. Fowler's network analysis tools can be downloaded.

A free program "KeyPlayer" by Stephen Borgatti is intended to identify,

> an optimal set of nodes in a network for one of two basic purposes: (a) crippling the network by removing key nodes, and (b) selecting which nodes to either keep under surveillance or to try to influence via some kind of intervention. The two purposes are different and require different procedures. KeyPlayer 1.4 provides two approaches for the first goal, and one approach for the second.[11]

"KeyPlayer" is based on his general interest in measures of centrality in networks and is developed in two journal articles (Borgatti 2006; Borgatti 2003). The work was supported by the Office of Naval Research, though other than an interest in national security expressed on Borgatti's website, there is no evidence of other work by him in this area.

The combination of intelligence-community work, possibly classified, with publicly available papers and software developed by the investigators is relatively new and represents an attempt to compromise between perceived needs of national security and the more usual ethics of scientific research. This was not the case in the 1970s, at least not in my personal experience. In the early 1970s, a research firm that was engaged in classified research for the intelligence community wished to expand its work into the social network field and approached me through a mutual friend. With the aid of NSF and Department of Education grants for which I was the principal investigator, we had developed several social network programs capable of handling very large matrixes on mainframe computers (Alba 1973; Alba and Guttman 1972). I suppose this made me attractive to the intelligence community. I turned them down. In the late 1970s, I inquired via a colleague well connected to the intelligence community into progress the intelligence services might have made in handling large social networks. I had hoped that they might share some of their technical computer work or at least some general ideas. Alba and my work was of course in the public domain. My colleague reported that for the first time in his life, he met a stone wall. I suppose the intelligence community had indeed made some progress but did not want anyone to know about it. This unilateral approach was not very useful for scientific research nor, ultimately, for progress and, also I believe, was unethical. Recent developments described earlier have made social networks research more collaborative and closer to straddling the line between secrecy and disclosure to the scientific community.

There remains a problem that is salient to organization research but also very relevant to national security research. This has to do with data error as well as unethical data collection. At a conference on data mining and national security, the CASOS group noted, "Social network analysis has been a prominent tool in investigating an adversarial organization. However, it is also susceptible from errors embedded in the given network structure. Therefore, reorganizing the links is required to perform analysis correctly. This reorganization is often done by human analysts" (Moon, Carley, and Levis 2008). But data and information in national security and Department of Defense investigations are classified and available on a "need to know" basis. Network analysts, even when they search for errors, are not in control of the data, nor do they know whether the data were collected under conditions that they would consider ethical.

The motivations of the sources of network data may also be a factor in distorted or inaccurate depictions of networks. The issues were well expressed by Elin Waring in a Social Network Listserv posting on August 5, 2004. Professor Waring, an expert on criminal social networks, has published articles and books in this area (Finckenauer and Waring 1998, 1997; Waring 2002). She observed, "I personally think that networks are the way to look at the organization of crime, and many SNA [Social Network Analysis] tools are helpful for this, but I would be very, very cautious." She added,

> The issue with most organized crime and terrorist network analysis, as has already been pointed out, is that the data that are available tend to reflect the story that particular actors, usually prosecutors or reporters, want to tell. So newspaper reports tend to produce small networks with dramatic connections often to famous people. Court records produce discrete and highly structured small networks that make for good cases. If the OC [organized crime] people from the FBI are involved the networks will almost inevitably look like 5 hierarchical families. If you get less processed data (such as phone calls or surveillance reports), the world will look messier and less structured. Almost everyone will end up in one big component (which is of course interesting) but it will look more like the regular crime networks.[12]

In my own work, whatever the setting and whomever the client, I have the following principles. The data are always under my direct control, must be collected under guidelines that I describe, and must reside on my computers, as are the names associated with the data. Confidentiality is always guaranteed. The network data are never the property of the organization that has commissioned the research or for whom I am a consultant, although the organizations generally own the survey data they had commissioned.[13] Names are never associated with network graphs or with network indices and are never revealed to officials, management, or employees. Rather, general patterns are described and used to suggest the ways in which things currently flow and/or might be changed. The flows studied depend on the purpose of the investigation—communication, prestige, authority, and even friendship. National security work cannot meet these conditions, and so I do not do it. Others apparently feel that the risks to national security outweigh the need for the protection of the subjects under investigation, some of whom are said to be "bad guys."

Conclusion: More Complicated than the Belmont Report

It is clear that the Belmont Report and federal IRB regulations merely scratch the surface of the complexities of the ethics of network research. One way of summarizing these issues is once more to raise the question, "Who benefits?"

Though what constitutes harm can be a matter of serious controversy, I find it easier to address the benefit issue since if the benefits are substantial, they will usually outweigh whatever minimal harm is engendered by carefully managed network data and analysis. But benefits are a tricky subject. Often we attempt to persuade our subjects and respondents that what they are doing will be of benefit to humanity. This is a general assumption of science and especially invoked in medical research. Even though the individual subject may not directly benefit from the research and the greatest harm to him/her is simply inconvenience, lives may eventually be saved by his/her participation in the research. This is especially evident in epidemiology. Neither science nor humanity in the abstract, however, is the direct beneficiary in academic research. Rather, the investigators are the beneficiaries: their ego, prestige, science citation index, and/or salaries are at stake. Those who teach may gain the added advantage of a live example for their classes. This is not to be deplored, for it underlies the institutional structure of science. I do not necessarily advocate changing our more abstract appeal to reflect this reality (though graduate students and PhD candidates can be effective in directly appealing to subjects to help the researchers pass their course requirements or to further their PhDs), but it is worth putting the matter of benefits into its proper context. We academics are often the prime beneficiaries.

There are also benefits to particular collectivities. In organization research on behalf of clients, the organization benefits if the research fulfills its objectives. To the extent that organizational benefits are shared with employees—it becomes a better place to work, life is made more rational or easier, or everyone makes more money—this is fine. If the benefits accrue only to management or worse, to particular managers, then the researcher might carefully consider the ethics of the situation. Network research into criminals or terrorists is supposed to benefit the nation or the state. In this case, not only do the individual subjects not benefit, they are intentionally put in harm's way. As noted above, there are three ethical issues at stake: the first is whether or not network "fingering" will be subject to judicial review; second, the extent to which the data are reliable with the accuracy necessary when people's lives are at stake—either the individual's or the collectivities; third, whether the data were collected in an ethical fashion (in national security cases this has unfortunately come to mean that respondents were not tortured). The first and third issues are not discussed in this chapter, though many will have strong opinions on it; regarding the second, my opinion is that the data are rarely of sufficient quality for life-and-death decisions, or even for purposes of incarceration. The issues are linked, however. Open court judicial review in an adversarial procedure can assess the accuracy of the network data and their admissibility as evidence, as happens with other data in court procedures (surveys introduced into evidence are carefully scrutinized), but such reviews are rarely invoked in procedures against terrorists or invoked after accusations have been publicly leaked.

Benefits to second parties are critical in epidemiological investigations. Second parties can become aware that they are at risk for a disease, though at a cost to respondents who may be "outed," if this concept is applied to any carrier of a disorder or possessor of a socially undesirable characteristic or behavior such as adultery. On the other hand, the benefits to society of containing disease are enormous.

Finally, there are direct benefits to individual respondents, though I believe these situations are relatively rare. Moreno's original situation with the girls in the cottages was "win-win." The girls could live with people they liked, and the general obstreperousness of the cottages was reduced. But the second benefit was one that accrued to the management of the institution and so belongs to the category of benefit to the collectivity. Most gains for individual respondents are distributed gains that come about as a result of a gain to the collectivity. In network snowball sampling (asking a respondent to name others with similar characteristics or which whom they interact with the promise of a gift to the nominated), however, respondents may directly gain the credit of having given nominees a gift.

The reader will have noticed that I may have raised more questions than I have answered. I think this is a requirement of discussions of ethics.

12 Coda
TEN MASTER IDEAS OF SOCIAL NETWORKS

Introduction

When I was a beginning social researcher at Columbia University's Bureau of Social Research, the director, who was wise in the ways of government bureaucracies and research grant writing, explained to me the following formula for a year-end report and or a grant proposal: "Much has been done, but much remains to be accomplished." This is a good mantra for a concluding chapter. Network theory and analysis have made great strides since 1736 when mathematician Leonhard Euler resolved a famous puzzle by drawing what may have been the first network diagram. In the twentieth century, the idea that social relations consisted of webs of affiliations and networks of interaction was turned from a metaphor into a set of specific concepts, theories, and operations.[1] The success of network graphs developed by psychiatrist Jacob Moreno in the 1930s, which he called "sociograms," and the subsequent development of graph theory and other mathematical tools for the analysis of networks, has culminated recently with mathematical statistical "hard science" physicists' heightened interest in networks. This history has reinforced the impression that the social network field is mainly concerned with methodology. In this book, we have attempted to counter this notion by focusing on concepts and theories. To be sure, in social science, as in the "hard sciences," the development of theories and findings go hand-in-hand with the development of methods to solve the theoretical puzzles; the methods in turn suggest new theoretical issues. But in our case, we have tried to focus on the theoretical ideas and basic concepts, while noting the mathematical underpinnings and continuing puzzles that need to be solved.

As the social network field began to mature in the latter part of the twentieth century, one view held that the detailed study of social relations in the form of social networks, through both qualitative and quantitative means, lay at the heart of sociology and would eventually replace classic ideas of status, roles, norms, values, and institutions. Another view, with which I agree, is what has been recently called the "double embeddedness" aspect of social networks: networks are embedded within a system of social institutions which in turn are embedded in a system of social networks, thus creating a constant feedback mechanism between networks and institutions. In this review, I will concentrate on ten "master ideas" that lay out essential features of network concepts, theory, and analysis. Since the network project is an ongoing one, each master idea has associated with it a number of unsolved problems. My hope is that some readers will become sufficiently interested in social networks to tackle some of these problems themselves.

The Ten Master Ideas

1. *Interaction and relatedness.* Social network theory is about describing, accounting for, or even predicting interactions between social units that could be people, groups, organizations, countries, ideas, social roles, or just about any social entity that can be named. As such, social network theories and ideas can be applied to any social level. For example, diffusion principles can apply to the spread of disease between people or innovations between companies. Likewise, people, companies, and nations all have social capital. But social networks differ from physical networks, such as power grids, even though some network concepts and findings apply to both physical and social networks.

    Social networks are driven by motivations, expectations, and cognitive limitations. They are influenced by and responsive to social norms and institutions. Through repeated interactions, new norms and institutions are created. As physical objects, electrical transformers do not create new power grids nor do they have motives.Social networks are also characterized by *multiplexity*—having more than one relationship among the social units. Networks can be "stacked" by creating matrixes of more than one relationship. It is not uncommon in modern life for people to be friends, coworkers, and neighbors. A boss-subordinate relationship on the job and a friendship outside of the office can complicate organizational life or enhance it. The way in which these overlapping relationships are viewed can also differ by cultural context. In traditional authority systems, nepotism is a normative way of gaining loyalty and compliance, but in rational-legal systems it contravenes the norms and is sometimes against the law. Organizations too often connect with one another in varying ways. They may be customers of one another, regularly hire from one another, or share clients through referral networks. Multiplexity is a fruitful avenue for further research and has important practical applications. Methodologically, however, analyzing multiple relationships remains something of a challenge.

Because repeated social interactions can change social systems, it is tempting to derive the nature of existing social systems by postulating repeated social interactions that develop into organized systems. Social authority systems, for example, can be derived from the elements of triadic interactions. While we cannot directly observe repeated interactions over the cycle of many years, we can simulate such cycles through computer models. These simulations are often theoretically informative. But pushed too far, this practice can lead to the "fallacy of origins" that has plagued social science for 200 years. It is tempting to speculate about the origins of current religions by looking at the practices of preliterate tribes, but modern scholarship is dubious about these ascriptions. The origins of military systems of authority might be derived from basic rules of interaction. We were not there at the time of origin, when military authority systems were first developed, however. While interaction is involved in all organizations and in all forms of authority, institutions have their own convoluted histories. Nonetheless, network structures of all kinds do develop from repeated interactions over time. There are some new ideas and tools in this field, and it will be interesting to see how this work develops.

2. *Displaying social networks as graphs and diagrams called sociograms.* This perhaps has caught the most attention. Network pictures can be dramatic but they are also problematic. An early Moreno sociogram in 1934 graphed the relation between ten babies in a nursery, based on the extent to which they paid attention to one another. The sociogram was laid out and drawn by hand. It was easy to interpret. However, once one gets past 15 or so points, the placement of the individuals in a graph and drawing connections between them becomes difficult, arbitrary, and prone to error. Interpretation becomes equally arbitrary. Modern networks can contain thousands of points; no one can draw the network by hand. Three methods of dealing with this problem exist. First, networks can be displayed by computers using various mathematical algorithms. Some displays are in 3D, and some are "movies" that show changes over time in networks. "Movies," which are of course not available for the printed page, are striking in displaying change over time in networks. We have used some of the results of these programs in this book, and the field is still developing. Second, there are a number of ways of partitioning networks or chopping them into meaningful, manageable pieces. Complicating this maneuver, however, is the fact that social groups tend to overlap. The parts or segments of a network can be graphed and displayed so that one does not have to deal with enormous networks; the partitioned segments are themselves indicative of the various communities and groups contained in the larger networks. Partitioning and segmenting networks has captured the attention of people beyond the social

network field, including physicists and other "hard" scientists. Third, and of major importance, mathematical models can compare observed relationships with those that might occur through mere chance, thereby moving the interpretation of networks away from arbitrary intuitions.

Visualizing, partitioning, and hypothesizing are often used simultaneously to gain a better understanding of the properties and meanings of networks. The power of these methods and the clear break with the intuitive interpretations of networks has led to the perception that social networks are "merely" a methodology. But all three methods depend on ideas, concepts, and theories of networks. For example, consider the following issues. What constitutes an interaction so that one can graph it? What is the nature of cohesion, and what are its effects? Theories of cohesion are the basis of algorithms used to partition a network into segments. What are the appropriate minimum network units or "molecules?" The methods also alter and develop the very network theories on which they are based. In this book, we have left detailed explication of the methods to the specialists, though we hope that the methods we discussed are sufficiently open-ended and suggestive of further development to interest readers who want further to advance the study of social networks.

3. *Homophily.* This is the "birds of a feather flock together" principle and moves us directly into considerations of social systems. The question of what constitutes similarity and how it is signaled is critical. While we tend to think of homophily in terms of people, network principles apply to collectivities as well. Homophily occurs through simple propinquity, common statuses, or other socially defined attributes (including contested attributes, such as skin color) or simply being in the same place at the same time. Homophily is a process as well as an outcome. People with the same values and attitudes tend to associate with one another. Interaction, in turn, leads to a greater likelihood of common values. People in the same structural position, for example, the same class, occupation, and education, tend to have the same values and engage in common activities and so come to associate with one another. Interaction can also lead to influence over the ideas and values of interaction partners. Sorting out what causes what has been a concern since the term homophily was introduced in 1955. Recently developed large-scale data sets that have a number of time points may help to resolve some of these questions, but at this date the questions are largely unanswered. Finally, one must remember that homophily is not necessarily a "good thing." Social networks based on homophily may be fundamentally "unfair"; homophily makes segregation and racial prejudice notoriously difficult for social planners to overcome.

4. *Triads* are the true start of a social system. Triads are the molecules of networks. While there are 16 possible combinations of triads, most are quite rare because relationships tend to be in balance. It is difficult to sustain a relationship with a friend whom another friend dislikes. Secrecy and relations between lovers, not to mention many other matters, are altered when a third party is

brought in. By observing the prevalence of different types of triads in different social networks under varying conditions, statisticians can tell a great deal about the nature of the underlying social network. Statistical models that predict the distribution of various types of triads and dyads, especially over time, are just coming into wider use. It will be interesting to see how this field develops and whether it will become as common a method as ordinary regression in data analysis. Some of the findings we cited on homophily were derived from this kind of analysis. This is an area ripe for further exploration.

5. *Motivation*. Basic human motivation corresponds to two fundamental aspects of social networks. One is *density*—a large number of connections between members of a network. As in a person's family of origin, density arises from *the motivational need for safety and social support*. The second related aspect of social networks corresponds to bridging or making connections between parts of a network, *structural holes* that might not otherwise be connected. At some point, to be effective, one has to reach out to others and move beyond one's comfort zone. The dual motivations of safety and effectiveness are present in all social networks. Entrepreneurs gain a profit from bridging structural holes and acting as "brokers" but also must have a home base of support. These dualities play out in small groups, organizations, and at every social level. The useful balance of closure and density on the one hand, and bridging structural holes on the other, is still being explored and is especially pertinent to organization studies. The idea of "making a profit" from making connections is intriguing. The profit may consist of gaining advancement in an organization, gaining an advantage in the political arena, or infamously, making someone "an offer they can't refuse." Networks also can create their own motivation; we look to others in a similar position and try to keep up with them.

6. *Position* in a network is the sixth master idea. Position has a number of aspects. The most straightforward is *degree*—the number of nominations a person or other social unit receives which puts them at the top of the heap. But this is not all there is to leadership. Who makes the nomination is important. Nominations from those who themselves are often named are obviously more important than nominations from the unpopular and are more indicative of power than a simple count of popularity. Position is easiest to study in a small group. Small group members tend to balance safety and effectance. One tries to associate with people who have more of whatever the group values. But the need for safety means that there is a tendency to nominate people who have just a bit more value than one possesses. People want to "have their phone calls returned." Reaching out to the top invites a non-response. The balance between needing support by one's peers and reaching beyond one's rank results in a stable ranking within the group, and oddly, also conforms to the proposition that leaders initiate more interaction with non-leaders than followers initiate with leaders.

Betweenness is a measure of a position that serves as a switching point or a gateway between different parts of a network. This is different from degree.

Persons who have a high betweenness rank are those who mediate between different parts of a network; one has to go through them to get to other positions. A person can be an important bridge between parts of a network yet be directly connected to only a few persons. Both betweenness and power are important factors in *diffusion*—another master idea that will be discussed later. *Distance* or closeness from one person to another in a network is involved in measuring betweenness. Distance is usually measured as the shortest non-redundant path between units or persons. Not that redundancy is necessarily inefficient: we sometimes have to hear the same thing several times to grasp its meaning or be convinced. Empirically, the influence of other persons or units on the focal person vastly declines somewhere between two and three steps out. It is not clear theoretically why this is true. This is a puzzle that remains to be solved.

The *strength of weak ties* is a striking aspect of bridging and betweenness. To break out of a dense set of relationships, to get new ideas or new jobs not available in one's immediate social environment, requires connections with others one does not know very well, does not see often, or is not bound to by many dense relations. Through two or three steps, one can encounter worlds that one might not otherwise know. This is a non-obvious proposition: if you are looking for a new job do not ask the people you know well, ask them to ask someone who is more removed from your immediate circle.

Networks can be *partitioned* because whole networks are often difficult to grasp and understand. One way to partition a network is to group people together who have similar relationships to other people, for example, the people who look up to the "leading crowd" even though they may not have much to do with one another. People grouped together on this basis are the network equivalent of a social *role*. A socially instituted role, such as a teacher-student role relation, both describes and prescribes how teachers relate to students and vice versa. There are cultural and social norms about these relations. The network partitioning analogue, "block models" describe roles from the point of view of the observer of the network. The content of the roles is inferred from other aspects of the situation. One type of partitioning is the core-periphery model. There are many examples of such situations, including trade relations between the "first world" core and the "third world" periphery.

Just as the block model idea builds on the preexisting sociological concept of a role, other partitioning ideas come from the concept of a *clique*—people who hang out more with each other than they hang out with individuals who are not in the clique. While this seems like a simple idea and concurs with both long-held sociological ideas as well as with common-sense observations, it is difficult systematically to maximize internal density and minimize external connections if one does not know from prior knowledge where the lines are to be drawn. The principle of *modularity* has been recently developed. The method is a rule of thumb or algorithm that successively compares the number of connections within a "community" or group with the number of connections in some equivalent randomized network. The algorithm continues to make dichotomous splits until there is no statistical difference between the observed partition and the one with the same points randomly connected. But this is a non-social system view, and we know that in social systems, groups tend to overlap. For example, methods based on group cohesion that test whether a group falls apart if a given member is dropped seem to conform better to social systems and can also produce hierarchically overlapping groups common to them. Both modularity methods and group cohesion methods are relatively new, and there is much work that needs to be done in exploring network position and partitions and their substantive implications. Recently, Facebook claimed it had explored various algorithms for clustering circles of friends but found them wanting. It is still trying.

Part of the problem of partitioning is reflected by the traditional sociological problem of "membership." The question of who is really part of a group or an organization is not as clear is it might seem. There are "members" but also "hangers on" and "fellow travelers" in most informal groups and voluntary organizations. For-profit organizations must constantly face the "make or buy" decision. They ask, shall we make the part ourselves or buy it from suppliers; when shall we rely on inside legal counsel and when we should go to an outside firm; and, should we make our own website or rely on others to produce one through "cloud computing"? Firms in many industries could not exist without the support of an "external economy" that provides goods and services essential to running the firm, even though the suppliers of these goods or services are not members of the firm. Organizations that make consumer products sometimes speak of their "franchise"—meaning regular buyers of their products. The networks that connect firms and organizations with other firms and organizations, with their customers and their clients, and with the larger social environment are important not only in advancing theory, but as a practical matter for each organization. There is a great deal of applied work in this area that ranges from traditional market research to developing organizational strategy. Most of this work is being done in business schools. Courses called "Strategy" are often taught by faculty in the network field.

7. *Organizational authority.* Social networks can be arranged as hierarchical systems. As we saw from considering leadership in small groups, some of the ranking is caused by processes endemic to social interaction. But much of the ranking is conferred by forces exogenous to the network. Nowhere is this more apparent than in formal organizations, all of which involve some kind of hierarchical authority system. Organization theorists of modern organizations believe that, in addition to the compliance that is derived from force, acceptance of the hierarchical structure occurs through acquiescence of the relationship by those lower in the hierarchy. This is the basic "contract" of organizational life. The worker accepts the organization supervisor's wishes and demands

within the boundaries of the organization; the organization reciprocates by paying the workers. Relationships in an organization can thus best be understood in network terms. Network analysis notes that in addition to compliance and formally mandated interactions, there are continuously occurring informal interactions. These additional interactions "short circuit" the formal power structure and change it, sometimes to the benefit but other times to the detriment of the organization. These additional interactions, made visible by network analysis, alter the power structure, laterally connect parts of the organization where no formal circuits are part of the design, and change leadership on the shop floor. Discovered very early in the history of social network analysis, these informal patterns have spurred an industry of organization consultants seeking to help organizations understand what takes place within their ranks and have contributed to the placement of social network experts in business schools. Nonetheless, the art, and perhaps science, of aligning informal leadership with the aims of an organization remains elusive.

8. *Small World.* This master idea has perhaps caught the most attention of the general public. The idea that networks connect the entire world, social as well as physical, seems on at least second thought to be entirely plausible. More surprising is the claim that a relatively small number of steps, small considering that a network might contain millions or even billions of units, connects the entire world. Small can be startlingly small. The simple arithmetic is straightforward. If each person had a circle of acquaintances of 100 people, then in three steps a population of 100,000, 000 can be reached. But this outcome depends on there being no overlap between each circle of friends, an unrealistic assumption given the fact that social networks are clustered. *Social circles*, loose networks formed by people whose friendships, interests, and values overlap, typical of metropolitan areas, are an important element in social network clustering. The result of this and other homophily situations are that the actual number of steps from one person to another in the small world is greater than the three or four that are expected by the mathematics of chance. An early experiment that used chain letters to reach a designated target found the famous "six degrees of separation," though in fact many chains were not completed. The quest to nail down and explicate the length of small world chains has resulted in much research. One avenue has been to account for the size of people's interpersonal environment. A large number obviously increases the likelihood of connections. It has been estimated that the average person in the modern world knows at least 300 persons; the growth of social networking sites may make this number much larger. But in all social networks, the distribution is highly skewed, with a small tail knowing as many as 5,000 people or more. The utility of estimating this number goes beyond small world theory. If one works backward from this number and determines, through a survey, the number of persons each respondent knows in a population of otherwise unknown size—such as the number of persons who are HIV

positive or who are heroin users—the size of that population can be estimated. Much more research is needed here. Among other matters, it is not known which characteristics determine the size of a person's interpersonal environment.

A completely different approach models very large networks as a series of "caves" or social circles, with each circle connected to an adjacent one, resulting in potentially long paths to circles that are not adjacent. But the models show that it takes but a few "short circuits" to connect all the social circuits, resulting in the small world phenomenon. Though there are examples of very large physical networks, there is still a paucity of real data for very large social networks, for example, all the people in a large city, making it difficult to test the models on real data. Two mechanisms have been proposed for accounting for those who connect more dense regions or social circles. One is a cumulative advantage, a version of the biblical observation that "to he who hath shall be given." Single stars are the link to people who themselves have few connections. The other is called assortative distribution—connections between elites or other persons of similar characteristics, each of whom has many connections. Though the small world is a catchy idea, a great deal of additional technical and theoretical work remains. First, the implications of the small world for macro sociological theory have been barely explored. Is a reconceptualization or revision of propositions about connections between different aspects of social systems required? What are the implications of new technologies such as Facebook, which explicitly aims to create small world graphs as a vast network connecting members with each other? The mechanisms of connections, or the lack of them, need to be explored. This would help our theoretical understanding of the implications of the small world. We know very little about who the key linkers are and how they came be in that position.

9. *Diffusion.* This master idea lies at the heart of social networks because the very basis of a social network is that something passes or flows from one unit to the other: for example, friendship, love, money, ideas, opinions, and disease. The shape of the network, its density, the number of alternate paths from one person to the other, the extent to which interactions are concurrent, the existence of hierarchy in which some network members are leaders and others followers, as well as the size of the network, are all factors in diffusion. Weak ties and bridging points are essential to diffusing something from an inner circle to a wider world. In general, diffusion follows an S-shaped curve: a few people join early; through various interaction patterns those individuals "infect" or enlist a few others; the number of adopters or the "infected" rises rapidly; and finally the growth tapers off because the available pool of potential adopters or those at risk for a new infection grows ever smaller. The model can vary in various ways, including the possibility that people are cured, forget, or need to be reminded. At some point in the process there is a *tipping point* when the diffusion appears to take off on its own

without any further input from the outside. No further inducements are required. Forecasting the tipping point is the "golden fleece" of marketing and a concern to public health officials. The former wants to know how to get products to take off while the latter seeks to cut off the growth of disease. Unfortunately, with present knowledge, tipping points are best found in retrospect and are almost impossible to forecast. With wide applications from epidemiology to opinion formation, market research, and intellectual history, diffusion is a "hot" topic. The models are complex, the ideas deceptively simple but hard to implement, and the rewards for furthering a better understanding of the field are great.

10. *Social Capital*. Intended as a partial analogue to financial capital, social capital looks to the consequences, generally positive but sometimes negative, of social networks. Social capital is a loose concept defined differently by various investigators. On the individual level, social capital can mean that people who have a large number and/or a wide range of friends in different occupations, or who have friends in high-ranked occupations, have better occupational outcomes. It is not clear that people must actually activate these connections to achieve good outcomes or that they consciously "invest" in them. Among those who do are social climbers who, despite the generally low societal regard in which their actions are viewed, try to gain the right kinds of friends in order to accrue later advantages. One thing most investigators agree upon, though they may not state this explicitly, is that like financial capital, social capital can reproduce itself, leading to still more social capital. At the community level, social capital has been conceptualized as a rich set of social networks comprised of both individual ties and organizational ties. These social relations are said to lead to greater social trust, which leads to practices such as sharing childcare and enforceable handshake business deals. Among many other outcomes, there are also health benefits and more effective democratic institutions. Dense social relations of course have a downside, including limiting opportunities outside of the community and reducing openness to new ideas. Importantly, social capital is both micro and macro at the same time. Individual social networks have community and group outcomes; overall community networks have both direct and indirect implications for individuals. This kind of cross-level and multi-level analysis is at the heart of modern social theory. Working out the implications of community networks will help specify the meaning and utility of the still diffuse concept of social capital.

There is another aspect of social capital, however, that has not been the province of classic social theory: making money from the very idea of a social network. This is the notion that underlies social networking sites such as Facebook. While the entrepreneurs of Facebook and similar sites have not fully realized their hopes of making quarterly profits from these sites (which are free to the users but earn money from advertisements or product referrals), the capitalized value of them is in the multi-millions. The main value currently in social networking sites comes from Initial Public Offerings (IPO's) or their anticipation. Essential to realizing profits from social network sites is the rapid apparent decline in cherished rights of privacy, making short shrift of the right to restrict information about one's own network. As the *New York Times* put it, "Not that long ago, many were leery of using their real names on the Web, let alone sharing potentially embarrassing personal details about their shopping and lifestyle habits... To Silicon Valley's deep thinkers, this is all part of one big trend: People are becoming more relaxed about privacy... companies are betting they [can] take this data, monetize it or resell it" (Stone 2010, A1).

The monetization of social networks, that is, turning social networks into financial capital, has led major figures in the academic study of networks to leave their academic positions for employment in the corporate sector or spend a good deal of their time consulting for computer, internet, and other firms, and for government, civilian, and defense agencies in an effort to capitalize on their own personal investments in network theory and analysis. This is not necessarily an activity based on financial greed. There are also intellectual rewards. As social networks, either within firms, between firms, or globally, have come to have demonstrable value, access to them for research purposes has become more difficult and available only to insiders who, however, can publish their work with appropriate pseudonyms or other restrictions.

The world has changed from the days in which the study of social networks was literally a "cottage industry" in which social networks of adolescent delinquent girls living in cottages were the subject matter. Globalization and the emergence of instant, massive, networked communication heighten the need to better understand that which was once an arcane interest of a few mathematicians and social theorists.

This is the conclusion of this book, but the field of social network analysis is a work in progress. In the years 2009 to 2010, *Science Citation* found over 3,500 articles under the search term "social network*" (the * indicates a "wild card," meaning the search included social network or social networks). Since the time the reader has started this book and arrived at its end, there have no doubt been a number of new developments in social network analysis and its applications. So has the reader wasted her/his time on this book? Are the findings in the book doomed to obsolescence before one has even started to read it? Robert K. Merton coined the apt phrase, "The fallacy of the latest word" (Merton 1984), meaning that although the most recent work appears to supersede previous research, theories, and findings, this is not necessarily true. In the network field, it is not so much a case of incorrectly falsifying previous findings, Merton's main concern, though this does occur, but rather the development of new methods that lead to new findings, the typical situation of a dynamic field. This book has therefore concentrated on basic concepts and theories that are less likely to be quickly superseded and illustrated them with findings that stem from the ten master ideas of social networks outlined in this chapter. My hope is that the reader has absorbed these ideas, but become convinced that they are merely the foundation for engaging in further discovery. If I have persuaded a few of you that you have a future in unraveling the many continuing puzzles and conundrums of social networks, then the book has succeeded.

Notes

CHAPTER 1

1. Barry Wellman has been consistently warning that "community lost" is a false idea. He instead promotes "community found" through social networks of all kinds (Wellman 1979).

2. The word is anathema to network scholars, however.

3. Pew Internet and American Life Project's December 2008 tracking survey, http://www.pewinternet.org/Reports/2009/Adults-and-Social-Network-Websites.aspx.

4. Pew Internet Project Memo, January 14, 2009.

5. Their business model is another story.

6. http://www.orgnet.com/divided.html.

7. Former United States Senator George J. Mitchell's twenty-month investigation into the use of anabolic steroids and human growth hormone (HGH) in Major League Baseball (MLB), released on December 13, 2007.

8. *Associated Press*, June 8, 2009, *Boyle v. U.S.*, 07-1309.

9. Two dissenting justices thought the statue indeed had intended formal organizations.

10. http://www.thenetworkthinkers.com/2009/2008/no-tweets-for-you.html

11. Whether the similarity of networked people is caused by homophily or influence is difficult to unentangle. Christakis and Fowler favor influence as an explanation.

12. For a similar point, see Martin (2009).

CHAPTER 2

1. Useful works are Newman 2010; Nooy, Mrvar, and Batagelj 2005; Wasserman and Faust 1997.

2. For an elegant analysis of basic network relations, see Martin 2009, chapters 1 and 2.

3. A classic study in the social network field is Claude Fischer's *To dwell among friends* (Fischer 1982).

4. The caveat of "other things being equal" is well illustrated, however, by the following example: "[T]he Middle East does not constitute a 'natural' trading bloc. The region's trade with Turkey indicates that complementarities in production matters more than cultural affinities, or even physical proximity, in promoting trade between countries"(Kleiman 1998).

5. Claude Fischer, personal communication.

6. Transaction costs are the costs occasioned by the friction that occurs when one buys or sells something, or when one imports something from another division or part of the same firm. This is a complicated topic that will be addressed in the chapter on organization.

7. Paul Krugman won a Nobel Prize for work in this field.

8. James Moody, personal communication.

9. See Martin 2009, chapters 2 and 3 for interesting analyses of the limits of balance and transitivity as he builds more complex networks from simple relationships.

10. This is only a heuristic. Martin follows this heuristic, but one can equally argue the reverse: that small networks are dependent upon the larger structures of which they are a part.

CHAPTER 3

1. There are many ways of graphing or displaying a network as a sociogram and a number of different ways of laying it out, and computer graphing has a distinct advantage over doing it by hand. Some have even created "movies" of networks that rotate them in various ways in three dimensions. Nonetheless, the challenge remains to find a way of depicting large social networks so that they can be read in a two-dimensional medium such as a piece of paper.

2. Granovetter's article is a "citation classic" with 2024 citations as compared with Milgram's 194 citations as of May 1, 2007.

3. National Estimates, http://www.census.gov/popest/archives/pre-1980/PE-11.html.

4. Claude Fischer (Fischer 1982, 143–157) finds no association between urban and less urban residence in the Bay Area and multiplexity after appropriate controls.

5. Recently a class of models related to logit regressions has been developed that can analyze some consequences of different ties between the same nodes in a network, but there are as yet relatively few applications (Koehly and Pattison 2005). If one wishes to compare total networks composed of the same nodes but different relations, then it is possible to correlate to the two matrixes (Borgatti, Everett, and Freeman 2004; Hubert and Schultz 1976), but it is not easy to condition this correlation on various attributes that might characterize the total network.

6. Merton distinguishes between a named position, which he calls "status," and relationships between statuses. A status may have "role relationships" between it and the other statuses with which it relates by virtue of structure and norms. A teacher (a named status) has a role relationship to students, other teachers, parents, principles, and so on. All the role relationships that a status enters into as a part of the definition of the particular status are called a "role set." An individual may have a number of different statuses. For example, besides "teacher," the person may also be "father." The set of all statuses that an individual inhabits is called a "status set" (Merton 1968b). I find this terminology less confusing and more precise than one that uses "role" for both position and relationships between positions. For propositions using this framework that have much in common with network concepts, see Coser 1975. The network field however seems to use "role" for both position and relationship, and I will conform to this usage.

7. As with the status/role distinction, the emic/etic conceptualization is also subject to various usages. (See Headland, Pike, and Harris 1990 for an extended discussion.)

8. More recently, though the notion of position is maintained, the concept of "role" has been dropped in considering "generalized" blockmodeling. The intent is to cluster networks such that units are said to be "equivalent if they link in equivalent ways to other units that are also equivalent" (Doreian, Batagelj, and Ferligoj 2005, 82). We will take up the clustering of networks below.

CHAPTER 4

1. An algorithm is a procedure, like a recipe. First do this, then that, perhaps check to see how things look, and then do another thing. This is different from an algebraic solution in which a set of equations are solved. There are many situations in which a set of equations cannot be solved, or it is unclear how to even write them. Following an algorithm by hand can be extremely tedious and error-prone, but computers can do them very quickly. This has introduced an entirely new approach to problem solving, and algorithms have become the heart of modern statistics and a crucial technique in network analysis.

2. I am indebted to Daniel Bell (personal communication) for the concept of the "C's."

3. In an aural presentation at the 2011 Sunbelt Network Meetings, augmented by personal communication, Lin Freeman pointed out modularity was introduced as a way of determining how "good" a given structural form is—the degree to which the clusters, groups or communities it examines display the properties expected of such structures. Now "Q" is used most often as an optimizing criterion in algorithms designed to find clusters, groups or communities. But while Newman and Girvan claim that it varies between 0 and 1, Freeman showed that it actually varies between -0.50 and 1 and Q is not properly scaled. The upper limit of Q is a function of the number n of clusters, groups or communities on which it is calculated. It is always equal to (n-1)/n. Furthermore, the expectations used in Q are not strictly random. They are conditional on the degrees of all vertices in the graph under consideration. As I note, clustering of networks into communities or groups is a work in progress.

4. The algebra of block manipulation is beyond the scope of this elementary presentation.

5. See the discussion in White, Boorman, and Breiger (1976).

6. Coleman (1961) describes the "leading crowd" in high schools at some length and decries their influence on intellectual achievement.

7. We are using the abstractions of block models to depict types of non-overlapping networks segments, regardless of the actual algorithms or techniques that were used to discover them. It is easiest to discuss the core/periphery model in terms of absolutes or abstractions; in actual practice, being in the core or the periphery can be a matter of degree.

8. For a similar point, see Borgatti and Everett (1999).

CHAPTER 5

This chapter is a substantially revised version of Charles Kadushin, "The motivational foundation of social networks," *Social Networks* 24 (2002): 79–91. The comments and contributions of Richard Alba, H. Russell Bernard, and James Moody are gratefully acknowledged.

1. The original article reported 44 completed chains, but a somewhat modified version (published in Milgram 1969) reports 42 completed chains. I assume the revised version has the correct figure.

2. Ronald Fairbairn was a Scottish psychoanalyst who in the 1940s developed theories that were more concerned with relations between people than motivational drives. He was influential on the British object-relations theorists and later on American relational theorists, with whom Greenberg was identified.

3. But note the famous case of Rosa Parks who paid her fare, refused to give up her seat for a white person, and was arrested. At that time there was no trust between African Americans and southern whites.

4. Greenberg (1991) interprets conflict between a boy and his father not in terms of classic Oedipal theories, but rather in terms of balancing safety and effectiveness in a network that includes the mother. Suppose, for example, that the boy wins a tennis match with his father. "The boy is attached to his father by needs of various kinds (that is, needs for all the feelings of security that come from being a father's son) as well as by virtue of his love, loyalty and concern...At the same time...the boy is ambitious and wants to be competent, he is competitive and wants to win, he resents the years of subordination to the father and wants revenge...[but] the mother's role colors all that has happened ...Winning attaches him to his mother...or winning is a submission—in the act of winning the boy feels that he loses his autonomy by serving his mother's purpose." (16–17), depending on how the mother feels about the father. Note the complexity in Greenberg's formulation. The father-son-mother triangle contains both competition and support. In competing with the father, the son makes himself structurally similar to the father. The outcome of this competition eventually depends on the relation the two have to the mother. But regardless of whether support or efficacy is primary, the other is always present and so the outcome is necessarily conflictual.

5. The envy is not necessarily of the sibling. Psychological theory suggests that the parents in the family of origin are also envied for their power and omnipotence. One need not have a sibling to generate this motive. See the example from Greenberg in the previous footnote.

6. A search for "social support" recently produced over 43,000 items indexed on the "Northern Light" search engine that includes its special collections in sociology (564 items), health psychology (187 items), and mental health (2,704 items). Reviews include: Coyne and Downey 1991; Cohen and Herbert 1996; House, Umberson, and Landis 1988.

7. This schematic is my interpretation of Burt's diagram in *Brokerage and closure: An introduction to social capital* (2005, 226) and is based on a cumulative logistic function $z = lcf(x,0,1)/2+lcf(y,0,1)$ that may correspond to the model he has in mind.

8. This point was suggested by Bonnie Erickson, personal communication.

CHAPTER 6

This is a revision of Charles Kadushin, "Networks and small groups," *Structure and Dynamics: eJournal of Anthropological and Related Sciences* 1, no.1 (2005c): Article 5. S. D. Berkowitz edited an early draft that he had solicited for a reedited volume of *Social structure: A network approach*. H. Russell Bernard contributed insightful editing and trenchant comments. Linton Freeman made useful comments, as did Richard Alba. Douglas R. White corrected some errors and recomputed the Freeman graphs. Three anonymous reviewers for *Structure and dynamics* contributed important comments. The author is of course responsible for any remaining errors.

1. "For the purpose of theorizing, it is useful to start with a setting where no role (or status) differentiation exists. The imagery is one of undifferentiated actors milling about, waiting and watching for a directed action to occur" (Leifer and Rajah 2000, 255).

2. As will be recalled (chapter 3), "clique" is a well-worn sociological term that means some cluster in which the nodes are more connected with one another than they are with other nodes in the graph. As was pointed out in chapter 3, identifying cliques in this sense is hard to achieve with a network algorithm that works under all circumstances.

3. Some research finds similar characteristics in non-human groups (Faust and Skvoretz 2002 and the references they cite).

4. Some might argue that the very definition of informal political processes within organizations and in society generally is that they have limited visibility. Lifting the veil of invisibility is in part what both "muckraking" and organizational analysis have in common.

5. The Bank Wiring Room was an experimental room of 14 workmen who assembled sets of central office telephone switches or "banks." It was intensively observed for a period of six and one-half months from November 1931 to May 1932 by a research team at the Hawthorne plant of Western Electric and reported in 1939. The report contained detailed sociograms as well as detailed qualitative observations that Homans re-analyzed in his *Human Group* (1950), chapter 3, "The Bank Wiring Observation Room." The Bank Wiring Room will be further analyzed in the next chapter on organizations.

6. On the strategies of initiating and receiving interactions in groups in which clear roles have not yet been developed, see (Leifer and Rajah 2000).

7. In the Bank Wiring Room, for example, wiremen attached wires and then handed over the bank to a solderman who applied the final touch of fusing the connections. The wiremen initiated the interaction. It was not symmetrical.

8. Jacob Moreno (1953 [1934]) artificially constructed primary groups of adolescent delinquent girls who were incarcerated in an institution that housed them in separate cottages. Using the techniques of sociometry, he placed girls who liked one another into the same cottage rather than having cottages populated by warring cliques. When grouped into cottages with greater group cohesion, the girls were less likely to be cantankerous.

9. See chapter 3 for statuses or position with names.

10. See the explanation of "algorithm" in endnote 1, chapter 4.

11. For a comparative assessment of differing analyses of this dataset see Freeman 2003

12. Douglas White pointed out that Freeman's corresponding fig. 6.3 needed correction: #16 does not attend 4 events with #11, #12, or #13 (she goes to only two events herself), and similarly for #12 with #15, who coattend 3 events. The present figures have been re-graphed by White.

13. The classic graph-theoretic definition of a clique is too restrictive because it implies complete connectivity and is not the one used here. Rather, the intuitive sociological definition tends to correspond to the idea that members of a clique interact more with one another than they interact with others who are not in the clique, but while this seems simple enough, this idea is difficult to implement as discussed in chapter 3.

14. This is obviously true of "networks in a box" but is also true of some open systems. Examples include the production of scientific knowledge in which people cite each other's works; in the production system of scholarly books in which the readers, the writers and the editors are all part of the same social circle (Coser, Kadushin, and Powell 1982); in systems of power elites (Higley et al. 1991); and in inter-organizational relations.

15. Martin offers a dissenting view: "The quest for status [in gangs], far from leading to an ordering of members and ritualized signals of subordination, instead leads members to *deemphasize* whatever status differences there are" (Martin 2009, 141, italics in the original). Martin also interprets (Whyte 1943) and Homans's analysis of the "Norton Street Gang" as an authority tree and an incipient formal organization rather than a basic informal group.

16. Empirical tests of some of the propositions on real group data are congruent with Gould's mathematical predictions; proofs of the equations are found in Gould's appendix.

17. H. Russell Bernard (personal communication) points out that the leadership paradox relates to a problem in anthropology: How did pre-state chieftainship emerge? In chiefdoms, the chief can wind up being impoverished because he has to give so much to his constituents. This is illustrated by the phenomenon of "big men" in Malaysia (Sillitoe 1998).

18. In a similar process, as explained by Feld (1991) most people believe others have more friends than they do. The explanation is straightforward. People who have many friends are necessarily more likely to be in one's interpersonal environment than people who have few friends. So looking at my interpersonal environment, I come to the conclusion that most people have more friends than I do.

CHAPTER 7

This chapter has benefited from the comments of Michael Brimm, Cynthia Epstein, Bethamie Horowitz, Dani Maman, Amalya Oliver, Stuart Pizer, and Ted Sasson.

1. More recently, Mintzberg recognizes that conscious organizational designs succumb to "emergent strategies" in which organizations change their designs by observing what works in actual practice (Mintzberg 1994) These emergent forms are justified in ways reminiscent of the "garbage can" theory of organizational rationale in which solutions are justified after the fact (March, Simon, and Guetzkow 1993).

2. The importance of including nonhuman objects as actors in a social network is pointed out by Actor Network Theory (ANT; Latour 2005), which I otherwise find to be neither about networks nor theory.

3. The methodology and the conclusions of the Hawthorne studies have been criticized for a number of years, as reviewed by Jeffrey (1985). The present use of the findings, not necessarily the intent of the original researchers, is I believe not affected by the critique.

4. For a critique see Perrow (1986), his chapter 3.

5. In a recent review of networks and organizations (Brass et al. 2004), I have been able to find but one study of a simple factory floor-like organization. The propositions in that review, though cast in general terms, actually refer only to more complex organizations.

6. Punishing the organizational innovator is not uncommon (see Brimm 1988).

7. I am indebted to Amalya Oliver for this point, based on her observations of the complexities of the bio-tech industry.

8. "Need to know" is a principle not only in military and espionage organizations but also in corporate information and innovation-driven organizations.

9. The application of the idea of double bind to modern management was developed in an unpublished paper by Charles Kadushin and Michael Brimm.

10. Markets are an intriguing form of network, and if the hand that guides them is invisible, as Adam Smith would have it, there are important network laws and propositions about markets (White 2002).

11. Gossip columnists thrive on the situations in which friendship and trust break down, in some ways highlighting its importance.

12. Both the "markets and hierarchies" and "external economy" set of concepts are due to the school of institutional economics most prominently associated with (Commons 1934) and specifically for the theory of the firm in (Coase 1952 [1937]). These theories were the precursors of theories of network embeddedness.

13. Michael Brimm, who is based in Paris, contributed this point about bazaars and Paris. I have enjoyed watching him shop in local markets.

14. There is a veritable social network industry devoted to the topic of joint publication and citation. (See, for example, Alesia [2006].)

15. The Clustering Coefficient is the number of ties divided by the total number of possible ties that could exist (Watts and Strogatz 1998). The mean density is the average of the number of ties divided by the number of pairs in each ego network.

CHAPTER 8

One of the topics of this chapter, the small world and very large-scale networks, has been the subject of several books and many articles written in recent years by physicists and mathematicians. The articles are virtually unreadable by the average social scientist. At the same time, the books written for a general audience are necessarily behind some very rapid developments in this field and suffer from a "gee whiz" look-what-we-invented syndrome and tend not to be sociologically literate. The result is that these books alienate many social scientists. An exception, though already out of date, is the literate and sociologically aware review article by Duncan J. Watts (2004). The article summarizes his key findings in ways that many readers will find accessible. I am indebted to H. Russell Bernard, Tom Snijders, Barry Wellman, and Douglas R. White for comments on various parts of this chapter. They are of course not responsible for errors of omission or commission that I have committed.

1. For using "small world" methods to estimate the number of HIV-positive individuals, see Shelley et al. (2006). For finding heroin users, see Kadushin et al. (2006).

2. The U.S. Census cites 4,075,682 individuals whose first name is Michael. It is the fourth most popular name. There is even a web site that allows one to find these numbers: http://howmanyofme.com/.

3. We will henceforth call these power distributions rather than power law distributions because the term "law" carries more connotations than seem appropriate.

4. Adapted from Hamill and Gilbert (2009).

5. There are several network clustering algorithms based on this form of agglutination. (For an early attempt see Alba and Kadushin [1976].)

6. The title of the TV series "Madmen" is based on the idea that in the '60s the advertising industry was centered on Madison Avenue in New York. Today, most of the agencies are not located on Madison Avenue. BBDO, founded in 1928 is now BBDO World Wide with offices in 79 countries. Its headquarters is located on the Avenue of the Americas (Sixth Avenue in Madmen's era). The many offices reflect the need for face-to-face contact with clients.

7. The details of the algorithm and its relationship to other methods of finding positions and relations within networks are described in Moody and White (2003).

8. Actually, this is not correct. Milgram's published *success* rate from the Omaha sample was 0.25; recalculations have shown it to be 0.18. For the purposes of the model, this does not really matter.

CHAPTER 9

This chapter has benefited greatly from discussion with Thomas Valente who also generously allowed me to draw upon the manuscript of his book, *Social networks and health: Models, methods, and applications* (2010). Gary Robins added some important points. Cynthia Epstein helped to clarify the ideas.

1. Goldenweiser used the term mainly in a cultural context. In lectures, Robert Merton offered the oar and paddle example.

2. Now that AT&T is no longer a monopoly, it has to compete in the marketplace. AT&T now has an active and innovative consumer research program that includes the study of social networks.

3. Recent work has developed models for the simultaneous operation of social influence and tie selection (homophilous or otherwise). See Steglich, Snijders, and Pearson (2010). But Snijders in an email circulated to the Social Networks Association list (reproduced with his permission), notes that "Disentangling selection and influence is possible only under the assumption that the available observed networks and individual variables contain all the variables that play a role in the causal process, and if moreover a number of distributional assumptions are made...The sensitivity to the distributional assumptions is a serious question, and this is a topic that should and will be investigated. The assumption that all relevant variables are observed is always questionable, but statistical inference very often is done under such assumptions...As the great statistician R. A. Fisher said when asked how to make observational studies more likely to yield causal answers: 'Make your theories elaborate'".

4. "Economists Craig Garthwaite and Timothy Moore of the University of Maryland, College Park, contend that Ms. (Oprah) Winfrey's endorsement of Barack Obama last year gave him about one million votes in the primaries and caucuses." Brian Stelter, *New York Times*, Monday, August 11, 2008, C4.

5. Allen is better known for the "Allen Curve" which identifies the optimal distance between physical distance and communication in engineering labs—less than 50 meters.

6. To be sure, despite public health laws, individuals are reluctant to contact their partners or to provide information to public health authorities for these diseases as well, but the stakes and the laws are quite different than for HIV: "Case-finding has been a key component of tuberculosis control programs and contact tracing an important tool for active case-finding for many years" (Klovdahl et al. 2001).

7. For a general mathematical treatment of these methods see Meyers (2007).

8. Though it may be "obvious" the concept of resistance had not previously entered any of the diffusion models we have discussed. Contrast this with Dubos (1959) who makes resistance to germs a centerpiece of his theory. In this view, germs do not automatically lead to disease, and the so-called "germ theory of disease" needs to take this into account. Organizational innovation though lauded in theory is actually subjected to much resistance and the innovators are rarely rewarded (Brimm 1988).

9. The idea of threshold also fits the previously noted importance of resistance to a disease. The threshold of resistance must be overcome.

10. Opinion leadership has a more complicated relationship to threshold, however, since opinion leaders cannot get too far ahead of their peers because then they will not be listened to or be appropriate role models. It depends on the nature of the external influences and the phase of adoption of the entire network in ways we cannot get into here.

11. For the do-it-yourself devotees, try http://ccl.northwestern.edu/netlogo/docs/, which is a guide to the free NetLogo system. A more network-based ABM is Construct http://www. casos.cs.cmu.edu/projects/construct/software.php.

CHAPTER 10

This chapter has benefited from the comments of James Moody, Robert Putnam, and a close reading by Cynthia Epstein. The chapter is based in part on (Kadushin 2004).

1. An informative review of the history of the concept of social capital and some of its virtues and problems is Portes (1998). See also Moody and Paxton (2009) and the volume 4, issues 11 and 12 of *American Behavioral Scientist*.

2. See Bjarnason (2009) for a recent conceptual analysis.

3. Despite or because of the plethora of definitions, sociologists tend to use the word "community" loosely, often as an undefined "primitive" (in the logical sense of primitive). The ASA Section on Community and Urban Society as well as the journal *City & Community* define community through its extensions, that is, give examples of the kinds of communities they have in mind but do not offer a formal definition. Psychologists define community loosely as "people in their environment," meaning people in their natural settings (Riger 2001).

4. Current findings suggest that social networking sites and internet use create a "digital divide" in social capital between those adept with these media and those who are not (Hargittai 2008).

5. "It is a metaphor that misleads: Where can I borrow social capital? What is the going interest rate? Can I move some of my social capital off-shore?" (Fischer 2005).

6. "Though the low-income societies obtain most of the gains from self-enforcing trades... they do not have the institutions that enforce contracts impartially, and so they lose most of the largest gains.... They do not have institutions that make property rights secure in the long run, so they lose most of the gains from capital-intensive production.... The intricate social cooperation that emerges when there is a sophisticated array of markets requires far better institutions and economic policies than most countries have. The effective correction of market failures is even more difficult" (Olson 1996, 22).

7. Bourdieu's first use of the concept was in 1980 (Bourdieu 1980).

8. Putnam uses "or that you can't be too careful in dealing with people?" as does the European Social Survey which began in 2001. The question was first used in this form by Almond and Verba as, "Some people say that most people can be trusted. Others say you can't be too careful in your dealings with people. How do you feel about it?" (Almond and Verba 1963). The question derives from "Most people can be trusted" used in the original "F" scale by Adorno (1950).

9. Especially when individual-level social capital indicators are correlated with self-reported health, there is a possibility that a halo effect is responsible for the correlation. Respondents who report one "good" thing also report another.

CHAPTER 11

This chapter draws on text and material presented in my article (Kadushin 2005b). It has benefited from comments by Leonard Saxe and Andrew Braun.

1. The NORC General Social Survey module on social networks asks "Who are the people with whom you discuss an important personal matter.... Just tell me their first name or initial." One-tenth of 1% did not answer, while 2.3% of respondents did not answer the income question and an additional 0.7% claimed they did not know

2. Andrew Braun, former Director of Biological Safety for Harvard Medical School, concurs and feels that the privacy rules are irrelevant today (personal communication).

3. "Statistical confidentiality is an essential principle of modern demographic and economic data-gathering and related statistical research. Today, the term 'statistical confidentiality' encompasses in shorthand form a bundle of now widely-recognized activities. These may include legal protections, standards of professional conduct, a set of non-disclosure assurances provided to respondents, or compilation and dissemination practices designed to protect data providers from improper use of their answers" (Anderson and Seltzer 2009).

4. The Brandeis University Cohen Center for Modern Jewish Studies, with which I am affiliated, has placed the following notice on its web-based surveys: "This survey is anonymous. The record kept of your survey responses does not contain any identifying information about you unless a specific question in the survey has asked for this. If you have responded to a survey

that used an identifying token to allow you to access the survey, you can be rest assured that the identifying token is not kept with your responses. It is managed in a separate database, and will only be updated to indicate that you have (or haven't) completed this survey. There is no way of matching identification tokens with survey responses in this survey."

5. In the days before computer databases, it was almost totally impractical to check up on any one respondent. Now, with computers and linked files, it is easy enough if the links can be made, but from a practical point of view still useless to the researcher, though valuable to a law enforcement agency that may wish to discover who, for example, are using illegal drugs, if that is the topic of the survey. Public-use micro-data sets such as health surveys usually have simulated demographic data so as to make identification of respondents virtually impossible. It is important, however, that groundbreaking network findings from the Framingham study would not have been possible had key tracing data with names and addresses been not available. They were not originally, however, in machine readable format (Fowler and Christakis 2008). IRBs were not in place when the original study was started but in any case, respondents agreed that they could and would be traced for follow-up purposes.

6. See editorial, *New York Times*, July 16, 2009.

7. All these are publicly acknowledged. http://www.casos.cs.cmu.edu/projects/ora/sponsors.php, accessed June 28, 2011.

8. http://www.casos.cs.cmu.edu/projects/ora/, accessed June 28, 2011.

9. http://www.casos.cs.cmu.edu/projects/DyNet/dynet_info.html, accessed June 28, 2011. Both *ORA and DyNet have the following disclaimer: "The software is experimental only and has not been designed for, tested or approved for hazardous use. The use of the software is at the user's own risk. Any conclusions you may draw based on the software or its use are your own. We expressly disclaim any responsibility or liability for any and all adverse effects, including personal, bodily, property or business injury, and for damages or loss of any kind whatsoever, resulting directly or indirectly, whether from negligence, intent or otherwise, from the use or disuse of the software, from errors in the software, or from misunderstandings arising from the software itself, its use or its documentation."

10. http://www.casos.cs.cmu.edu/projects/NetEst/netest_info.html , accessed June 28, 2011.

11. http://www.analytictech.com/keyplayer/keyplayer.htm, accessed June 28, 2011.

12. SOCNET listserv, http://lists.ufl.edu/cgi-bin/wa?A1=ind0408&L=SOCNET, August 4, 2004. Copied with Waring's permission.

13. If the work is being done through an academic research institute, the rules of the academy apply. Generally, most universities require that all reports be published or available on the Web, and that the data be publically available through such data banks as ICPSR, with identifying information removed.

CHAPTER 12

1. For an excellent history of social networks see Freeman (2004).

Bibliography

Adamic, Lada, and Eytan Adar. 2005. How to search a social network. *Social Networks* 27 (3): 187–203.

Adorno, Theodor W. 1950. *The authoritarian personality, studies in prejudice: The American Jewish Committee* Social studies series, publication no. 3. New York: Harper.

Alba, Richard D. 1973. A graph-theoretic definition of a sociometric clique. *Journal of Mathematical Sociology* 3:113–126.

———, and Myron Guttman. 1972. SOCK: A sociometric analysis system. *Behavioral Science* 17:326.

Alba, Richard D., and Charles Kadushin. 1976. The intersection of social circles: A new measure of social proximity in networks. *Sociological Methods and Research* 5 (1): 77–102.

Alba, Richard D., and Gwen Moore. 1978. Elite social circles. *Sociological Methods and Research* 7 (November): 167–188.

Alesia, Zuccala. 2006. Modeling the invisible college. *Journal of the American Society for Information Science and Technology* 57 (2): 152–168.

Allen, Stephen. 1978. Organizational choices and general management influence networks in divisionalized companies. *Academy of Management Journal* (September): 341–365.

Allen, Thomas J. 1977. The role of person to person communication networks in the dissemination of industrial technology. Cambridge, Mass.: MIT Working Paper.

———, and Stephen I. Cohen. 1969. Information flow in research and development laboratories. *Administrative Science Quarterly* 14 (1): 12–19.

Almond, Gabriel A., and Sidney Verba. 1963. *The civic culture: Political attitudes and democracy in five nations*. Princeton, N.J.: Princeton University Press.

Amos, C., G. Holmes, and D. Strutton. 2008. Exploring the relationship between celebrity endorser effects and advertising effectiveness: A quantitative synthesis of effect size. *International Journal of Advertising* 27 (2): 209–234.

Anderson, Margo, and William Seltzer. 2009. Federal statistical confidentiality and business data: Twentieth-century challenges and continuing issues. *Journal of Privacy and Confidentiality* 1 (1): 7–52.

Antal, T., P. L. Krapivsky, and S. Redner. 2006. Social balance on networks: The dynamics of friendship and enmity. *Physica D: Nonlinear Phenomena* 224 (1–2): 130–136.

Aral, Sinan, and Marshall W. Van Alstyne. 2008. Networks, information and brokerage: The diversity-bandwidth tradeoff (formerly titled "Network structure and information advantage"). Workshop on Information Systems Economics 2006, International Conference on Network Science 2007, Academy of Management Conference 2007.

Armelagos, George J., and Kristin N. Harper. 2005. Genomics at the origins of agriculture, part two. *Evolutionary Anthropology: Issues, News, and Reviews* 14 (3): 109–121.

Asch, Solomon E. 1951. Effects of group pressure upon the modification and distortion of judgments. In *Groups, leadership and men: Research in human relations*, edited by H. S. Guetzkow. Pittsburgh, Pa.: Carnegie Press.

Bailey, Stefanie, and Peter V. Marsden. 1999. Interpretation and interview context: Examining the General Social Survey name generator using cognitive methods. *Social Networks* 21 (3): 287.

Baker, Wayne, and Robert R. Faulkner. 1991. Role as resource in the Hollywood film industry. *American Journal of Sociology* 97 (2): 279–309.

———. 1993. The social organization of conspiracy: Illegal networks in the heavy electrical equipment industry. *American Sociological Review* 58:837–860.

———. 2009. Social capital, double embeddedness, and mechanisms of stability and change. *American Behavioral Scientist* 52 (11): 1531–1555.

Baldassarri, Delia, and Mario Diani. 2007. The integrative power of civic networks. *American Journal of Sociology* 113 (3): 735–780.

Barabási, Albert-Laszló. 2002. *Linked: The new science of networks*. Cambridge, Mass.: Perseus Publishing Co.

Barabási, A. L., and R. Albert. 1999. Emergence of scaling in random networks. *Science* 286 (5439): 509–512.

Barnard, Chester I. 1938. *The functions of the executive*. Cambridge, Mass.: Harvard University Press.

Barnes, J. A. 1972. Social networks. In *Module* 26, edited by J. B. Casagrande, W. Goodenough, and E. Hammel. Boston: Addison-Wesley.

Bateson, Gregory. 1972. Double bind, 1969. In *Steps to an ecology of mind*, edited by G. Bateson. New York: Ballentine.

Bavelas, Alex. 1948. A mathematical model for small group structures. *Human Organization* 7:16–30.

Beatles, The. 1967. *Sgt. Pepper's lonely heart's club band: With a little help from my friends*. Los Angeles: Capital Records.

Becker, Gary Stanley. 1964. *Human capital: A theoretical and empirical analysis, with special reference to education, National Bureau of Economic Research: General series*. New York: National Bureau of Economic Research; distributed by Columbia University Press.

Beggs, John J., Valerie A. Haines, and Jeanne S. Hurlbert. 1996. Revisiting the rural-urban contrast: Personal networks in nonmetropolitan and metropolitan settings. *Rural Sociology* 61 (2): 306–325.

Berelson, Bernard , Paul F. Lazarsfeld, and William N. McPhee. 1954. *Voting: A study of opinion formation in a presidential campaign*. Chicago: University of Chicago Press.

Berkowitz, Bill. 2001. Studying the outcomes of community-based coalitions. *American Journal of Community Psychology* 29 (2): 213–227.

Bernard, H. Russell, and Peter D. Killworth. 1979. Why are there no social physics. *Journal of the Steward Anthropological Society* 11 (1): 33–58.

Bernard, H. Russell, Eugene C. Johnsen, Peter D. Killworth, and Scott Robinson. 1989. Estimating the size of an average personal network and of an event subpopulation. In *The small world*, edited by M. Kochen. Norwood, N.J.: Ablex Publishing Co.

Bjarnason, Thoroddur. 2009. Anomie among European adolescents: Conceptual and empirical clarification of a multilevel sociological concept. *Sociological Forum* 24 (1): 135–161.

Blau, Peter Michael. 1955. *The Dynamics of bureaucracy*. Glencoe, Ill: Free Press.

———. 1964. *Exchange and power in social life*. New York: Wiley.

———, and Joseph E. Schwartz. 1984. *Crosscutting social circles: Testing a macrostructural theory of intergroup relations*. New York: Academic Press.

———, and W. Richard Scott. 1962. *Formal organizations: A comparative approach*. Chandler publications in anthropology. San Francisco: Chandler Publishing Co.

Boase, Jeffrey, John B. Horrigan, Barrry Wellman, and Lee Rainie. 2006. The strength of Internet ties. Washington, D.C.: Pew Internet and American Life Project.

Boissevain, Jeremy. 1974. *Friends of friends: Networks, manipulators and coalitions*. London: Basil Blackwell.

Borgatti, Stephen P. 2006. Identifying sets of key players in a social network. *Computational and Mathematical Organization Theory* 12 (1): 21–34.

———. 2003. The key player problem. In *Dynamic social network modeling and analysis: Workshop summary and papers*, edited by R. Breiger, K. Carley and P. Pattison. Washington, D.C.: National Academy of Sciences Press.

———, and Martin G. Everett. 1992. Notions of position in social network analysis. *Sociological Methodology* 22:1–35.

———. 1999. Models of core/periphery structure. *Social Networks* 21 (4): 375–395.

———, and Linton C. Freeman. 2004. *UCINET 6 for Windows: Software for social network analysis*. Analytic Technologies, Harvard, Cambridge, Mass.

Borgatti, Stephen P., and Pacey C. Foster. 2003. The network paradigm in organizational research: A review and typology. *Journal of Management* 29 (6): 991–1013.

———, and José-Luis Molina 2003. Ethical and strategic issues in organizational social network analysis. *Journal of Applied Behavioral Science* 39 (3): 337–350.

———. 2005. Toward ethical guidelines for network research in organizations. *Social Networks* 27 (2): 107–117.

Bourdieu, Pierre. 1980. Le capital social: Notes provisoires. *Actes de la recherche en sciences sociales* 31 (January): 2–3.

———. 1985. The forms of capital. In *Handbook of Theory and Research for the Sociology of Education*, edited by J. G. Richardson. New York: Greenwood.

———, and Loïc J. D. Wacquant. 1992. *An invitation to reflexive sociology*. Chicago: University of Chicago Press.

boyd, danah michele. 2008. *Taken out of context: American teen sociality in networked publics*. PhD diss., Information Management and Systems, University of California, Berkeley.

Brass, Daniel J., Joseph Galaskiewicz, Henrich R. Greve, and Tsai Wenpin. 2004. Taking stock of networks and organizations: A multilevel perspective. *Academy of Management Journal* 47 (6): 795–817.

Breiger, Ronald. 1974. The duality of persons and groups. *Social Forces* 53:181–190.

———, Scott A. Boorman, and P. Arabie. 1975. An algorithm for clustering relational data, with applications to social network analysis and comparison with multi-dimensional scaling. *Journal of Mathematical Psychology* 12:328–383.

Brimm, I. Michael. 1988. Risky business: Why sponsoring innovations may be hazardous to career health. *Organizational Dynamics* 16 (3): 28–41.

Brown, Timothy T., Richard M. Scheffler, Sukyong Seo, and Mary Reed. 2006. The empirical relationship between community social capital and the demand for cigarettes. *Health Economics* 15 (11): 1159–1172.

Browning, Christopher R. 2009. Illuminating the downside of social capital: Negotiated coexistence, property crime, and disorder in urban neighborhoods. *American Behavioral Scientist* 52 (11): 1556–1578.

Burns, T., and G. M. Stalker. 1961. *The management of innovation*. London: Tavistock Publications.

Burt, Ronald S. 1982. *Toward a structural theory of action: Network models of social structure, perception and action*. New York: Academic Press.

———. 1984. Network items and the General Social Survey. *Social Networks* 6:293–339.

———. 1987. Social contagion and innovation: Cohesion versus structural equivalence. *American Journal of Sociology* 92:1287–1355.

———. 1992. *Structural holes: The social structure of competition*. Cambridge, Mass.: Harvard University Press.

———. 1999. The social capital of opinion leaders. *Annals of the American Academy of Political and Social Science* 566 (1): 37–54.

———. 2000. The network structure of social capital. In *Research in organizational behavior*, edited by R. I. Sutton and B. M. Staw. Greenwich, Conn.: JAI Press.

———. 2002. Bridge decay. *Social Networks* 24 (4): 333–363.

———. 2005. *Brokerage and closure: An introduction to social capital*. Oxford: Oxford University Press.

———. 2006. Closure and stability: Persistent reputation and enduring relations among bankers and analysts. In *Formation and Decay of Economic Networks*, edited by J. E. Rauch. New York: Russell Sage.

———, Joseph E. Jannotta, and James T. Mahoney. 1998. Personality correlates of structural holes. *Social Networks* 20:63–87.

Buskens, Vincent, and Arnout van de Rijt. 2008. Dynamics of Networks if Everyone Strives for Structural Holes. *American Journal of Sociology* 114 (2): 371–407.

Camitz, Martin, and Fredrik Liljeros. 2006. The effect of travel restrictions on the spread of a moderately contagious disease. *BMC Medicine* 4 (1): 32.

Carley, Kathleen, Jeffrey Reminga, and Natasha Kamneva. 2003. Destabilizing terrorist networks. Pittsburgh, Pa.: Carnegie Mellon University, Institute for Software Research International.

Centers for Disease, Control, and Prevention. 2005. Guidelines for the investigation of contacts of persons with infectious tuberculosis. *Morbidity and Mortality Weekly Report* 54 (RR 15): 1–47.

———. 2010. Epi glossary. http://www.cdc.gov/reproductivehealth/Data_Stats/Glossary.htm#E (accessed September 2010).

Chandler, Alfred. 1977. *The visible hand*. Cambridge, Mass.: Belknap Press.

Charuvastra, Anthony, and Marylene Cloitre. 2008. Social bonds and posttraumatic stress disorder. *Annual Review of Psychology* 59 (1): 301–328.

Chiang, Yen-Sheng. 2007. Birds of moderately different feathers: Bandwagon dynamics and the threshold heterogeneity of network neighbors. *Journal of Mathematical Sociology* 31 (1): 47–69.

Christakis, Nicholas A., and James H. Fowler. 2007. The spread of obesity in a large social network over 32 years. *New England Journal of Medicine* 357 (4): 370–379.

Clauset, Aaron, Cosma Rohilla Shalizi, and M. E. J. Newman. 2009. Power-law distributions in empirical data. *arXiv:0706.1062v1 [physics.data-an]*.

Coase, Ronald H. 1952 (1937). The nature of the firm. In *Readings in price theory*, edited by G. J. Stigler and K. E. Boulding. Homewood, Ill.: Irwin.

Cohen, Sheldon, and S. Leonard Syme. 1985. *Social support and health*. Orlando, Fla.: Academic Press.

———, and Tracy B. Herbert. 1996. Health psychology: psychological factors and physical disease from the perspective of psychoneuroimmunology. *Annual Review of Psychology* 47:113–142.

Coleman, James S. 1957. *Community conflict*. Glencoe, Ill.: Free Press.

———. 1961. *The adolescent society: The social life of the teenager and its impact on education*. New York: Free Press.

———. 1990. *Foundations of social theory*. Cambridge, Mass.: Harvard University Press.

———, Elihu Katz, and Herbert Menzel. 1966. *Medical innovation: A diffusion study*. New York: Bobbs Merril.

Colizza, Vittoria, Alain Barrat, Marc Barthelemy, and Alessandro Vespignani. 2006. The role of the airline transportation network in the prediction and predictability of global epidemics. *Proceedings of the National Academy of Sciences of the United States of America* 103 (7): 2015–2020.

Commons, John Rogers. 1934. *Institutional economics: Its place in political economy*. New York: Macmillan.

Conti, Norman, and Patrick Doreian. 2010. Social network engineering and race in a police academy: A longitudinal analysis. *Social Networks* 32 (1): 30–43.

Cook, Karen S. 2001. *Trust in society, Russell Sage Foundation series on trust*. New York: Russell Sage Foundation.

Cooley, Charles Horton. 1909. *Social organization*. New York: Charles Scribner's Sons.

Coser, Lewis A., Charles Kadushin, and Walter A. Powell. 1982. *Books: The culture and commerce of publishing*. New York: Basic Books.

Coser, Rose Laub. 1975. The complexity of roles as a seedbed of individual autonomy. In *The idea of social structure: Papers in honor of Robert K. Merton*, edited by L. A. Coser. New York: Harcourt Brace Jovanovich.

Cote, Rochelle R., and Bonnie H. Erickson. 2009. Untangling the roots of tolerance: How forms of social capital shape attitudes toward ethnic minorities and immigrants. *American Behavioral Scientist* 52 (12): 1664–1689.

Council, National Research. 2003. *Protecting participants and facilitating social and behavioral sciences research*. Washington, D.C.: National Academies Press.

Coyne, J. C., and G. Downey. 1991. Social factors and psychopathology: Stress, social support, and coping processes. *Annual Review of Psychology* 42:401–425.

Craven, Paul, and Barry Wellman. 1973. The network city. *Sociological Inquiry* 43:57–88.

Cross, Jennifer L. Moren, and Nan Lin. 2008. Access to social capital and status attainment in the United States: Racial/ethnic and gender differences. In *Social capital: An international research program*, edited by N. Lin and B. H. Erickson. Oxford: Oxford University Press.

Cross, Rob, Stephen P. Borgatti, and Andrew Parker. 2001. Beyond answers: Dimensions of the advice network. *Social Networks* 23 (3): 215–235.

Dahl, Robert A. 1961. *Who governs?* New Haven, Conn.: Yale University Press.

Davis, Allison, Burleigh B. Gardner, and Mary R. Gardner. 1941. *Deep South, a social anthropological study of caste and class*. Chicago: University of Chicago Press.

Davis, Kingsley, and Wilbert E. Moore. 1945. Some principles of stratification. *American Sociological Review* 10 (2): 242–249.

De, Prithwish, Joseph Cox, Jean-François Boivin, Robert W. Platt, and Ann M. Jolly. 2007. The importance of social networks in their association to drug equipment sharing among injection drug users: A review. *Addiction* 102 (11): 1730–1739.

Dean, Dwane Hal. 1999. Brand endorsement, popularity, and event sponsorship as advertising cues affecting consumer pre-purchase attitudes. *Journal of Advertising* 28 (3): 1–12.

Dictionary, Oxford English. Networking, n. http://www.oed.com/viewdictionaryentry/Entry/235272 (accessed June 29, 2011).

Dodds, P. S., R. Muhamad, and D. J. Watts. 2003. An experimental study of search in global social networks. *Science* 301 (5634): 827–829.

Domhoff, G. William. 1967. *Who rules America?* Englewood Cliffs, N.J.: Prentice-Hall.

———. 1978. *Who really rules? New Haven and community power reexamined*. New Brunswick, N.J.: Transaction Books.

Donne, John. 1999 [1624]. Meditation XVII. In *Devotions upon emergent occasions*. New York: Random House.

Doreian, Patrick, Vladimir Batagelj, and Anuška Ferligoj. 2005. Positional analyses of sociometric data. In *Models and methods in social network analysis*, edited by P. Carrington, J. Scott, and S. Wasserman. New York: Cambridge University Press.

Dubos, René J. 1959. *Mirage of health: Utopias, progress, and biological change*. 1st ed., *World perspectives*. New York: Harper.

Dufur, Mikaela J., Toby L. Parcel, and Benjamin A. McKune. 2008. Capital and context: Using social capital at home and at school to predict child social adjustment. *Journal of Health and Social Behavior* 49:146–161.

Dunbar, R. I. M. 1993. Coevolution of neocortical size, group size and language in humans. *Behavioral and Brain Sciences* 16:681–694.

Durkheim, Émile. 1951 [1897]. *Suicide: A study in sociology*. Glencoe, Ill.: Free Press.

———. 1947 [1902]. *The division of labor in society*. Glencoe, Ill: Free Press.

Eccles, Robert G., and Dwight B. Crane. 1988. *Doing deals: Investment banks at work*. Boston, Mass.: Harvard Business School Press.

Edin, Per-Anders, Peter Fredriksson, and Olof Åslund. 2003. Ethnic enclaves and the economic success of immigrants: Evidence from a natural experiment. *Quarterly Journal of Economics* 118 (1): 329–357.

Editorial, *New York Times*. July 16, 2009. Illegal and pointless. *New York Times*, http://www.nytimes.com/2009/07/17/opinion/17fri1.html?_r=1&hpw (accessed July 17, 2009).

Egan, Matt, Carol Tannahill, Mark Petticrew, and Sian Thomas. 2008. Psychosocial risk factors in home and community settings and their associations with population health and health inequalities: A systematic meta-review. *BMC Public Health* 8 (1): 239.

Ekeh, Peter P. 1974. *Social exchange theory: The two traditions*. Cambridge, Mass.: Harvard University Press.

Epstein, Jason. 2010. Publishing: The revolutionary future. *New York Review of Books* 57 (4): http://www.nybooks.com/articles/23683.

Erickson, Bonnie H. 1988. The relational basis of attitudes. In *Social structures: A network approach*, edited by B. Wellman and S. D. Berkowitz. New York: Cambridge University Press.

———. 1996. Culture, class and connections. *American Journal of Sociology* 102 (1): 217–251.

Erikson, Kai. 1976. *Everything in its path: Destruction of community in the Buffalo Creek flood.* New York: Simon and Schuster.

Etzioni, Amitai. 1961. *A comparative analysis of complex organizations: On power, involvement, and their correlates.* New York: Free Press of Glencoe.

Farrell, Michael B. August 21, 2009 Facebook faces (another) challenge over users' privacy. *Christian Science Monitor*, http://www.csmonitor.com/Innovation/Tech-Culture/2009/0821/facebook-faces-another-challenge-over-users-privacy (accessed June 28, 2011).

Faulkner, Robert. 1980. In *Centrality in a freelance social structure: Social networks in big Hollywood.* New Brunswick, N.J.: Transaction Books.

Faust, Katherine. 2007. Very local structure in social networks. *Sociological Methodology* 37:209–256.

———, and J. Skvoretz. 2002. Comparing networks across space and time, size and species. *Sociological Methodology* 32:267–299.

Feld, Scott L. 1981. The focused organization of social ties. *American Journal of Sociology* 86 (5): 1015–1035.

———. 1991. Why your friends have more friends than you do. *American Journal of Sociology* 96 (6): 1464–1477.

———, and William C. Carter. 1998. Foci of activities as changing contexts for friendship. In *Placing friendship in context*, edited by R. G. Adams and G. Allan. Cambridge: Cambridge University Press.

Feldman, Tine Rossing, and Susan Assaf. 1999. Social capital: Conceptual frameworks and empirical evidence: An annotated bibliography. Social Capital Initiative Working Paper 5. Washington, D.C.: World Bank.

Fernandez, Roberto M., and Emillio Castilla. 2001. How much is that network worth? Social capital in employee referral networks. In *Social capital: Theory and research*, edited by N. Lin, K. Cook and R. S. Burt. New York: Aldine de Gruyter.

Fernandez, Roberto M., and M. Lourdes Sosa. 2005. Gendering the job: Networks and recruitment at a call center. *American Journal of Sociology* 111 (3): 859

Festinger, L., S. Schacter, and K. Back. 1950. *Social pressures in informal groups: A study of human factors in housing.* Stanford, Calif.: Stanford University Press.

Finckenauer, James, and Elin Waring. 1997. Russian emigre crime in the U.S.: Organized crime or crime that is organized? In *Russian organized crime: The new threat?* edited by P. Williams. London: Frank Cass.

———. 1998. *Russian mafia in America: Crime, immigration, and culture.* Boston: Northeastern University Press.

Fischer, Claude S. 1982. *To dwell among friends.* Chicago: University of Chicago Press.

———. 1992. *America calling: A social history of the telephone to 1940.* Berkeley and Los Angeles: University of California Press.

———. 2005. *Bowling Alone*: What's the score? *Social Networks* 27 (2): 155–167.

Fowler, James H., and Nicholas A. Christakis. 2008. *Supplementary online material for: Dynamic spread of happiness in a large social network: Longitudinal analysis over 20 years in the Framingham heart study.* Available from http://jhfowler.ucsd.edu/dynamic_spread_of_happiness_supplement.pdff.

Frank, Kenneth A. 2009. Quasi-Ties: Directing resources to members of a collective. *American Behavioral Scientist* 52 (12): 1613–1645.

———, Chandra Muller, Kathryn S. Schiller, Catherine Riegle-Crumb, Anna Strassmann Mueller, Robert Crosnoe, and Jennifer Pearson. 2008. The social dynamics of mathematics course taking in high school. *American Journal of Sociology* 113 (6): 1645–1696.

———, and Jeffrey Y. Yasumoto. 1998. Linking action to social structure within a system: Social capital within and between subgroups. *American Journal of Sociology* 104 (3): 642–686.

Freeman, Linton. 1979. Centrality in social networks: I. Conceptual clarification. *Social Networks* 1:215–239.

———. 1992. The sociological concept of "group": An empirical test of two models. *American Journal of Sociology* 98 (1): 152–166.

———. 2003. Finding groups: A meta-analysis of the southern women data. In *Dynamic Social Network Modeling and Analysis*, edited by R. Breiger, K. Carley and P. E. Pattison. Washington, D.C.: The National Academies Press.

———. 2004. *The development of social network analysis: A study in the sociology of science*. Vancouver, B.C.: Empirical Press.

Friedkin, Noah E., and Karen S. Cook. 1990. Peer group influence. *Sociological Methods Research* 19 (1): 122–143.

Friedman, Samuel R., Melissa Bolyard, Pedro Mateu-Gelabert, Paula Goltzman, Maria Pia Pawlowicz, Dhan Zunino Singh, Graciela Touze, Diana Rossi, Carey Maslow, Milagros Sandoval, and Peter L. Flom. 2007. Some data-driven reflections on priorities in AIDS network research. *AIDS and Behavior* 11 (5): 641–651.

Fromm, Erich. 1941. *Escape from freedom*. New York: Holt, Rinehart and Winston.

Gabbay, Shaul M., Ilan Talmud, and Ornit Raz. 2001. Corporate social capital and strategic isomorphism: The case of the Israeli software industry. In *Social capital of organizations*, edited by S. M. Gabbay and R. T. A. J. Leenders. Oxford: Elsevier.

Galaskiewicz, Joseph, Wolfgang Bielefeld, and Myron Dowell. 2006. Networks and organizational growth: A study of community based nonprofits. *Administrative Science Quarterly* 51 (3): 337–380.

Garfinkel, Harold. 1967. *Studies in ethnomethodology*. Englewood Cliffs, N.J.: Prentice-Hall.

Garip, Filiz. 2008. Social capital and migration: How do similar resources lead to divergent outcomes? *Demography* 45 (3): 591–617.

Gautreau, Aurélien, Alain Barrat, and Marc Barthélemy. 2008. Global disease spread: Statistics and estimation of arrival times. *Journal of Theoretical Biology* 251 (3): 509–522.

General Electric Company. 2000. Annual Report 1999. Fairfield, Conn.: General Electric Company.

Geroski, P. A. 2000. Models of technology diffusion. *Research Policy* 29 (4–5): 603–625.

Gertner, Jon. 2003. The 3rd annual year in ideas. *New York Times*, December 14, 2003, Sunday, 92.

Gillies, Donald. 2008. Review of *Hasok Chang, Inventing temperature: Measurement and scientific progress*. *British Journal for the Philosophy of Science* 60 (1): 221–228.

Girvan, M., and M. E. J. Newman. 2002. Community structure in social and biological networks. *Proceedings of the National Academy of Sciences of the United States of America* 99 (12): 7821–7826.

Gladwell, Malcom. 2000. *The tipping point: How little things can make a big difference*. New York: Little, Brown & Co.

Glanville, Jennifer L., and Elisa Jayne Bienenstock. 2009. A typology for understanding the connections among different forms of social capital. *American Behavioral Scientist* 52 (11): 1507–1530.

Goffman, Erving. 1967. *Interaction ritual: Essays on face-to-face behavior*. 1st ed. Garden City, N.Y.: Anchor Books.

Goldenweiser, Alexander. 1922. *Early civilization: An introduction to anthropology*. New York: A. A. Knopf.

Goodman, Paul. 1959. *The empire city*. Indianapolis, Ind.: Bobbs-Merrill.

Gould, Roger V. 2002. The origins of status hierarchies: A formal theory and empirical test. *American Journal of Sociology* 107 (5): 1143–1178.

Granovetter, Mark S. 1973. The strength of weak ties. *American Journal of Sociology* 78:1360–1380.

———. 1978. Threshold models of collective behavior. *American Journal of Sociology* 83 (6): 1420–1443.

———. 1982. The strength of weak ties: A network theory revisited. In *Social structure and network analysis*, edited by P. Marsden and N. Linn. Beverly Hills, Calif.: Sage.

———, and Roland Soong. 1983. Threshold models of diffusion and collective behavior. *Journal of Mathematical Sociology* 9:165–179.

Greenberg, Jay. 1991. *Oedipus and beyond: A clinical theory*. Cambridge, Mass.: Harvard University Press.

Haidt, Jonathan, and Judith Rodin. 1999. Control and efficacy as interdisciplinary bridges. *Review of General Psychology* 3 (4): 317–337.

Hall, Alan, and Barry Wellman, 1985. Social networks and social support. In *Social support and health*, edited by Sheldon Cohen and S. Leonard Syme. Orlando: Academic Press.

Hallinan, Maureen T. 1982. Classroom racial composition and children's friendships. *Social Forces* 61:56–72.

———, and Richard Williams. 1989. Interracial friendship choices in secondary schools. *American Sociological Review* 54:67–78.

Hamill, Lynne, and Nigel Gilbert. 2009. Social circles: A simple structure for agent-based social network models. *Journal of Artificial Societies and Social Simulation* 12 (2): 3.

Hannan, Michael T., and John Freeman. 1989. *Organizational ecology*. Cambridge, Mass.: Harvard University Press.

Hansen, Morton T., Joel M. Podolny, and Jeffrey Pfeffer. 2001. So many ties, so little time: A task contingency perspective on social capital in organizations. In *Social capital of organizations*, edited by S. M. Gabbay and R. T. A. J. Leenders. Oxford: Elsevier.

Harary, Frank, Robert Z. Norman, and Dorwin Cartrwright. 1965. *Structural models: An introduction to the theory of directed graphs*. New York: Wiley.

Hargittai, Eszter. 2008. The digital reproduction of inequality. In *Social Stratification*, edited by D. Grusky. Boulder, Colo.: Westview Press.

Harrington, Brooke. 2001. Organizational performance and corporate social capital: A contingency model. In *Social capital of organizations*, edited by S. M. Gabbay and R. T. A. J. Leenders. Oxford: Elsevier.

Hartvigsen, G., J. M. Dresch, A. L. Zielinski, A. J. Macula, and C. C. Leary. 2007. Network structure, and vaccination strategy and effort interact to affect the dynamics of influenza epidemics. *Journal of Theoretical Biology* 246 (2): 205–213.

Hauhart, Robert. 2003. The Davis–Moore theory of stratification: The life course of a socially constructed classic. *American Sociologist* 34 (4): 5–24.

Haynie, Dana L. 2001. Delinquent peers revisited: Does network structure matter? *American Journal of Sociology* 106 (4): 1013–1057.

Headland, Thomas N., Kenneth A. Pike, and Marvin Harris. 1990. *Emics and etics: The insider/outsider debate, frontiers of anthropology*. Newbury Park, Calif.: Sage Publications.

Heider, Fritz. 1946. Attitudes and cognitive organization. *Journal of Psychology* 21:107–112.

Hendrick, Ives. 1942. Instinct and the ego during infancy. *Psychoanalytic Quarterly* 11:33–58.

Higley, John, and Gwen Moore. 1981. Elite integration in the United States and Australia. *American Political Science Review* 75 (3): 581–597.

Higley, John, Ursula Hoffmann-Lange, Charles Kadushin, and Gwen Moore. 1991. Elite integration in stable democracies: A reconsideration. *European Sociological Review* 7 (1): 35–53.

Hill, R. A., and R. I. M. Dunbar. 2003. Social network size in humans. *Human Nature* 14:53–72.

Homans, George Casper. 1950. *The human group*. New York: Harcourt, Brace.

———, and David M. Schneider. 1955. *Marriage, authority and final causes*. Glencoe, Ill.: Free Press.

Hoover, Edgar M., and Raymond Vernon. 1962. *Anatomy of a metropolis: The changing distribution of people and jobs within the New York metropolitan region*. New York: Anchor Books.

House, James S., Karl R. Landis, and Debra Umberson. 1988. Social relationships and health. *Science* 241 (July 29, 1988): 540–545.

Huberman, B. A., C. H. Loch, and A. Onculer. 2004. Status as a valued resource. *Social Psychology Quarterly* 67 (1): 103–114.

Hubert, Lawrence, and James Schultz. 1976. Quadratic assignment as a general data analysis strategy. *British Journal of Mathematics, Statistics and Psychology* 29:190–241.

Hunter, Floyd. 1953. *Community power structure*. Durham: University of North Carolina Press.

Hurlbert, Jeanne S., John J. Beggs, and Valerie Haines. 2001. Social networks and social capital in extreme environments. In *Social capital theory and research*, edited by N. Lin, K. S. Cook, and R. S. Burt. New York: Aldine de Gruyter.

Hutchinson, Delyse, and Ronald M. Raspee. 2007. Do friends share similar body image and eating problems? The role of social networks and peer influences in early adolescence. *Behaviour Research and Therapy* 45:1557–1577.

Ibarra, Herminia, Martin Kilduff, and Tsai Wenpin. 2005. Zooming in and out: Connecting individuals and collectivities at the frontiers of organizational network research. *Organization Science* 16 (4): 359–371.

Institutes of Health, National. 1997. *The Adolescent Health Study* NIH. Cited August 25, 2008. Available from http:// www.nih.gov/news/pr/sept97/chd-09.htm.

Jaques, Elliott. 1976. *A general theory of bureaucracy*. London, New York: Heinemann; Halsted Press.

Jeffrey, A. Sonnenfeld. 1985. Shedding light on the Hawthorne studies. *Journal of Organizational Behavior* 6 (2): 111–130.

Johanson, Jan-Erik. 2001. The balance of corporate social capital. In *Social capital of organizations*, edited by S. M. Gabbay and R. T. A. J. Leenders. Oxford: Elsevier.

Jure, Leskovec, A. Adamic Lada, and A. Huberman Bernardo. 2007. The dynamics of viral marketing. *ACM TransActions on the Web* 1 (1): 5.

Kadushin, Charles. 1966. The friends and supporters of psychotherapy: On social circles in urban life. *American Sociological Review* 31:786–802.

———. 1968a. Power, influence and social circles: A new methodology for studying opinion-makers. *American Sociological Review* 33:685–699.

———. 1968b. Reason analysis. In *International encyclopedia of the social sciences*, edited by D. L. Sills. New York: Macmillan, Free Press.

———. 1969. The professional self-concept of music students. *American Journal of Sociology* 75 (3): 389–404.

———. 1976. Networks and circles in the production of culture. *American Behavioral Scientist* 19:769–784.

———. 1981. Notes on the expectations of reward in n-person networks. In *Continuities in structural inquiry*, edited by P. Blau and R. K. Merton. London: Sage.

———. 1995. Friendship among the French financial elite. *American Sociological Review* 60 (2): 202–221.

———. 2004. Too much investment in social capital? *Social Networks* 26:75–90.

———. 2005a. *The American intellectual elite: Republication of the 1974 edition, with a new introduction*. Sommerset, N.J.: Transaction.

———. 2005b. Who benefits from network analysis: Ethics of social network research. *Social Networks* 27 (2): 139–153.

———. 2005c. Networks and small groups. *Structure and Dynamics: eJournal of Anthropological and Related Sciences* 1 (1): Article 5.

———. 2006 [1969]. *Why people go to psychiatrists*. New Brunswick: Aldine Transaction [originally published by Atherton].

———, and Peter Abrams. 1973a. Opinion-making elites in Yugoslavia. Part 1, Informal leadership. In *Social structure of Yugoslav opinion-makers.*, edited by A. Barton, B. Denitch and C. Kadushin. New York: Praeger.

———. 1973b. Social structure of Yugoslav opinion-makers. Part 2, Formal and informal influences and their consequences for opinion. In *Opinion-making elites in Yugoslavia*, edited by A. Barton, B. Denitch, and C. Kadushin. New York: Praeger.

Kadushin, Charles, and Delmos Jones. 1992. Social networks and urban neighborhoods in New York City. *City & Society* 6 (1): 58–75.

Kadushin, Charles, Peter D. Killworth, H. Russell Bernard, and Andrew Beveridge. 2006. Scale-up methods as applied to estimates of heroin use. *Journal of Drug Issues* 36 (2): 417–439.

Kadushin, Charles, Matthew Lindholm, Dan Ryan, Archie Brodsky, and Leonard Saxe. 2005. Why it is so difficult to form effective community coalitions. *City & Community* 4 (3): 255–275.

Kalish, Yuval, and Garry Robins. 2006. Psychological predispositions and network structure: The relationship between individual predispositions, structural holes and network closure. *Social Networks* 28:56–84.

Karlsson, Diana, Andreas Jansson, Birgitta Normark, and Patric Nilsson. 2008. An individual-based network model to evaluate interventions for controlling pneumococcal transmission. *BMC Infectious Diseases* 8 (1): 1–10.

Kashima, Yoshisia, Emiko S. Kashima, Paul Bain, Anthony Lyons, R. Scott Tindale, Garry Robins, Cedric Vears, and Jennifer Whelan. 2010. Communication and essentialism: Grounding the shared reality of a social category. *Social Cognition* 28 (3): 306–328.

Katz, Elihu. 1957. The 2-step flow of communication: An up-to-date report on an hypothesis. *Public Opinion Quarterly* 21 (1): 61–78.

———. 1960. Communication research and the image of society: Convergence of two traditions. *The American Journal of Sociology* 65 (5): 435–440.

———, and Paul F. Lazarsfeld. 1955. *Personal influence*. New York: Free Press.

Killworth, Peter D., and H. Russell Bernard. 1978. The reverse small-world experiment. *Social Networks* 1:159–192.

Killworth, Peter D., Eugene C. Johnsen, H. Russell Bernard, Gene Anne Shelley, and Christopher McCarty. 1990. Estimating the size of personal networks. *Social Networks* 12:289–312.

Killworth, P. D., C. McCarty, E. C. Johnsen, H. R. Bernard, and G. A. Shelley. 2006. Investigating the variation of personal network size under unknown error conditions. *Sociological Methods & Research* 35 (1): 84–112.

Klausner, Samuel Z. 1964. On some differences in modes of research among psychologists and sociologists. In *Transactions of the fifth world congress of sociology*. Vol. 4, 209–235.Washington, D.C: International Sociological Association.

Kleiman, Ephraim. 1998. The role of geography, culture and religion in Middle East trade. In *Lessons from East Asia for the development of the Middle East in the era of peace*, edited by E. Ben-Ari. Jerusalem: Harry S. Truman Institute for the Advancement of Peace.

Kleinberg, Jon. 2003. An impossibility theorem for clustering. In *Advances in Neural Information Processing Systems 15. Proceedings of the 15th Conference on Neural Information Processing Systems*, edited by S. Becker, S. Thrun, and K. Obermayer. Cambridge, Mass.: MIT Press.

Klovdahl, Alden S. 1985. Social networks and the spread of infectious diseases: The AIDS example. *Social Science & Medicine* 21 (11): 1203–1216.

———. 2005. Social network research and human subjects protection: Towards more effective infectious disease control. *Social Networks* 27 (2): 119–137.

Klovdahl, A. S., E. A. Graviss, A. Yaganehdoost, M. W. Ross, A. Wanger, G. J. Adams, and J. M. Musser. 2001. Networks and tuberculosis: An undetected community outbreak involving public places. *Social Science & Medicine* 52 (5): 681–694.

Klovdahl, A. S., J. J. Potterat, D. E. Woodhouse, J. B. Muth, S. Q. Muth, and W. W. Darrow. 1994. Social networks and infectious disease: The Colorado Springs study. *Social Science & Medicine* 38 (1): 79–88.

Koehly, Laura M., and Phillipa Pattison. 2005. Random graph models for social networks: Multiple relations or multiple raters. In *Models and methods in social network analysis*, edited by P. J. Carrington, J. Scott, and S. Wasserman. New York: Cambridge University Press.

Kono, Clifford, Donald Palmer, Roger Friedland, and Matthew Zafonte. 1998. Lost in space: The geography of corporate interlocking directorates. *American Journal of Sociology* 103 (4): 863–911.

Kornhauser, Arthur, and Paul F. Lazarsfeld. 1955 (1935). The analysis of consumer actions. In *The language of social research*, edited by P. F. Lazarsfeld and M. Rosenberg. Glencoe, Ill.: Free Press.

Kornish, Laura J. 2006. Technology choice and timing with positive network effects. *European Journal of Operational Research* 173 (1): 268–282.

Kossinets, Gueorgi, and Duncan J. Watts. 2009. Origins of homophily in an evolving social network. *American Journal of Sociology* 115 (2): 405–450.

Krebs, Valdis E. 2002. *Uncloaking terrorist networks*. Available from http://firstmonday.org/htbin/cgiwrap/bin/ojs/index.php/fm/article/view/941/863%20/.

———. 2004. Power in networks. Available from http://www.orgnet.com/PowerInNetworks.pdf.

———. 2008. Connecting the dots. *Orgnet.com*, http://www.orgnet.com/tnet.html (accessed June 28, 2011).

Kroeber, A. L. 1948. *Anthropology: Race, language, culture, psychology, prehistory*. Rev. ed. New York: Harcourt, Brace.

Krugman, Paul R., and Maurice Obstfeld. 2000. *International economics: Theory and policy*. Reading, Mass.: Addison-Wesley.

Lang, Kurt, and Gladys Engel Lang. 2006. Personal influence and the new paradigm: Some inadvertent consequences. *Annals of the American Academy of Political and Social Science* 608 (1): 157–178.

Latour, Bruno. 2005. *Reassembling the social: An introduction to actor-network-theory.* Clarendon lectures in management studies. Oxford: Oxford University Press.

Laumann, Edward O., and David Knoke. 1987. *The organizational state: Social choice in national policy domains.* Madison: University of Wisconsin Press.

Laumann, Edward O., and Franz U. Pappi. 1976. *Networks of collective action: A perspective on community influence systems.* New York: Academic Press.

Lazarsfeld, Paul F. 1972 [1934]. The art of asking why: Three principles underlying the formulation of questionnaires. In *Qualitative Analysis: Historical and Critical Essays,* edited by P. F. Lazarsfeld. Boston: Allyn and Bacon. Original edition, *The National Marketing Review,* now defunct.

———, Bernard Berelson, and Hazel Gaudet. 1948. *The people's choice: How the voter makes up his mind in a presidential campaign.* New York: Columbia University Press.

Lazarsfeld, Paul F., and Robert K. Merton. 1978 [1955]. Freedom and control in modern society. In *Friendship as a social process: A substantive and methodological analysis,* edited by M. Berger, T. Abel, and C. H. Page. New York: Octagon Books.

Lazega, E., and P. E. Pattison. 1999. Multiplexity, generalized exchange and cooperation in organizations: A case study. *Social Networks* 21 (1): 67–90.

Leavitt, Harold J. 1951. Some effects of certain communication patterns on group performance. *Journal of Abnormal and Social Psychology* 46:38–50.

Leifer, Eric M. 1988. Interaction preludes to role setting: Exploratory local action. *American Sociological Review* 53 (6): 865–878.

———, and Valli Rajah. 2000. Getting observations: Strategic ambiguities in social interaction. *Soziale Systeme* 6 (2): 252–267.

Lerer, Nava, and Charles Kadushin. 1986. Effects of group cohesion on posttraumatic stress disorder. In *The Vietnam veteran redefined: Fact and fiction,* edited by G. Boulanger and C. Kadushin. Hillsdale, N.J.: Lawrence Erlbaum.

Lévi-Strauss, Claude. 1969. *The elementary structures of kinship.* Boston, Mass.: Beacon Press.

Lin, Nan. 2001. *Social capital: A theory of social structure and action.* New York: Cambridge University Press.

———, and Mary Dumin. 1986. Access to occupations through social ties. *Social Networks* 8 (4): 365–385.

Lin, Nan, Karen S. Cook, and Ronald S. Burt. 2001. *Social capital theory and research.* Sociology and economics, ed. P. England, G. Farkas, and K. Lang. New York: Aldine de Gruyter.

Lin, Nan, and Bonnie H. Erickson. 2008a. Theory, measurement, and the research enterprise on social capital. In *Social capital: An international research program,* edited by N. Lin and B. H. Erickson. Oxford; New York: Oxford University Press.

———, eds. 2008b. *Social capital: An international research program.* Oxford; New York: Oxford University Press.

Lincoln, James R., Michael L. Gerlach, and Peggy Takahshi. 1992. *Keiretsu* networks in the Japanese economy: A dyad analysis of intercorporate ties. *American Sociological Review* 57 (5): 561–585.

Linton, Ralph. 1936. *The study of man: An introduction.* New York; London: D. Appleton-Century Company.

Lipsman, Andrew. June 15, 2011. The Network Effect: Facebook, Linkedin, Twitter & Tumblr Reach New Heights in May. *comScore Blog*, http://blog.comscore.com/2011/06/facebook_linkedin_twitter_tumblr.html (accessed June 30, 2011).

Luce, R. Duncan., and A. D. Perry. 1949. A method of matrix analysis of group structure. *Psychometrika* 14 (1): 95–116.

Luke, D. A., and J. K. Harris. 2007. Network analysis in public health: History, methods, and applications. *Annual Review of Public Health* 28:69–93.

Lyons, Pat. 2009. *Mass and elite attitudes during the Prague Spring era: Importance and legacy.* Prague: Institute of Sociology, Academy of Sciences of the Czech Republic.

Malinowski, Bronislaw. 1922. *Argonauts of the Western Pacific.* London: Routledege Kegan Paul.

———. 1959 [1926]. *Crime and custom in savage society.* Patterson, N.J.: Littlefield, Adams & Co.

Maman, Daniel. 1997. The power lies in the structure: Economic policy forum networks in Israel. *British Journal of Sociology* 48 (2): 267–285.

Mandel, Micha. 2000. Measuring tendency towards mutuality in a social network. *Social Networks* 22:285–298.

March, James G., Herbert Alexander Simon, and Harold Steere Guetzkow. 1993. *Organizations.* Vol. 2. Cambridge, Mass.: Blackwell.

Markus, Hazel Rose, and Shinobu Kitayama. 1998. The cultural psychology of personality. *Journal of Cross-Cultural Psychology* 29 (1): 63–87.

———. 2003. Models of Agency: Sociocultural Diversity in the Construction of Action. *Nebraska Symposium on Motivation* 49:1–57.

Marsden, Peter V. 1987. Core discussion networks of Americans. *American Sociological Review* 52 (1): 122–131.

———. 1990. Network data and measurement. *Annual Review of Sociology* 16:435–463.

———. 2005. Recent developments in network measurement. In *Models and methods in social network analysis*, edited by P. J. Carrington, J. Scott, and S. Wasserman. New York: Cambridge University Press.

———, and Jeanne S. Hurlburt. 1988. Social resources and mobility outcomes: A replication and extension. *Social Forces* 66:1038–1059.

Martin, John Levi. 2009. *Social structures.* Princeton, N.J.: Princeton University Press.

Marx, Groucho. 1959. *Groucho and me.* New York: B. Geis Associates; distributed by Random House.

McCain, Roger Ashton, III. 2002. *Essential principles of economics: A hypermedia text.* 2nd rev. ed. Drexel University. Available from http:// william-king.www.drexel.edu/top/prin/txt/EcoToC.html (cited October 10, 2002).

McPherson, Miller. 2004. A Blau space primer: Prolegomenon to an ecology of affiliation. *Industrial and Corporate Change* 13 (1): 263–280.

———, Lynn Smith-Lovin, and James M. Cook. 2001. Birds of a feather: Homophily in social networks. *Annual Review of Sociology* 27:415–444.

Merton, Robert K. 1968a. The Matthew effect in science. *Science* 159 (3810): 56–63.

———. 1968b. *Social theory and social structure.* Glencoe, Ill.: Free Press.

———. 1973. *The sociology of science: Theoretical and empirical investigations.* Chicago: University of Chicago Press.

———. 1984. The fallacy of the latest word: The case of pietism and science. *American Journal of Sociology* 89 (5): 1091–1121.

———. 1993. *On the shoulders of giants: A Shandean postscript*. Post-Italianate ed. Chicago: University of Chicago Press.

Meyer, John, and Brian Rowan. 1991. Institutionalized organizations: Formal structure as myth and ceremony. In *The new institutionalism in organizational analysis*, edited by W. W. Powell and P. J. DiMaggio. Chicago: University of Chicago Press.

Meyers, L. 2007. Contact network epidemiology: Bond percolation applied to infectious disease prediction and control. *Bulletin of the American Mathematical Society*, n.s., 44 (1): 63–86.

Milgram, Stanley. 1967. The small-world problem. *Psychology Today* 1 (1): 62–67.

———. 1969. Interdisciplinary thinking and the small world problem. In *Interdisciplinary relationships in the social sciences*, edited by M. Sherif and C. W. Sherif. Chicago: Aldine.

———. 1974. *Obedience to authority: An experimental view*. 1st ed. New York: Harper & Row.

Mills, C. Wright. 1959. *The power elite*. New York: Oxford University Press.

Mintz, Beth, and Michael Schwartz. 1985. *The power structure of American business*. Chicago: University of Chicago Press.

Mintzberg, Henry. 1979. *The structuring of organizations: A synthesis of the research*. Englewood Cliffs, N.J.: Prentice Hall.

———. 1994. *The rise and fall of strategic planning*. New York: The Free Press.

Mitchell, J. Clyde. 1969. The concept and use of social networks In *Social networks in urban situations*, edited by J. C. Mitchell. Manchester: University of Manchester Press.

Mitchell, Stephen A. 1993. *Hope and dread in psychoanalysis*. New York: Basic Books.

Mizruchi, Mark S., and Michael Schwartz. 1987. *Intercorporate relations: The structural analysis of business*. Cambridge: Cambridge University Press.

Mokken, R. J. 1979. Cliques, clubs and clans. *Quality & Quantity* 13 (2): 161–173.

Molm, Linda D., Nobuyuki Takahashi, and Gretchen Peterson. 2000. Risk and trust in social exchange: An experimental test of a classical proposition. *American Journal of Sociology* 105 (5): 1396–1427.

Monge, Peter, and Sorin Adam Matei. 2004. The role of the global telecommunications network in bridging economic and political divides, 1989 to 1999. *Journal of Communication* 54 (3): 511–531.

Moody, James. 2001. Race, school integration, and friendship segregation in America. *American Journal of Sociology* 107 (3): 679–716.

———, and Pamela Paxton. 2009. Building bridges: Linking social capital and social networks to improve theory and research. *American Behavioral Scientist* 52 (11): 1491–1506.

Moody, James, and Douglas R. White. 2003. Structural cohesion and embeddedness: A hierarchical concept of social groups. *American Sociological Review* 68 (1): 103–127.

Moon, Il-Chul, Kathleen Carley, and Alexander Levis. 2008. Vulnerability assessment on adversarial organization: Unifying command and control structure analysis and social network analysis. In *SIAM International Conference on Data Mining, Workshop on Link Analysis, Counterterrorism and Security*. Atlanta, Georgia.

Moore, Gwen. 1979. The structure of a national elite network. *American Sociological Review* 44:673–692.

Moore, Joan. 1961. Patterns of women's participation in voluntary associations. *American Journal of Sociology* 66:592–598.

Moreno, Jacob L. 1953. *Who shall survive? Foundations of sociometry, group psychotherapy and sociodrama*. New York: Beacon House. [Originally published as Nervous and Mental Disease Monograph 58, Washington, D.C., 1934.]

Morris, Martina, ed. 2004. *Network epidemiology: A handbook for survey design and data collection, International studies in demography*. Oxford: Oxford University Press.

———, Mark S. Handcock, William C. Miller, Myron S. Cohen, Carol A. Ford, John L. Schmitz, Marcia M. Hobbs, Kathleen M. Harris, and J. Richard Udry. 2006. Prevalence of HIV infection among young adults in the United States: Results from the Add Health Study. *American Journal of Public Health* 96 (6): 1091–1097.

Morris, Martina, and Mirjam Kretzschmar. 1997. Concurrent partnerships and the spread of HIV AIDS. *AIDS* 11 (5): 641–648.

Morris, Martina, Ann E. Kurth, Deven T. Hamilton, James Moody, and Steve Wakefield. 2009. Concurrent partnerships and HIV prevalence disparities by race: Linking science and public health practice. *American Journal Public Health* 99 (6): 1023–1031.

Mosca, Gaetano. 1939 [1923]. *The ruling class (Elimenti di scienza politica)*. New York: McGraw-Hill.

Mouw, Ted. 2006. Estimating the causal effect of social capital: A review of recent research. *Annual Review of Sociology* 32 (1): 79–102.

Morozov, Evgeny. July 13, 2009. Foreign policy: Iran's terrifying Facebook police. *Foreign Policy*, http://www.npr.org/templates/story/story.php?storyId=106535773 (accessed June 28, 2011).

Nannestad, Peter. 2008. What have we learned about generalized trust, if anything? *Annual Review of Political Science* 11 (1): 413–436.

National Commission for the Protection of Human Subjects of Biomedical and Behavioral Research. 1979. The Belmont Report: Ethical principles and guidelines for the protection of human subjects of research. Bethesda, Md.: National Institutes of Health: Department of Health, Education, and Welfare.

Neaigus, Alan, Samuel R. Friedman, Marjorie Goldstein, Gilbert Ildefonso, Richard Curtis, and Benny Jose. 1995. Using dyadic data for a network analysis of HIV infection and risk behaviors among injecting drug users. In *Social Networks, Drug Abuse, and HIV Transmission*, edited by R. H. Needle, S. L. Coyle, S. G. Genser, and R. T. I. Trotter. Rockville, Md.: U.S. Department of Health and Human Services, Public Health Service, National Institutes of Health.

Needham, Rodney. 1962. *Structure and sentiment: A test case in social anthropology*. Chicago: University of Chicago Press.

Newman, M. E. J. 2003. The structure and function of complex networks. *SIAM Review* 45:167–256.

———. 2006a. Finding community structure in networks using the eigenvectors of matrices. *Physical Review E* 74 (3): 036104-1–036104-19.

———. 2006b. Modularity and community structure in networks. *PNAS* 103 (23): 8577–8582.

———. 2010. *Networks: An introduction*. Oxford, UK: Oxford University Press.

———, and Juyong Park. 2003. Why social networks are different from other types of networks. *Physical Review E* 68 (3): 036122.

———, and M. Girvan. 2004. Finding and evaluating community structure in networks. *Physical Review E* 69 (2): 026113.

Nisbet, Erik C. 2006. The engagement model of opinion leadership: Testing validity within a European context. *International Journal of Public Opinion Research* 18 (1): 3–30.

Nooy, Wouter de, Andrej Mrvar, and Vladimir Batagelj. 2005. *Exploratory social network analysis with Pajek. Structural analysis in the social sciences*. New York: Cambridge University Press.

Olguín, Daniel Olguín, Benjamin N. Waber, Taemie Kim, Akshay Mohan, Koji Ara, and Alex (Sandy) Pentland. 2009. Sensible organizations: Technology and methodology for automatically measuring organizational behavior. *EEE transactions on systems, man, and cybernetics—Part b: Cybernetics* 39 (1): 1–12.

Oliver, Amalya L. 2004. Biotechnology entrepreneurial scientists and their collaborations. *Research Policy* 33 (4): 583–597.

———, and Julia Porter Liebeskind. 1997. Three levels of networking for sourcing intellectual capital in biotechnology: Implications for studying interorganizational networks. *International Studies of Management & Organization* 27 (4): 76–103.

Olson, Mansur, Jr. 1996. Distinguished lecture on economics in government: Big bills left on the sidewalk: Why some nations are rich and others poor. *Journal of Economic Perspectives* 10 (2): 3–24.

Owen-Smith, Jason, and Walter W. Powell. 2004. Knowledge networks as channels and conduits: The effects of spillovers in the Boston biotechnology community. *Organization Science* 15 (1): 5–21.

Padgett, John F. 2001. Networks and markets. In *Organizational genesis, identity, and control: The transformation of banking in Renaissance Florence*, edited by J. E. Rauch and A. Casella. New York: Russell Sage Foundation.

———, and Christopher K. Ansell. 1993. Robust action and the rise of the Medici, 1400–1434. *American Journal of Sociology* 98 (6): 1259–1319.

Pareto, Vilfredo. 1896. *Cours d'économie politique professé à l'Université de Lausanne*. 2 vols. Lausanne, Paris: F. Rouge; Pichon.

Parsons, Talcott. 1951. *The social system*. Glencoe, Ill.: Free Press.

Perrow, Charles. 1986. *Complex organizations: A critical essay*. New York. Random House.

Phillips, Fred. 2007. On S-curves and tipping points. *Technological Forecasting and Social Change* 74 (6): 715–730.

Pinhasi, Ron, Joaquim Fort, and Albert J. Ammerman. 2005. Tracing the origin and spread of agriculture in Europe. *PLoS Biology* 3 (12): e410.

Podolny, Joel M. 2005. *Status signals: A sociological study of market competition*. Princeton, N.J.: Princeton University Press.

———, and James N. Baron. 1997. Resources and relationships: Social networks and mobility in the workplace. *American Sociological Review* 62 (5): 673–693.

Podolny, Joel M., and Karen L. Page. 1998. Network forms of organizations. *Annual Review of Sociology* 24 (1): 57.

Pool, Ithiel de Sola, and Manfred Kochen. 1978. Contacts and influence. *Social Networks* 1 (1): 5–51.

Portes, Alejandro. 1998. Social capital: Its origins and applications in modern sociology. *Annual Review of Sociology* 24 (1): 1.

———, and Julia Sensenbrenner. 1993. Embeddedness and immigration: Notes on the social determinates of economic action. *American Journal of Sociology* 98 (6): 1320–1350.

Powell, Walter W. 1990. Neither market nor hierarchy: Network forms of organization. *Research in Organizational Behavior* 12:295–336.

———, and Laurel Smith-Doerr. 2005. Networks and economic life. In *The handbook of economic sociology*, edited by N. J. Smelser and R. Swedberg. Princeton, N.J.: Princeton University Press.

Powell, W. W., D. R. White, K. W. Koput, and J. Owen-Smith. 2005. Network dynamics and field evolution: The growth of interorganizational collaboration in the life sciences. *American Journal of Sociology* 110 (4): 1132–1205.

Price, D. J. D. 1976. General theory of bibliometric and other cumulative advantage processes. *Journal of the American Society for Information Science* 27 (5–6): 292–306.

Pronyk, Paul M., Trudy Harpham, Joanna Busza, Godfrey Phetla, Linda A. Morison, James R. Hargreaves, Julia C. Kim, Charlotte H. Watts, and John D. Porter. 2008. Can social capital be intentionally generated? A randomized trial from rural South Africa. *Social Science & Medicine* 67 (10): 1559–1570.

Provan, Keith G., Amy Fish, and Joerg Sydow. 2007. Interorganizational networks at the network level: A review of the empirical literature on whole networks. *Journal of Management* 33 (3): 479–516.

Putnam, Robert D. 2000. *Bowling alone: The collapse and revival of American community*. New York: Simon and Schuster.

———. 2008. *Social capital primer*. Available from http://www.hks.harvard.edu/saguaro/primer.htm (cited January 3 2009).

———, Robert Leonardi, and Raffaella Nanetti. 1993. *Making democracy work: Civic traditions in modern Italy*. Princeton, N.J.: Princeton University Press.

Quételet, Adolphe. 1969. *A treatise on man and the development of his faculties. A facsimile reproduction of the* 1842 *English translation of* Sur l'homme et le développement de ses facultés. History of psychology series. Gainesville, Fla.: Scholars' Facsimiles & Reprints.

Rapoport, Anatol. 1954. Spread of information through a population with sociostructual bias. III. Suggested experimental procedures. *Bulletin of Mathematical Biophysics* 16:75–81.

Raudenbush, Stephen W., and Anthony S. Bryk. 2002. *Hierarchical linear models: Applications and data analysis methods*. 2nd ed. Newbury Park, Calif.: Sage Publications.

Regulations, Code of Federal. 2010. Protection of human subjects, title 45, Vol. 1 — Public welfare, CFR Part 46, subpart A, B, C, D, E. Washington, D.C.: U.S. Government Printing Office.

Riger, Stephanie. 2001. Transforming community psychology. *American Journal of Community Psychology* 29 (1): 69–81.

Roberts, S. G. B., R. I. M. Dunbar, T. V. Pollet, and T. Kuppens. 2009. Exploring variation in active network size: Constraints and ego characteristics. *Social Networks* 31:138–146.

Robins, Garry, and Phillipa Pattison. 2005. Interdependencies and social processes: Dependence graphs and generalized dependence structures. In *Models and methods in social network analysis*, edited by P. Carrington, J. Scott, and S. Wasserman. New York: Cambridge University Press.

Robinson, William S. 1950. Ecological correlations and the behavior of individuals. *American Sociological Review* 15 (3): 351–357.

Roethlisberger, Fritz Jules, and William John Dickson. 1939. *Management and the worker*. Cambridge, Mass.: Harvard University Press.

Rogers, Everett M., and D. Lawrence Kincaid. 1981. *Communications networks: Toward a new paradigm for research*. New York: Free Press.

Rosenblum, Stephanie. 2011. Got Twitter? You've been scored. *New York Times*, June 26th, 2011, SR8.

Rossi, Peter W. 1966. Research strategies in measuring peer group influences. In *College Peer Groups*, edited by T. M. Newcomb and E. K. Wilson. Chicago: Aldine.

Roth, Camille, and Jean-Philippe Cointet. 2010. Social and semantic coevolution in knowledge networks. *Social Networks* 32 (1): 16–29.

Rothenberg, Richard. 2007. The relevance of social epidemiology in HIV/AIDS and drug abuse research. *American Journal of Preventive Medicine* 32 (6, suppl. 1): S147–S153.

———, Claire Sterk, Kathleen E. Toomey, John J. Potterat, David Johnson, Mark Schrader, and Stefani Hatch. 1998. Using social network and ethnographic tools to evaluate syphilis transmission. *Sexually Transmitted Diseases* 25 (March): 154–160.

Rousseau, Denise M., Sim B. Sitkin, Ronald S. Burt, and Colin Camerer. 1998. Not so different after all: A cross-discipline view of trust. *Academy of Management Review* 23 (3): 393–404.

Sampson, Robert J., and Corina Graif. 2009. Neighborhood social capital as differential social organization: Resident and leadership dimensions. *American Behavioral Scientist* 52 (11): 1579–1605.

Sandfleur, Rebecca L., and Edward O. Laumann. 1998. A paradigm for social capital. *Rationality and Society* 10:481–501.

Saxenian, AnnaLee. 1994. *Regional advantage: Culture and competition in Silicon Valley and Route 128.* Cambridge, Mass.: Harvard University Press.

———. 2006. *The new argonauts: Regional advantage in a global economy.* Cambridge, Mass.: Harvard University Press.

Schaefer, David R., John M. Light, Richard A. Fabes, Laura D. Hanish, and Carol Lynn Martin. 2010. Fundamental principles of network formation among preschool children. *Social Networks* 32 (1): 61–71.

Scheffler, Richard M., Timothy T. Brown, Leonard Syme, Ichiro Kawachi, Irina Tolstykh, and Carlos Iribarren. 2008. Community-level social capital and recurrence of acute coronary syndrome. *Social Science & Medicine* 66 (7): 1603–1613.

Schegloff, Emanuel A. 1999. What next? Language and social interaction at the century's turn. *Research on Language and Social Interaction* 32 (1–2): 141–148.

Schumacher, Ernst Friedrich. 1973. *Small is beautiful: A study of economics as if people mattered.* New York: Harper & Row.

Schumpeter, Joseph Alois. 1934. *The theory of economic development: An inquiry into profits, capital, credit, interest, and the business cycle.* Cambridge, Mass.: Harvard University Press.

Shelley, G. A., P. A. Killworth, H. R. Bernard, C. McCarty, E. C. Johnsen, and R. E. Rice. 2006. Who knows your HIV status II?. Information propagation within social networks of sero-positive people. *Human Organization* 65 (4): 430–444.

Shrum, Wesley, Neil H. Cheek, Jr., and Saundra MacD. Hunter. 1988. Friendship in school: Gender and racial homophily. *Sociology of Education* 61 (4): 227–239.

Sillitoe, Paul. 1998. *An introduction to the anthropology of Melanesia. Culture and tradition.* Cambridge: Cambridge University Press.

Simmel, Georg. 1950 [1903]. The metropolis and mental life. In *The sociology of Georg Simmel*, edited by K. Wolff. New York: Free Press.

———. 1950. *The sociology of Georg Simmel.* New York: Free Press.

———. 1955 [1922]. *Conflict and the web of group affiliations.* Glencoe, Ill.: Free Press.

Simon, Herbert Alexander. 1947. *Administrative behavior: A study of decision-making processes in administrative organization.* New York: Macmillan Co.

Smangs, Mattias. 2006. The nature of the business group: A social network perspective. *Organization* 13 (6): 889–909.

Smith, Adam. 1778. *An inquiry into the nature and causes of the wealth of nations.* 2nd ed. London: Printed for W. Strahan and T. Cadell.

Smith, Kirsten P., and Nicholas A. Christakis. 2008. Social networks and health. *Annual Review of Sociology* 34 (1): 405–429.

Snijders, Tom A. B., Gerhard G. van de Bunt, and Christian E. G. Steglich. 2010. Introduction to stochastic actor-based models for network dynamics. *Social Networks* 32 (1): 44–60.

Snyder, David, and Edward L. Kick. 1979. Structural position in the world system and economic growth, 1955–1970: A multiple-network analysis of transnational interactions. *American Journal of Sociology* 84 (5): 1096–1126.

Son, Joonmo, and Nan Lin. 2008. Social capital and civic action: A network-based approach. *Social Science Research* 37 (1): 330–349.

Steglich, Christian, Tom Snijders, and Michael Pearson. 2010. Dynamic networks and behavior: Separating selection from influence. *Sociological Methodology* 40:329–392.

Steinfels, Peter. 1979. *The neoconservatives: The men who are changing America's politics*. New York: Simon and Schuster.

Stiller, J. and R. I. M. Dunbar. 2007. Perspective-taking and memory capacity predict social network size. *Social Networks* 29:93–104.

Stinchcombe, Arthur L. 1959. Bureaucratic and craft administration of production: A comparative study. *Administrative Science Quarterly* 4 (2): 168–187.

Stern, Daniel N. 1985. *The interpersonal world of the infant: A view from psychoanalysis and developmental psychology*. New York: Basic Books.

Stone, Brad. 2010. For web's new wave, sharing details Is the point. *New York Times*, April 23, 1.

Subrahmanyam, Kaveri, and Patricia Greenfield. 2008. Virtual worlds in development: Implications of social networking sites. *Journal of Applied Developmental Psychology* 29:417–419.

Sykes, Gresham M. 1958. *The society of captives: A study of maximum security prison*. Princeton, N.J.: Princeton University Press.

Talmud, Ilan, and Gustavo S. Mesch. 1997. Market embeddedness and corporate instability: The ecology of inter-industrial networks. *Social Science Research* 26:419–441.

Tatge, Mark. 2004. How Madison, Wis., became a hotbed of biocapitalism. *Forbes*, May 24.

Thoits, Peggy A. 1995. Stress, coping and social support processes: Where are we? What next? *Journal of Health and Social Behavior* 35: Extra Issue: Forty Years of Medical Sociology: The State of the Art and Directions for the Future 53–79.

Tichy, Noel M., and Charles Fombrun. 1979. Network analysis in organizational settings. *Human Relations* 32:923–965.

Tichy, Noel M., and Stratford Sherman. 1993. *Control your destiny or someone else will: How Jack Welch is making General Electric the world's most competitive corporation*. New York: Doubleday/Currency.

Tilly, Charles. 2007. Trust networks in transnational migration. *Sociological Forum* 22 (1): 3–24.

Travers, Jeffery, and Stanley Milgram. 1969. An experimental study of the small world problem. *Sociometry* 32 (4): 425–443.

Uehara, Edwina. 1990. Dual exchange theory, social networks, and informal social support. *American Journal of Sociology* 96 (3): 521–557.

Useem, Michael. 1980. Corporations and the corporate elite. *Annual Review of Sociology* 6:41–77.

———. 1984. *The inner circle: Large corporations and the rise of business political activity in the U.S. and U.K.* New York: Oxford University Press.

Uzzi, Brian. 1996. The sources and consequences of embeddedness for the economic performance of organizations: The network effect. *American Sociological Review* 61:674–698.

———. 1999. Embeddedness in the making of financial capital: How social relations and networks benefit firms seeking financing. *American Sociological Review* 64 (4): 481–505.

Vajja, Anju, and Howard White. 2008. Can the World Bank build social capital? The experience of social funds in Malawi and Zambia. *Journal of Development Studies* 44 (8): 1145–1168.

Valente, Thomas W. 1995. *Network models of the diffusion of innovations*. Cresskill, N.J.: Hampton Press.

————. 1996. Social network thresholds in the diffusion of innovations. *Social Networks* 18:69–89.

————. 2007. Networks and public health: A review of *Network epidemiology: A handbook for survey design and data collection*, M. Morris (Ed.). *Social Networks* 29:154–159.

————. 2010. *Social networks and health: Models, methods, and applications*. New York: Oxford University Press.

————, and Patchareeya Pumpuang. 2007. Identifying opinion leaders to promote behavior change. *Health Education Behavior* 34 (6): 881–896.

Valente, Thomas W., and David Valahov. 2001. Selective risk taking among needle exchange participants: Implications for supplemental interventions. *American Journal of Public Health* 91 (3): 406–410.

van den Bulte, Christophe, and Gary L. Lilien. 2001. Medical innovation revisited: Social contagion versus marketing effort. *American Journal of Sociology* 106 (5): 1409–1435.

van den Bulte, Christophe, and Yogesh V. Joshivan. 2007. New product diffusion with influentials and imitators. *Marketing Science* 26 (3): 400–421.

van der Gaag, Martin, Tom A. B. Snijders, and Henk Flap. 2008. Position generator measures and their relationship to other social capital measures. In *Social capital: An international research program*, edited by N. Lin and B. H. Erickson. Oxford: Oxford University Press.

van Hooijdonk, Carolien, Mariel Droomers, Ingeborg M. Deerenberg, Johan P. Mackenbach, and Anton E. Kunst. 2008. The diversity in associations between community social capital and health per health outcome, population group and location studied. *International. Journal of Epidemiology* 37 (6): 1384–1392.

Verbrugge, Lois M. 1977. The structure of adult friendship choices. *Social Forces* 56:576–597.

Volker, Nitsch. 2000. National borders and international trade: Evidence from the European Union. *Canadian Journal of Economics* 33 (4): 1091–1105.

Waber, Benjamin N., Daniel Olguín Olguín, Taemie Kim, and Alex (Sandy) Pentland. 2008. Understanding organizational behavior with wearable sensing technology. Paper presented at the *Academy of Management Annual Meeting*. Anaheim, Calif.

Waldinger, Roger. 1996. *Still the promised city? African-Americans and new immigrants in postindustrial New York*. Cambridge, Mass.: Harvard University Press.

Walker, Gordon, and David Weber. 1984. A transaction cost approach to make-or-buy decisions. *Administrative Science Quarterly* 29:373–391.

Wallace, Walter L. 1966. *Student culture: Social structure and continuity in a liberal arts college*. Chicago: Aldine.

Waring, Elin. 2002. Conceptualizing co-offending: A network form of organization. In *Crime and social organization: Advances in criminological theory*, edited by E. Waring and D. Weisburd. Rutgers, N.J.: Transaction Publishers.

Wasserman, Stanley, and Katherine Faust. 1997. *Social network analysis: Methods and applications*. Cambridge: Cambridge University Press.

Wasserman, Stanley, and Garry Robins. 2005. An introduction to random graphs, dependence graphs, and p*. In *Models and methods in social network analysis*, edited by P. Carrington, J. Scott, and S. Wasserman. New York: Cambridge University Press.

Watts, Duncan J. 2003. *Six degrees: The science of a connected age*. New York: W.W. Norton.

————. 2004. The "new" science of networks. *Annual Review of Sociology* 30 (1): 243–270.

————, and P. S. Dodds. 2007. Influentials, networks, and public opinion formation. *Journal of Consumer Research* 34 (4): 441–458.

————, and M. E. J. Newman. 2002. Identity and search in social networks. *Science* 296 (5571): 1302.

Watts, Duncan J., and Stephen H. Strogatz. 1998. Collective dynamics of "small-world" networks. *Nature* 393:440–442.

Weber, Max. 1946. *From Max Weber: Essays in sociology*. Translated, edited, and with an introduction by H. H. Gerth and C. Wright Mills. New York: Oxford University Press.

Weimann, Gabriel. 1994. *The influentials: People who influence people*. Albany: State University of New York Press.

————, D. H. Tustin, D. van Vuuren, and J. P. R. Joubert. 2007. Looking for opinion leaders: Traditional vs. modern measures in traditional societies. *International Journal of Public Opinion Research* 19 (2): 173–190.

Wellman, Barry. 1979. The community question: The intimate networks of East Yorkers. *American Journal of Sociology* 84 (5): 1201–1231.

————. 1993. An egocentric network tale: A comment on Bien et al. (1991). *Social Networks* 15 (4): 423–436.

————. 1999a. The network community: Introduction to networks in the global village. In *Networks in the global village: Life in contemporary communities*, edited by B. Wellman. Boulder, Colo.: Westview Press.

————. 1999b. *Networks in the global village: Life in contemporary communities*. Boulder, Colo.: Westview Press.

————, Peter J. Carrington, and Alan Hall. 1988. Networks as personal communities. In *Social structures: A network approach*, edited by B. Wellman and S. D. Berkowitz. New York: Cambridge University Press.

Wellman, Barry, Kenneth A. Frank, Nan Lin, Karen S. Cook, and Ronald S. Burt. 2001. Network capital in a multilevel world: Getting support from personal communities. In *Social capital theory and research*, edited by N. Lin, K. S. Cook, and R. S. Burt. New York: Aldine de Gruyter.

Wellman, Barrry, and Caroline Haythornthwaite. 2002. *The internet in everyday life*. Oxford: Blackwell.

White, Douglas R., and Frank Harary. 2001. The cohesiveness of blocks in social networks: Node connectivity and conditional density. *Sociological Methodology* 31:305–359.

White, Harrison C. 1963. *An anatomy of kinship: Mathematical models for structures of cumulated roles*. Engelwood Cliffs, N.J.: Prentice Hall.

————. 2002. *Markets from networks: Socioeconomic models of production*. Princeton, N.J.: Princeton University Press.

————, Scott A. Boorman, and Ronald L. Breiger. 1976. Social structure from multiple networks: Blockmodels of roles and positions. *American Journal of Sociology* 81:730–779.

Whyte, William Foote. 1943. *Street corner society: The social structure of an Italian slum*. Chicago: University of Chicago Press.

Williamson, Oliver E. 1975. *Markets and hierarchies: Analysis and antitrust implications, a study in the economics of internal organization*. New York: Free Press.

————. 1981. The economics of organizations: The transaction cost approach. *American Journal of Sociology* 87 (November): 548–577.

Winship, Christopher. 1977. A distance model for sociometric structure. *Journal of Mathematical Sociology* 5:21–39.

Zachary, Wayne W. 1977. An information flow model for conflict and fission in small group. *Journal of Anthropological Research* 33:452–473.

Zetterberg, Hans L. 2011. The Many-Splendored Society. Book 2. A Language-Based Edifice of Social Structures. 2nd ed. http://www.zetterberg.org/ (accessed June 23, 2011).

Zhao, Shanyang, and David Elesh. 2008. Copresence as "being with." *Information, Communication & Society* 11 (4): 565–583.

Zheng, Tian, Matthew J. Salganik, and Andrew Gelman. 2006. How many people do you know in prison? Using overdispersion in count data to estimate social structure in networks. *Journal of the American Statistical Association* 101:409–423.

Zipf, George Kingsley. 1949. *Human behavior and the principle of least effort: An introduction to human ecology.* Cambridge, Mass.: Addison-Wesley Press.

Index